Displacement

MANCHESTER
1824

Manchester University Press

Displacement

Global conversations on refuge

Edited by
Silvia Pasquetti and Romola Sanyal

Manchester University Press

Published by Manchester University Press
Oxford Road, Manchester M13 9PL
www.manchesteruniversitypress.co.uk

British Library Cataloguing-in-Publication Data
A catalogue record for this book is available from the British Library

ISBN 978 1 5261 2346 6 hardback
ISBN 978 1 5261 6029 4 paperback

First published 2020
Paperback published 2021

Typeset
by New Best-set Typesetters Ltd

Contents

List of figures

List of contributors

Diana Allan is an Assistant Professor in the Department of Anthropology and the Institute for the Study of International Development at McGill University and filmmaker. She is the author of *Refugees of the Revolution: Experiences of Palestinian Exile* (2014) and the co-founder of the Nakba Archive.

Cathrine Brun is Director of the Centre for Development and Emergency Practice (CENDEP) at Oxford Brookes University. She is a human geographer focusing on protracted displacement, the ethics and politics of humanitarianism and making home in displacement.

Jonathan Darling is an Assistant Professor in Human Geography at Durham University. His research focuses on the ethics and politics of forced migration, and considers how cities engage with questions of asylum and refuge.

Chiara Denaro is a Research Assistant in the Law and Criminology Department at Edge Hill University (UK).

Didier Fassin is Professor of Social Science at the Institute for Advanced Study in Princeton. Elected to the Annual Chair in Public Health at the Collège de France, he is the President of the French Medical Committee for Exiles. He recently authored *Life. A Critical User's Manual* (Polity, 2018) and edited *Deepening Divides. How Physical Borders and Social Boundaries Delineate Our World* (Pluto, 2019)

Konstantina Isidoros is a Research Affiliate of ISCA and Research Fellow of FRSG at the University of Oxford.

Caroline Wanjiku Kihato is a Visiting Research Fellow at the University of Oxford's Department of International Development and a Global Scholar at the Woodrow Wilson International Center for Scholars.

Loren B. Landau is Professor of Migration and Development at the University of Oxford and the South African Research Chair in Human Mobility and the Politics of Difference based at the University of the Witwatersrand's African Centre for Migration & Society. His interdisciplinary scholarship explores mobility, multi-scale governance, and the transformation of socio-political community across the Global South.

Ulrich Oslender is an Associate Professor of Geography at Florida International University in Miami. He is the author of *The Geographies of Social Movements: Afro-Colombian Mobilization and the Aquatic Space* (Duke University Press, 2016), and co-editor of *Bridging Scholarship and Activism: Reflections from the Frontlines of Collaborative Research* (Michigan State University Press, 2015).

Pei Palmgren is a PhD Candidate in Sociology at the University of California, Los Angeles. He is currently completing a comparative ethnography of labor migration regimes in Thailand and has previously published in the *Journal of Refugee Studies* and the *Journal of Ethnic and Migration Studies.*

Silvia Pasquetti is a Lecturer in Sociology at Newcastle University. Her work on forced displacement has appeared in *Theory & Society*, *Law & Society Review*, *IJURR*, and other interdisciplinary journals.

Tazreena Sajjad currently serves as Senior Professorial Lecturer in the Global Governance, Politics and Security (GGPS) Program in the School of International Service (SIS) at American University in Washington, D.C. Her areas of specialization include transitional justice, refugees and forced displacement, DDR, post-conflict governance, gender and conflict.

Romola Sanyal is an Associate Professor of Urban Geography at the London School of Economics. Her work focuses on forced migration, urbanization, urban politics and citizenship.

Ala Sirriyeh is a Senior Lecturer in Sociology at Lancaster University. Her research centres on migration, youth and activism.

Ragne Øwre Thorshaug is a geographer, and a PhD student at the Department for Architecture and Planning at NTNU Norwegian University of Science and Technology.

Chia Youyee Vang is Professor of History at the University of Wisconsin-Milwaukee. She is the author of *Fly Until You Die: An Oral History of Hmong Pilots in the Vietnam War* (Oxford University Press, 2019) and *Hmong America: Reconstructing Community in Diaspora* (University of Illinois Press, 2010), and co-editor of *Claiming Place: On the Agency of Hmong Women* (University of Minnesota Press, 2016).

Preface
The political geography and moral economy of asylum

Didier Fassin

The "refugee question" is one of the most vexing of our times. Not only is the number of forcibly displaced persons in the world the highest on record, according to the United Nations, with more than 70 million people affected, including 26 million refugees strictly speaking, but their fate is increasingly worrying, as growing levels of rejection and violence put to the test the very principles of the 1951 Geneva Convention on Refugees. Once under the aegis of international law, refugees have become more and more vulnerable as many states refuse to provide them with asylum, letting them die at their borders and abandoning them to criminal groups or undemocratic governments.

The category of refugee has itself come to be problematic. Whereas it is supposed to confer an official protective status in the host country to persons being persecuted, or fearing persecution, in their home country, they are actually, in many contexts, stigmatized, victimized, and discriminated against in the same way as undocumented migrants. The legal boundary that distinguishes them from *soit-disant* illegal aliens, ensuring them in principle a series of rights, tends to blur as they experience precarious conditions, suffer from xenophobic reactions by nationals, and are subjected to police harassment all the same. Besides, as states artificially separate refugees and migrants, or actual and bogus asylum seekers, simply by enforcing stricter criteria of recognition, they delegitimize an increasing proportion of claims and automatically reduce the number of those granted protection while augmenting the number of those in limbo. Therefore, rather than considering refugees in accordance with their official designation, which only reflects changing norms and practices, it could be more relevant to think of them under the generic and much broader category of forced nomads, including asylum seekers, economic migrants, and undocumented foreigners. I have elsewhere proposed to analyze this coerced migration as a form of life that puts in tension the universal of a condition and the specifics of circumstances, the biological of threatened existences and the biographical of eventful being-in-the-world, the exclusion by law and its circumvention by practice. This form of life under dire constraints should not, however, lead to overlooking or minimizing the power of expectations and imaginations, far from the bare life that has sometimes been ascribed to refugees by social scientists. *Displacement* can be read as a recognition of these tensions and an avoidance of these reifications.

In that regard, the wide range of situations examined by the authors distances them from the habitual ethnocentrism of public debates about the so-called refugee question, which is generally viewed through Western lenses in Western countries – in particular Southern Europe and the United States. The political geography of asylum is much richer. It shows that most displaced persons are on the African and Asian continents, and that not only is the distribution uneven across the planet, but it also takes distinct configurations. In the Global South, people in search of protection generally flee to a neighboring country: Zimbabweans in South Africa, Sudanese in Uganda, Somalians in Kenya, Rohingyas in Bangladesh, Afghans in Iran and Pakistan, Syrians in Jordan and Lebanon, Venezuelans in Colombia and Brazil. Although there are exceptions, in most cases, they are accommodated in large camps run by the United Nations or by local governments, the oldest of which are the Palestine refugee camps. Their registration generally suffices to grant them status and protection. In the Global North, by contrast, people who claim asylum often come from far away, having crossed numerous countries, encountered multiple obstacles, and spent considerable amounts of money to eventually find themselves stuck in a bureaucratic system in which officers and judges will decide whether they are granted refugee status or rejected as undocumented migrants. Each situation thus gives rise to a complex casuistry in which accounts, testimonies, documents, medical reports of body traces or psychic trauma, anthropological and geopolitical expertise about the home countries are mobilized. Most European countries proceed in this manner. In sum, one could speak of two forms of governmentality, with massive management in the South and individualized treatment in the North. Resettlement, favored by the United States, Australia, and Scandinavian countries, appears to be a sort of intermediate configuration. It consists of selecting refugees in camps of the Global South, generally on the basis of their vulnerability, to transfer them to the Global North. This simplified dual image is, however, rapidly changing. On the one hand, camps have multiplied in Southern Europe, where they are called hotspots, and the United States, where they are designated as detention centers; as well as on the other side of the borders in Morocco, Libya, and Turkey, in particular, as part of a process of externalization of the control of refugees in exchange for financial aid. On the other hand, asylum seeking is rapidly growing in Egypt, Uganda, Angola, and even more significantly South Africa, which at the peak of the so-called migrant crisis in 2015 notified more claimants than the entire European continent. Bringing together refugee camps and asylum seeking, internal displacement and international resettlement, local dwelling and global exile, this volume edited by Silvia Pasquetti and Romola Sanyal illustrates this diversity of situations and related stakes.

But this unequal distribution of refugees across the planet and the variety of corresponding forms of governmentality are underlain by a moral economy of asylum that rarely receives the attention it deserves. By moral economy, I mean the production, circulation, and appropriation, critical or not, of values and affects regarding both the politics of protection and the people to be protected. A historical perspective, on which the authors insist in their contributions, is certainly useful to apprehend the evolution of these values and affects as well as their changing tensions. We may have had the illusion that in the aftermath of the Second World War a combination of sense of responsibility, ideas of solidarity, and sentiments of empathy had led to the signing of international documents guaranteeing sanctuaries, in reference to the etymology of the word asylum, for people who are victims of persecution or flee the risk thereof. In fact, as historians have demonstrated, realpolitik has always prevailed over good will, and the apparent generosity from the 1950s to the 1970s was mostly the result of the need for a workforce in Western countries and of the ideological contention of the Cold War. The partial closing of borders to the labor force and soon afterwards to family reunification, followed by the fall of socialist regimes, revealed that generosity in protection was no more on the agenda. In Western Europe, in the 1970s, Chilean and Argentinian political opponents fleeing right-wing dictatorships aroused admiration, while Cambodian and Vietnamese boat people who had escaped communist repression and were rescued in the South China Sea stirred up compassion. The former were seen as heroic combatants; the latter as tragic victims. But these affects and depictions declined in the 2010s when the political opponents were Syrians seeking protection from the Baathist regime and the boat people were sub-Saharan Africans risking their lives across the Mediterranean. Mistrust became common among officers and judges in asylum procedures and, rather than heroes or victims, claimants were suspected of being false refugees or potential terrorists, often with racialist or even racist undertones. A new moral imagination has thus emerged, with the paradox that the increased severity in granting asylum is presented as a sign of respect for the preciously preserved refugee status. Moreover, when analyzing more closely the treatment over time of certain groups and their recognition as refugees, it is even possible to have a finer understanding of the changing moral economy of asylum. Children have long been a particular object of empathy, but as they are now administratively designated as unaccompanied minors, the obsessive verification of their age attests to an increasing suspicion. Women have recently been acknowledged as a special social group in certain circumstances when they are considered to be at risk of what is defined as forced marriage or genital mutilation, and so have gay people submitted to stigmatization and violence in homophobic environments. In the meantime, traditional criteria of recognition of asylum for political, religious, ethnic, or racial reasons have lost some of their effectiveness in the assessments of claims. Moral hierarchies are therefore implicitly established among causes of persecution and among suffering subjects. They reflect not only the representations one has of others in peril but also those one wants to give of oneself. The authors of the present volume provide multiple case studies exemplifying these processes.

A great merit of *Displacement* is indeed to offer an exploration, in various historical contexts, of the multiple issues involved in the management of forced nomads beyond the spectacular images and disparaging discourses through which they are generally represented. The contributors thus allow the reader to perceive each situation under a new light yet from an open perspective, and to realize that this form of life has become one of the most acute prisms to apprehend the disquieting evolution of contemporary societies, as it is often from the margins of social worlds that their logics at work become visible.

Acknowledgements

This monograph is very much a collective endeavour stemming from years of conversations with colleagues, students, practitioners, activists, and people involved in different contexts of displacement. While these acknowledgements cannot possibly do justice to all these indirect and long-term influences underpinning the development of our ideas, we would like to thank all those who have been part of this journey. And indeed it has been a journey, as many life events amongst many of us have punctuated the making of this book.

We would like to thank the authors who believed in our project and contributed their work to this book through their busy schedules and different challenges. Their collective contribution has been crucial for generating the new cross-regional and cross-disciplinary conversations on displacement, global humanitarianism, and refugee lives that we advocate for in this book. We are inspired by their work and their dedication to this project.

We are also deeply grateful to Tom Dark, the acquiring editor for Manchester University Press, who has believed in our idea since we outlined it to him in a meeting four years ago. Tom has encouraged us through the ebbs and flows of the book's development and his continued support has been crucial for ensuring the successful completion of this project. We also thank the press and especially Lianne Slavin for bringing this book to its final iteration. In addition, we thank Meredith Whitten for preparing the index of the book and Saurja Sen for generously volunteering his time to copy-edit the entire manuscript.

Among her colleagues and friends, Silvia owes a special thanks to Didier Fassin, who generously volunteered feedback on her broader work on displacement and refugees during her in-residence fellowship at the Institute for Advanced Study in Princeton (2017–2018). At the IAS, she found an exciting environment of both intellectual engagement and support, which helped her work through her varied projects on displacement, including this one. She would also like to thank Loïc Wacquant for encouraging her to put refugees in dialogue with other "urban outcasts," interrogating the law and politics of control over them across different cities and regions. She is also grateful to the Newcastle School of Geography, Politics, and Sociology for being a supportive and engaging intellectual home.

Romola would like to thank her friends and colleagues, especially those at the LSE who have supported her through the work on this book.

Introduction: global conversations on refuge

Silvia Pasquetti and Romola Sanyal

The impetus for this volume came from conversations that we shared about our work in the Middle East, in Europe, and in South Asia, and across disciplinary divides. We came from backgrounds in architecture, planning, and geography, on the one hand, and urban ethnography and political sociology, on the other, and have utilized different theoretical and methodological lenses to study questions of governance, agency, and politics. Our conversations converged on the need for more productive, nuanced, and contextualized ways of "doing refugee studies" that were both attentive to histories of displacement and crossed disciplinary boundaries.

This book is thus a political project founded on an effort to create new avenues for theorizing about forced migration. Rather than summarizing developments around it, our aim is to encourage analyses of refugee situations that trace and compare historical trajectories of displacement and refuge, to promote interdisciplinary dialogue on the complex nature of forced migration, and to think more creatively about the processes, politics, and experiences of displacement. To this end, we went on a search for scholars across different disciplines, working in different regions and on creative analyses of displacement. We sought work that would utilize new theoretical frameworks to unpack processes of displacement, thus challenging more orthodox analyses of them.

Our goal was to problematize four entrenched patterns that have troubled us in our long engagement with studying refugees. First, we found in our own transnational and comparative work, that many studies on refugees remain within national, and regional, boundaries. Related to that, and perhaps given the urgency of current crises, we noted that a lot of scholarship tended towards a-historicism. Third, while some scholars have produced solid interdisciplinary work, we found that much work on refugees, particularly that rooted in specific academic disciplines, remains within its disciplinary siloes. Finally, and perhaps as a result of such narrow research agendas, it appeared to us that there was a theoretical impasse in much of the social science writing on refugees for the past twenty years. This, to us, stood in sharp contrast to the lively theoretical innovations in other fields such as urbanization, migration, and development.

These patterns are troubling because they stand in the way of understanding longer histories of displacement and their effects on places, the changing nature of the politics of displacement and aid, and the varied experiences of displacement that have resonances with other parts of the world. They prevent us from raising important questions about the uneven paths within the global humanitarian machine, including how it operates within different local contexts, about the connections between histories of colonialism and imperialism and the governance of refugees, about the different forms of refugee politics that emerge within and across global and local arenas, and about the different spaces that refugees inhabit and shape in their search for a dignified future. In other words, it detracts from a systemic and historic understanding of the politics of displacement and recovery.

Thus, for example, in reference to the argument above about the regional focus of forced migration, we note that there are often excellent academic analyses of local contexts, but that there are limited conversations across regional divides. Understanding how localized responses function in a larger humanitarian landscape and how they are tied to broader geopolitics of migration, humanitarian funding, and global practices of aid offers an important lens into the topological nature of displacement and humanitarianism. It breaks away from the potential to fetishize places as being "unique and different" because ultimately all displacements are unique and different – yet operate in relation to one another. Further, the risk for many scholars working on contemporary issues in forced migration in these localized contexts is to focus so much on present "crises" as to slip into a-historical analyses. Placing contemporary crises in longer trajectories of other geopolitical and geofinancial shifts, as well as in conversation with other regions where similar issues may be taking place, enables us to understand what, if any, shifts have taken place in relation to refugee protection. It helps us trace longer trajectories of imperialism, racism, and power that underpin many of the practices of hospitality, humanitarianism, and the portrayal of refugees today.

We can go further and take up the point about the field being largely trapped in disciplinary siloes. We recognize that there are scholars who have engaged in critical interdisciplinary work, but by and large the field tends to be dominated by particular disciplines and specialized conversations. The importance of interdisciplinary analyses cannot be overstated as different tools, methodologies, and conceptual frameworks allow us to advance the kind of theorization that we discuss above.

In our final intervention, we note the theoretical impasse discussed above. Here, we argue that, in the study of forced migration, the specter of bare life, space, and state of exception looms large. As Adam Ramadan (2013) suggests, Giorgio Agamben's work has become a hegemonic presence within this field. While it is important to acknowledge the importance of this work and its clear applicability to the study of forced migration, to remain captive within its orbit at the expense of exploring other theoretical concepts limits the intellectual expansion of this field.

So, how do we embark on this ambitious project to expand the boundaries of forced migration studies? One way to approach this is to consider what local–global conversations do to advance our political project. We ask ourselves: how do we bring the politics of refugee return, relief, and resettlement in the Middle East and South Asia into conversation with each other? How do these conversations help us unpack larger politics of decolonization, communalism, citizenship, and belonging? How do they help us advance an understanding of subaltern politics? Fields such as urban studies, with which we have engaged for years, have come to benefit significantly from transnational conversations. It seems that refugee and forced migration studies could equally advance from such endeavors rather than insisting on accentuating the distinctiveness of their situations. In doing so, the field could join other areas of research that have moved beyond treating the Global South as a site of empirical evidence toward seeing it as a site of theory as well. We can thus produce a "Southern turn" in forced migration studies that could challenge the dominance of theorizing refuge from the Global North.

Put differently, we note that other fields of inquiry – whether they are on urbanization, or gender, or migration – have developed diverse understandings of social worlds and human interactions and ask why the work around refugees has not evolved in the same way. Why do refugee studies and forced migration studies continue to be dominated by scholars writing from the Euro-American center? Returning to the earlier point about the possibility of a southern turn in forced migration studies, one must ask: is refugee studies in need of decolonizing? We feel that taking account of history and understanding the larger global landscape within which humanitarianism unfolds, as well as examining the productive, generative effects of forced displacement, are important in order to better understand how local practices of humanitarian intervention and resistance emerge.

Further, how can we connect refugee experiences to broader debates about human subjectivities and practices, especially at the bottom of societal hierarchies? How can we overcome the tendency to either theorize refugees and forced migrants in negative terms (as if the fundamental features of their lives are invariably what they lack vis-a-vis citizens) and in disconnection from broader societal processes and conflicts (as if they inhabit worlds apart), or celebrate their agency unproblematically? How can we bridge between these two approaches that seem to be stuck in a binary understanding of the world in which subjectivity of people is a zero-sum game: either one is able to exercise politics in ways understandable to Western audiences, or one is stripped of political life and turned into a subject of aid and control?

In this collection, we hope to offer a modest intervention of thinking about forced migration through interdisciplinary, transnational, and historical lenses. Through our collection of chapters that encompass different countries across the world, we hope to open up new conversations between places, and think about forced migration issues using new and different theoretical lenses. We hope the book offers an impetus to develop more dialogues across disciplines that enrich our understanding of displacement. Specifically, in this volume, we attempt to undertake a critical examination of the shifting mechanisms and unequal paths underpinning the global humanitarian management of displacement. We aim to generate global conversations on structures and experiences of refuge that articulate connections and mutual influences between broadly Northern and Southern formations of displacement without lumping them together in a-historical and ultimately implausible ways.

In doing so, we highlight the importance of context in understanding the emergence of specific forms of control and resistance. We also effectively address and show the connections between some of the most topical issues in the context of displacement today, including the increasing deferral of legal–moral responsibility toward refugees and the turn toward the externaliza-tion of asylum in the Global North, the coexistence of protracted encampment and urban refuge models in the Global South, the colonial and imperial dimensions of structures of control and care, the intersection of categories of displacement with axes of inclusion and exclusion such as "race" and nationhood, refugees' relationships with urban actors, and the potential and limits of refugees' transnational networks of solidarities.

The work that we support and advocate for in this monograph – geographical imagination and cross-regional dialogue, historical sensibilities, interdisciplinary efforts, and theoretical creativity beyond "bare life" – is also helpful for addressing other urgent issues of displacement that we do not directly discuss, such as climate-related displacement, statelessness, secondary and multiple displacement, and the feminization of displacement. Finally, the cumulative theoretical work that we produce in this monograph aims to encourage more interdisciplinary studies about how displacement shapes and is shaped by legal, political, and moral struggles over resources, rights, and belonging. This theoretical work is also oriented toward debates in social and political theory about issues of justice, recognition, and redistribution (e.g., Fraser and Honneth, 2003) that so far have not identified the role that displacement plays in structures and experiences of inclusion and exclusion.

Global conversations

In his theoretical reflections on how to produce "decolonial knowledge" about a certain topic, Walter Mignolo (2000, 2018: 149) argues that "it is not enough to change the content of the conversation (the domains, the enunciated); on the contrary it is of the essence to change the terms (regula-tions, assumptions, principles managed at the level of the enunciation) of the conversation." He highlights how the level of "the enunciated" is the level of "conceptual abstractions that posit an ontology in which there is no emotion" while the level of "the enunciation" is "where emotioning and reasoning take place ... the domains do not have their own emotions. Emotions lie within the actors of the enunciation who shape the enunciated: its domination, exploitation, conflicts." In this view, "decoloniality is one type of confrontation, or *speaking to*, that delinks from the dictates of imperial enunciations." Decolonizing movements in different disciplines therefore not only critique the veil of universalism placed by the Euro-American core, and interrogate the politics of knowledge stemming from it, but also turn toward knowing from elsewhere – i.e., knowledge production from and led by black and indigenous scholars (Noxolo, 2017). Our effort in this book to think about decolonization remains partial and incomplete but, as Noxolo (2017) notes, this must continue. We include a range of scholars who occupy varied positions in academia and come from different backgrounds with varying relationships to their research projects and sites. Building on that, the conversations that we propose in this book strive to disconnect the study of displacement "from the dictates of imperial enunciations" and to unsettle "the border thinking" that builds conceptual walls between both regions and disciplines in the study of refugees and forced migration.[1] Specifically, with our suggestion for "global conversations" on displacement and refuge we highlight three key analytical points.

First, we argue that transnational and transregional dialogue is a crucial first step towards decentering abstract ways of "doing theory" that silence "subjugated knowledges"[2] about displacement; for example, those "knowledges" about the geopolitical and geofinancial logics producing displacement that emerge from the cities and refugee camps of the Global South. In other words, transnational and transregional dialogue is crucial for shifting the terms of how we talk about displacement, thus legitimizing and mobilizing "subjugated knowledges" as full and crucial contributors to our conceptual understanding of how displacement is produced, managed, and experienced. Along these lines, we recognize and join recent efforts to better understand and theorize about displacement by studying it in a wide variety of regional, national, and local contexts (Bloch and Dona 2018; Feldman, 2018; Fiddian-Qasmiyeh et al., 2014; Fitzgerald and Arar, 2018). The juxtaposition of "unexpected" or neglected case studies with more familiar ones to Western audiences is a way to speak about displacement that makes new conceptual connections between displacement and the distribution of rights, power, and legitimate recognition across different scales of the global order. It is a way of speaking about displacement that is linked to new types of questions and conversations about displacement. Thus, for example, can the Colombian case that we include in this monograph helps us theorize the racial dimension of displacement both within and across borders? Can the case of the Hmong refugees in the United States help us dissect the imperial dimension of contemporary Northern formations of displacement? Can the case of the Rohingya refugees in Bangladesh help us develop new conceptual geographies of displacement and global and local power relations? Can the case of the internally displaced in post-Soviet Georgia push forward the interdisciplinary theorization of materiality in refugee studies? Similar "global conversations" on the political, the urban, and the everyday animate each chapter of this monograph.

Second, with "global conversations" we aim to take an analytical stance that strongly emphasizes relationships – convergences, tensions, flows, and conflicts – across scales of the global order. This is not necessarily a methodological stance advocating specific methodologies – for example, multi-sited ethnographies – for capturing global–local relationships. Rather, it is an epistemological perspective that traces connection across places and times, without the assumption that by doing so we can reach definitional or conceptual wholes. Put differently, we follow Anna Tsing's (2005: 5) suggestion that it is the "friction" produced by global–local interactions that leads to "new arrangements of culture and power." As she puts it: "rubbing two sticks together produces heat and light; one stick alone is just a stick." In each chapter of this monograph we see how this action of "rubbing two sticks" together plays out at different levels; for example, across state relationships, across state and urban configurations, in relationships between differently situated global and local actors – and in different histories – of (post)colonialism, of imperialism, of activism, and of survival.

Finally, with "global conversations" we aim to produce "relational" rather than group- or region-oriented approaches to displacement. We aim to unsettle "substantialist" assumptions about the exceptionality of certain cases and the representational power of other cases and problematize the tendency to look at case studies in isolation from others. This "relational" approach helps put in dialogue studies of displacement with other conversations about urban poverty, transnational solidarity, militarism, and imperialism. Thus, for example, as Darling's Chapter 9 on urban accommodation for refugees in the UK and Kihato and Landau's Chapter 10 on urban humanitarianism in Southern Africa show, the urban level emerges as a particularly important level for theorizing how displacement is managed and experienced and for interrogating the dilemmas of humanitarianism in increasingly militarized and unequal cities where the sources of marginality and dispossession vary significantly. Likewise, Isidoros' Chapter 8 on the interactions between Sahrawi people and mostly Western humanitarians in the Sahrawi refugee camps dotting the Algerian desert helps theorize tensions and possibly misunderstanding within transnational solidarity movements and networks. Isidoros argues that, while some of the humanitarians see the Sahrawi as refugees, the Sahrawi see themselves as "citizens-in-waiting." Further, given their familiarity with nomadic lifestyles, the Sahrawi do not necessarily experience the tent or the camp as spatial exceptionalities. This contrasts with humanitarians' spatial perceptions. The Sahrawi are not so concerned with the spatial dimension of their lives (the camp rather than the city, the tent rather than the house), but with its legal dimension: it is through the tools of international and human rights that they seek recognized statehood for the spaces they inhabit. The refugee category is thus a means to this end. This instrumentality is often lost in translation when they interact with the humanitarians who visit their camps. Complementing Isidoros' work, Denaro's Chapter 7 examines Syrian refugees' mobilization of networks of mostly European supporters while en route across the Mediterranean Sea and often across Italy toward Northern European destinations. Like Isidoros, Denaro shows how those categorized as refugees actively engage with a variety of social actors, modulating their voices and claims depending on the type of actor they interact with and the situation they find themselves in. Together, the two chapters help us theorize both the potential and the limits of transnational solidarities in complex refugee situations.

As these brief examples of "global conversations" show, the chapters we have included in this monograph can and should be read in dialogue with each other. While the contributors do not directly speak to one another, in this introduction we have identified and discussed how we have solicited and organized these chapters with several aims in mind: avoiding a-historical "presentism," promoting interdisciplinary dialogue, engaging in creative theorization about displacement that is sensitive to context, and connecting displacement to broader conversations about power, rights, redistribution, recognition, and justice and how to study them.

The global conversations that we propose in this volume aim to advance the work that still needs to be done to produce decolonial knowledge that, following the abovementioned point raised by Walter Mignolo, "delinks" the study of displacement "from the dictates of imperial enunciations." Specifically, these conversations aim to build new ways of "doing" refugee and forced migration studies that make and dissect connections across regional and local formations of displacement, that operate firmly within interdisciplinary perspectives, and that produce new integrated theoretical approaches to displacement, refuge, and humanitarianism.

Geographies of displacement: local contexts and scales of intervention

Across the social sciences, place is increasingly recognized as a key feature of social, political, and legal processes. For example, Gieryn (2000) has invited sociologists to "spatialize" their research. In other words, other social science disciplines are joining geography in its analytical attention to spatial approaches to migration, including asylum migration. Geographers have analyzed migration in myriad ways including through using these lenses of im/mobility, waiting, and "carceral geographies" (Bagelman, 2016; Darling, 2009, 2010; Hyndman and Giles, 2011; Hyndman and Mountz, 2008; Martin, 2012; Moran et al., 2018; Mountz et al., 2013). All of these have been important in understanding the power politics and effects of detention and offshoring that are becoming the central features of migration management. In this monograph, we adopt a broader perspective on spatial processes within and across formations of displacement, paying attention to local contexts and other scales of governance and being sensitive to how scales are not only invented, but also exist in relation to one another. We also acknowledge the vastly different geopolitical contexts within which hospitality unfolds – for example, how postcolonial environments present particular challenges and practices of hosting refugees different to those in contexts in the Global North (Landau, 2018). Thus, for example, Palmgren's Chapter 11 on Southeast Asia connects national and urban scales to provide a better understanding of how degrees and forms of humanitarian protection are offered in each, while Darling highlights the geopolitical dimension of the accommodation system for refugees in the UK in Chapter 9, and Kihato and Landau investigate how humanitarianism intersects with urban poverty in African cities in Chapter 10.

We aim to bring our work into conversation with that taking place within the "carceral geographies." That work has been an important lens by which to understand the evolution of the humanitarian system, the emergence of a securitized system where refugees are in fact stripped of their legal rights. Recognizing how imprisonment and decelerations function as an important part of the refugee management system offers an important entry point into how class, race, gender, and other identity attributes affect the texture of mobility. As Doreen Massey (2002) aptly noted in her work, globalization is experienced unevenly by different groups of people being shaped by and shaping power geometries. However, such practices are embedded within local politics and histories of understanding and managing migration. Further, there is a danger that such analyses of refugees and migrants as being voiceless victims immobilized within a larger oppressive humanitarian system that seeks to merely keep them alive, but not allow them to function as political agents, can be applied indiscriminately across the world. Indeed, some of the studies on camps seem to veer in this direction. Such theorization runs the danger of ignoring the complex nuances in each context and can lead to academic imperialism. On the other hand, we also do not intend to valorize refugees as agentive. Such romanticization of refugees or of the conditions under which they live can also be deeply problematic and inattentive to how humanitarianism can be a bureaucratic and oppressive system that does in fact function as a system of detention.

Along these lines, the monograph includes and, with this introduction, outlines connections between case studies drawn from different national, regional, and urban settings. However, we do not lump together these case studies, nor do we mobilize them to get closer to a presumably generaliz-able substantive approach to the "essence" of "camp formations," "refugee camps," or "securitized humanitarianism." By contrast, we empirically map convergences and divergences, as well as complementarities and contradictions within the global humanitarian machine. In line with our arguments against a-historical "presentism" and in favor of historical sensibility and contextualized dialogue between empirical and theoretical work, the monograph shows how categorization, control, and protection are geographically distributed and continuously renegotiated by global and local actors.

First, it highlights how the Global North's preference for regimes of individualized asylum cases and its reluctance to accept masses of refugees fleeing war and violence have produced the mass warehousing of refugees in the Global South (Fitzgerald, 2019). The shifting politics of donor countries to the United Nations High Commissioner for Refugees (UNHCR: the main UN agency responsible for refugees and forced migrants), located predominantly in the Global North, have also played a pivotal role in the ways in which those seeking safe havens have been classified and reclassified. Anxieties of immigration, xenophobia, and donor exhaustion have drawn ambiguous lines between "deserving" asylum seekers and "devious" economic migrants – categories that are clearly flimsy on close examination.

Further, in the Global South, protracted refugee situations and limited international aid and support have also led to shifts in policies and attitudes, creating new forms of disenfranchisement among refugees and other forced migrants. Moreover, at a time of increased securitization in many post 9/11 Northern states, and equally intensified existential anxieties in host states in the Global South, an increased number of stateless and internally displaced people have been left precariously suspended between global and local regimes of management. As Sajjad's Chapter 4 on the Rohingya refugees in Bangladesh shows, these entanglements have a salient impact on how different states address questions of security, refugee reception, and international law. Thus, the monograph approaches Southern and Northern formations of displacement – in both their variation and their scalar connections – along the lines of Comaroff and Comaroff's (2012: 47, emphasis in the original) argument about the Global South, and, by extension, the Global North, as a *"relation, not a thing in and of itself."*

Interdisciplinarity: beyond a fragmented approach to refugees

There is no dearth of works on refugees, asylum seekers, migrants, and the geopolitics surrounding their categorization, movement, and enclosure (Collyer, 2016; Hyndman, 2000; Hyndman, 2012; Malkki, 1995; Mountz, 2011; Zetter, 1991, 2018). Indeed, with the advent of the Syrian "crisis," the media, academic work, and policy work have been inundated with information and analyses of refugees and migrants. There appears to be interesting divergences in terms of academic work on refugees. There are, for example, more technical, practical discussions about humanitarian protection – such as providing ICT, water, sanitation, and other services to refugees. There are also volumes written on refugees that tend to be dominated by refugee studies scholars, legal scholars, and migration experts who have spent a lifetime understanding the nuances of the system. These works have been foundational to understanding how the global system operates, how the humanitarian system has developed, and how that gets translated into the evolution of rights of refugees as well (Calhoun, 2010; Milner and Wojnarowicz, 2017). Then, there are discrete pieces of work in history, for example, which work specifically on displacement, refugees, and migrants, but do not label themselves as being part of refugee studies (Bau, 1985; Chatterji, 2011; Kaur, 2007; Zamindar, 2007). These historical analyses offer important insights into how the management of refugees, resistances to the production of refugee labels, and emergence of refugee, local, and state politics emerges. In other words, they offer contextual readings that provide a nuanced understanding of how different parts of the world have grappled with questions of displacement. However, in being technical–practical or location specific, what gets lost is a broader understanding of the global humanitarian system. These are only some examples of a larger pattern of fragmentation in refugee studies, which, together with the relative isolation of the literature on refugees from cutting-edge theoretical developments in different disciplines, limits our understanding of the role of displacement in historical and comparative perspectives.

Our aim, then, was to bring these fragmented conversations together in order to dissect the complexity of displacement as both an object of institutional experimentation from above (by state or international agencies) and an experience that, like other human experiences, is imbued with different, context-specific emotions, desires, and actions from below. Further, as we will discuss in the next section, by connecting these conversations, our goal was to unsettle analyses of refugees, migrants, and other displaced persons as being "bare life" – subject to systems of oppression that offer them no way out. Instead, we sought to connect refugees to other social actors; for example, the urban dwellers among whom they settle in different cities across the world. While of course no single author can address all the different structural and experiential features of displacement, the monograph strongly emphasizes how old and new phenomena of displacement – from the formation of refugee camps in the Global South, to the securitization of refuge and the increased turn toward decampment in many countries of the world – do not develop in a political–moral vacuum. On the contrary, these – at times contradictory – trajectories of displacement are connected to broader global and local processes of distribution and contestation of power and struggles for access to material and symbolic resources. Through this perspective, we approach refugee studies as inherently interdisciplinary and open to the cross-fertilization of ideas and conversations emerging within different disciplines. We build on and push forward initial interdisciplinary attempts at analytical integration, such as Michel Agier's (2011) extension of urban anthropology to refugee camps and Didier Fassin's (2015) approach to refugees through an emerging moral anthropology of the state. Our own work is also driven by this interdisciplinary sensibility. For example, in our research we have striven to bridge the study of displacement with debates about urban informality and marginality, about securitization and militarism, and about the relationship between morality and the law (Pasquetti, 2019, 2015a, 2015b; Pasquetti and Picker, 2017; Picker and Pasquetti, 2015; Sanyal, 2018, 2014, 2011).

This interdisciplinary sensibility emerges from each of the three sections of this monograph. The first section operates at the intersection of political geography, the sociology of the state, the history of imperialism, and studies of securitization. It builds on some of the emerging conversations in these disciplines – for example, on the link between imperial histories, "race," and the state – to dissect how state institutions experiment with legal categorization and management of refugees at different global and local levels. Oslender's Chapter 3 on Colombia shows the importance of bridging migration studies and works on "race," recognizing how struggles over the official categorization of displaced people are closely linked to struggles over racial categorization. Interdisciplinarity also runs through the second section of the monograph, which brings together geographers, anthropologists, and sociologists using ethnographic methodologies to enrich our understanding of the experiential dimension of displacement. This section takes seriously how displacement is negotiated in everyday life examining, for instance, the role of material objects, refugees' production of practical maps of mobility beyond the ones dictated by legal regulations, and their often-troubled relationships not only with institutional management from above but also with dominant ethnonational narratives that render them invisible or essentialize their identities.

Along similar lines, the third section straddles the boundaries between geography, urban studies, and sociology to examine how different actors, from law-enforcement agencies to humanitarian NGOs, use a variety of tools – formal and informal mechanisms – to manage humanitarian situations at different scales from the global, to the regional, to the urban. This concluding part also raises questions about how state and international actors relate to moral–political responsibility (theirs and that of others) as they become involved in the management of humanitarian aid across these different scales of intervention.

Theorizing displacement: productive and agentive approaches

Transnational and transregional dialogues, attention to historical trajectories and legacies, and efforts toward interdisciplinarity are conducive to new ways of producing conceptual knowledge about displacement that unsettles longstanding assumptions about refugees as passive victims whose lives are deprived of political and historical texture by all-powerful structures of power. Established theoretical sources typically theorize forced displacement as a destructive force for the social lives and political subjectivities of forced migrants (Kleinman et al., 1997), and conceptualize the management of displacement as a top-down disempowering process that approximates what happens in what Ervin Goffman (1990 [1968]) calls "total institutions." For example, Hannah Arendt (1973: 297) theorizes refugees as people that, together with legal citizenship, have lost a protective political community. She opposes the "thinness" of human rights to the supposedly more solid protection given by legal citizenship. Building on that and the work of Carl Schmidt and Walter Benjamin, and with a focus on space, Agamben ([1995] 1998) theorizes camp formations as spaces that extinguish political life. Whether wrapped in the Agambian and Foucauldian conceptual language of "bare life," "governmentality," and "biopower," or more recently, in the concept of "necropower" (borrowed from Achille Mbembe, 2003), this emphasis on passive victimhood runs through most attempts at theorizing structures and experiences of refuge. Equally troubling is the opposite romanticized assumption about refugees' ability to reverse power relations and re-appropriate the meanings of the categories imposed on them. What is missing is a more systematic theorization of the productive powers of displacement: for example, how it creates new legal–political and moral dilemmas for state and global actors; how it interacts with other processes such as urban development; and how it is negotiated by displaced people in different contexts (e.g., in refugee camps, in cities, on the move, in their relationships with other segments of "the global poor," in their interaction with humanitarian institutions, and law-enforcement agencies, etc.); and how it impacts people and institutions in old and new places of refuge. Given that there is rich empirical work on many of these issues, there is an urgent need to match this up with the rich theorization of refuge and refugee beyond "bare life."

These theoretical sources are still very much relevant today, as they draw attention to the difficulties that refugees face in negotiating their lives in the context of complex bureaucracies and in a world of nation-states and national passports where non-citizens are increasingly perceived through security lenses (Coutin, 2011; Feldman, 2015; Torpey, 2000). Yet, they are not well equipped for developing productive and agentic approaches to displacement. Thus, we have encouraged contributors to creatively engage in a theoretical dialogue with their empirical materials. We did not have specific political or social theories in mind – such as postcolonial theory or theories of practice – though, as we discuss below when we specify what we mean by "global conversations," we do see the importance of integrating postcolonial and decolonial debates in refugee studies. In his layered reflections on theories that cross borders and travel to other places, Edward Said (1991 [1983]: 226–47, 2001 [2000]: 436–52) argues that travel can either tame or make theory more transgressive. Following this view, we did not assume that certain theories were more appropriate than others but, conversely, we pushed contributors to elaborate on how and why certain concepts were useful for understanding their case studies.

Even just a cursory look at the concepts and theories used by our contribu-tors shows how productive our approach has been. Ulrich Oslender does build on Hannah Arendt's work, but he turns to her less-known theorization of "thoughtlessness" to make sense of how state bureaucracies process people, in his case internally displaced people (IDPs) in Colombia. He also refreshingly excavates the distinct experiences of African-Caribbean IDPs within the "thoughtless" Colombian bureaucratic system. While Oslender develops a theoretical approach to categorization and management of IDPs along ethnoracial lines, Chia Youyee Vang ties together the histories of war, imperialism, and refuge that run through the lives of Hmong refugees resettled in the United States in the 1970s and 1980s. Her Chapter 1 shows the promise of a postcolonial approach sensitive to the interplay between local and global histories within refugee studies.

In Chapter 4 on the Rohingya refugees in Bangladesh, Tazreena Sajjad looks at how the Bangladeshi state questions and rejects the protracted reception of new waves of Rohingya refugees in connection to the restrictive policies increasingly adopted by states in the Global North. Her chapter thus raises the question of how the securitization of refuge that crosses different regions of the world further reinforces itself as a global trend because states observe other states' practices and discourses. Southeast Asia, especially Thailand and Malaysia, is also the empirical terrain from which Pei Palmgren theorizes about state involvement in informal and even illegal practices of control and containment of Rohingya at both the national and the urban levels (Chapter 11). By doing so, he highlights the role of the state in informality and illegality, situating his work within emerging debates about "informality from above" and "legal consciousness" under conditions of marginality and oppression.

Two other examples include Diana Allan's (Chapter 5) theorization of Palestinian aquatic identities – that is, Palestinian identities, including refugee ones, that are rooted to the sea, rather than, as traditionally conceptualized, rooted to land – and Jonathan Darling's (Chapter 9) use of Roberto Esposito's concept of "immunology" to examine how political–moral and even legal responsibilities toward refugees are muted and rejected in the policy arena in the contemporary UK. Further, Chiara Denaro (Chapter 7) uses Albert Hirschman's concepts of "voice" and "exit" to examine how Syrian refugees strove to have their voice heard while in transit. Cathrine Brun and Ragne Øwre Thorshaug theorize the role of buildings and material objects in the lives of IDPs in Georgia in Chapter 6. Caroline Kihato and Loren Landau theorize in-visibility and "stealth humanitarianism" in marginalized localities of urban refuge in the Global South (Chapter 10). Ala Sirriyeh gives attention to age as an axis that increasingly marks "innocent" refugee bodies, separating them from other refugee bodies in the Global North (Chapter 2). Kostantina Isidoros engages with theories of globalization, interrogating global and local identities, boundaries, and interactions from the standpoint of Saharawi refugees in the Algerian desert (Chapter 8). She shows the global dimension of the Sahrawi subjectivities and politics as they are expressed in their interactions with other "global actors" such as the humanitarians who visit their camps. The Sahrawi people treat these humanitarians as "guests" in need of help and orientation within the unfamiliar and harsh physical–political terrain of the Algerian desert.

These are just some examples of how the chapters offer rich and creative theorizing about displacement. The result is that, rather than having an integrated theoretical framework, the monograph has an eclectic but ultimately stimulating collection of theoretical sources. We hope that the cumulative theoretical work we have produced will inspire refugee studies to be more receptive to new theoretical developments in the social sciences. In this view, the monograph is in dialogue with recent theorizing of displacement, humanitarianism, and refugee lives, such as Fassin's (2009, 2011, 2013, 2015) work on humanitarianism, the state, and morality (see, for example, Darling's Chapter 9 on the asylum dispersal system in the UK), Monika Krause's (2014) and Julian Go's (2016) work on transnationalism, field theory, and humanitarian interventions (see, for example, the chapters on the global, state, and urban levels of humanitarian interventions), and Lucy Mayblin (2017) and Gurminder Bhambra's (2017) research on the colonial–historical genealogies of humanitarian regimes of management (see, for example, the chapters on Hmong refugees in the US and refugee children in the UK).

Structure of the book

The book is divided into three thematic sections, each composed of chapters drawing on cases from both the Global South and the Global North. The first section – "Experiments of categorizing and control" – draws on a variety of methodologies including historical archives, ethnography, and textual analysis of official discourses to examine the categorization of refugees as an arena of struggle and contestation connected with broader processes of control at the urban, regional, and global levels. The section shows how the categorization of refugees and other forced migrants is tied to the formal and informal distribution of symbolic and material resources as well as to the mobilization of moralizing evaluative categories by state institutions and also humanitarian organizations. It also ties displacement to other axes of inclusion and exclusion such as "race," nationhood, and age.

The second section – "Inhabiting displacement and crafting futures" – shifts attention to the experiential dimension of displacement in different contexts across the Global South and the Global North as refugees and other forced migrants make sense and act upon the experiments of categorization and control imposed on them. This section is interdisciplinary but methodologically more homogenous as it is centered on ethnographic methodology. It excavates distinct relationships between displacement and landed identities, between forced migrants and material objects, and between global forms of activism and refugee voices and claims. This section nicely connects with recent development across the social sciences on human senses, political subjectivities, and affective–moral connection with landscapes of war and militarism and with material objects.

The final section of the book – "Scales of intervention" – again crosses the Global South and the Global North to excavate how the global and local interact: mutually influence each other, converge, or clash. This is not just an effort to map different regional and local case studies but also highlights how being attentive to interactions across scales of intervention helps us understand structures and experiences of displacement in both their continuities and changes. This section gives particular attention to the urban level, showing how looking at global and state actors from an urban perspective raises interesting questions about the involvement of institutional actors in informality and even illegality as well as about the language and scope of humanitarian interventions at a time of increasingly fragmented sources of marginality, poverty, and dispossession across the citizen–refugee divide.

Taken as a whole, the conversations within and across the three sections offer ways of thinking about refugees not only from a securitized perspective, but also through thinking about their agency in relation to that and taking into consideration the scales at which humanitarian, security, and other processes operate. While the individual chapters remain grounded in their contexts, they offer the opportunity to think about the issues around the management of refuge and the practice of everyday life among refugees as relational across scales, regions, and disciplinary boundaries.

Experiments of categorizing and control

The first section begins with Chia Youyee Vang's Chapter 1 on the resettlement of Hmong refugees in the US in the 1970s and 1980s. Vang notes how Hmong refugees from Laos had supported American troops in Vietnam. In the aftermath of the US loss in Southeast Asia, many were resettled as refugees in the US – a program through which the US attempted to help those who had supported their campaign in the region. However, the process was fraught in many ways. Attempts at trying to mold refugees into willing subjects through language and acculturation programs were met with difficulties and resistance. Refugees are often seen as "speechless emissaries" (Malkki, 1996) and this chapter questions that assumption through investigating various processes. Vang documents the process of including refugees in the rolls of those being resettled in the US. She notes, for example, that many refugees persuaded others to whom they were not related to add them to their reset-tlement applications as sisters or widows or children. In the US, many who came struggled to find work and "assimilate" into society. The assistance provided to them also increased the resentment of those in the US who were also struggling with poverty. However, as she shows, the Hmong were not voiceless, passive, and grateful recipients of support and resettlement. Rather, they tried to subvert the system in different ways, including by refusing to take on jobs they were unhappy with and enrolling for welfare instead. The chapter highlights the complex nature of refugee resettlement in the US, illuminating not only the geopolitics of refugee resettlement schemes, but also how, when such programs are put into practice, they do not merely produce docile bodies, but rather create varied and often resistant subjects.

In Chapter 2 titled "Niche openings and compassionate exclusion: the reception of refugee children in the UK" Alaa Sirriyeh draws on the concept of "niche openings" to explore how the category of children is deployed in the increasingly restrictive asylum system in the UK. Her chapter shows how the UK has had a longer history of protecting children – for example, the Kindertransporters during the Second World War. The British have also exhibited a certain compassion for children, paying particular attention to their innocence and vulnerability. Children and childhood are seen to be categories and phases in life that ought to be protected, particularly in times of crises such as conflicts. Sirriyeh's chapter, however, draws attention to the varied ways in which the term children is understood. On the one hand, with the tragic death of toddler Aylan Kurdi, and the media's compassionate response to it, there was greater commitment by the British government (in principle) to bring child refugees into the UK and resettle them. On the other hand, Sirriyeh notes the complexities of understanding what a child is within these narratives. She notes how the imagination of a "child" is one that is younger, more vulnerable, versus many of the minors who have come over who are in their teens and are viewed with greater suspicion and contempt. Thus teenagers, who are still minors, occupy a precarious position, where they are legally classified as children and are vulnerable, but lack the social support by asylum-providing countries like the UK who see them as being less deserving than those who would be considerably younger and in supposedly greater need of protection. Sirriyeh's chapter thus offers a glimpse into the niche openings available to children looking for asylum in host countries, but is tempered through a sobering look at the laws and regulations that affect child protection regimes and general social attitudes towards children.

In Chapter 3 of this section, "The banality of displacement: re-reading Hannah Arendt to instil critical thought in the Colombian refugee crisis," Ulrich Oslender draws on Arendt's work on the banality of evil to construct a powerful critique of how the system of management of refugees and IDPs fails to take into consideration the many facets of their identities, especially in terms of their ethnoracial membership. Oslender engages in a critical reflection of the idea of banality, noting that as Arendt envisioned it, it was not about the commonplace or mundane but rather about thoughtlessness – specifically lacking critical thought. He argues that this thoughtlessness is not something that is simply there, but rather it is something that is actively produced. Oslender critiques the IDP protection system operating in Colombia in the process of developing his argument around the thoughtlessness that is embedded in the system. He argues that it is not just the violence of conflict that is thoughtless, but also the system of registration, the bureaucracy around the recognition of IDP status, and the provision of support that have at their heart institutional thoughtlessness that is problematic. For starters, there is the numbers game, where IDPs are reduced to figures and thus lose their complex identities. These numbers of IDPs are hotly disputed between the state, which attempts to play them down, and the non-governmental organizations (NGOs) such as the Consultancy for Human Rights and Displacement (CODHES), which indicate higher numbers. Second, he points out that while the constitution in Colombia recognizes African-Caribbeans as ethnoracial minorities in the country, figures collected about IDPs fail to account for ethnoracial differences. As a result, as he notes, *campesinos*, fisherfolks, black, indigenous, or *mestizo* – very varied groups of people – are subsumed under a single umbrella of IDP. Few, if any, statistics are kept on their ethnic differences. Thus, the system that attempts to protect IDPs in fact fails them. A useful illustration of this point is made through his discussion of diet – the provision of food for IDPs and the food that is provided which is not in line with the diet they are used to. Part of this stems from the fact that no data is available to know which ethnic group IDPs come from and thus to tailor humanitarian support accordingly. This brings us back to questions that lie at the heart of the humanitarian project. As recipients of humanitarian aid, are refugees only meant to be grateful and submissive? This is a question that Vang has also raised through her work in Chapter 1. What does it take for us to see refugees as unique humans and provide responses that are in line with that recognition? How do we, through our practice and academic work, re-humanize refugees and move away from a rhetoric in which they are seen to be nothing more than recipients of aid? This requires us to think about agency and identity more critically.

The first section concludes with Chapter 4 titled "Refugees welcome? The politics of repatriation and return in a global era of security." In this chapter, Tazreena Sajjad offers a refreshing Southern perspective on the debates about "crimmigration" and "securitization" of migration that are often centered on Northern states. She draws our attention to the politics of hosting refugees among Global South countries in an era of growing security concerns and the diminishing power of the UN to protect the rights of refugees. In particular, she focuses on how Bangladesh has hosted the Rohingya over the last several decades as Myanmar has engaged in repeated ethnic cleansing practices against them. Like other scholars working on the politics of hosting refugees in the Global South, such as B.S. Chimni, Sajjad draws our attention to the unevenness of the global humanitarian system whereby those countries who are often least equipped to host large numbers of refugees find themselves doing so over long periods of time (Chimni, 2000). This has become even more apparent since the end of the Cold War as refugees have begun to carry less and less political value. While countries in the Global South are tasked with hosting large numbers of refugees, their security concerns tend to be overlooked while those of countries in the Global North are amplified. The

UN, which is dependent on funding from donor countries in the Global North, plays a role in perpetuating this uneven system. What then do these countries in the Global South do? As with the work by Palmgren, Sajjad draws our attention to the questionable practices of states in the Global South. She looks at how, in countries such as Bangladesh – which has hosted Rohingyas since the 1980s – there are attempts to try to limit the numbers of refugees or repatriate them or resettle them in geographically problematic areas. As a result of the diminishing power of the UN, a change in the geopolitical landscape of the world, and the emphasis on security concerns, the rights of refugees continue to be eroded.

Inhabiting displacement and crafting futures

The first chapter of the second section focuses on the case of displaced Palestinians. In Chapter 5 titled "At sea: maritime Palestine displaced," Diana Allan takes us through a critical understanding of Palestinian identity and displacement and its relationship to the sea in her exquisitely written ethnographic chapter. Here, she challenges normative understandings of Palestinian refugees as coming from farming backgrounds (*fellaheen*), and shows us instead the lives of Palestinian refugees who were fishermen who were displaced to Lebanon. Her work not only illuminates the close relationship – both personal and professional – of these communities to the sea, but also the complex political negotiations they have to engage with in order to continue their trades and indeed stake a claim to territory through their nautical understandings. In a particularly telling example, she talks about how these fishermen have an intimate understand of the aquatic terrain, honed through generations of working in these trades, and how these are then mobilized to challenge other forms of territorial knowledge and disputes over having illegally crossed international waters. Allan's work is not only an original contribution to the understanding of Palestinian identity, but also of rethinking the identity of Palestinian refugees as *landed*. It offers an important lens with which to understand the geographies of forced migration, lending itself to the critical development of pathways taken to refuge (aquatic), the spaces of exile (as she notes, to move away from imagining refuge to be in the camp), and the kinds of work done in refuge (fishing and other maritime activities). As she notes "This chapter is a tentative attempt to reclaim and reconnect experiences of exodus, labor and resistance at sea – crosscutting past and present – through a body of water, where fishing is both subject and method." Indeed, as she asks, "What might forgotten Palestinian histories of maritime displacement yield?" In fact, such a question can and perhaps should be asked of many other displacements in various parts of the world.

In their Chapter 6 titled "Privatized housing and never-ending displacement: the temporality of dwelling for displaced Georgians," Cathrine Brun and Ragne Øwre Thorshaug explore displacement through a critical analysis of materiality and homemaking practices among internally displaced persons from Abkhazia to Georgia. Looking at collective shelters which until 2009 were used by the state to house IDPs, and were then privatized, the authors "analyze the experience of what happens when the status of the material shelter that forced migrants occupy changes from temporary to permanent living spaces through privatization, but people's displacement statuses do not change accordingly." These buildings are inhabited by IDPs, but they have been privatized since 2009 and so are no longer IDP housing but private residential structures like any other in cities like Tbilisi. The Georgian state allowed the privatization of the housing but did not change the status of the residents from IDPs to citizens as they continue to clash with Abkhazia over the latter's independence. The buildings and their residents play a key role in the continuation of claims of Georgia over the Abkhaz region.

Despite the status change of the buildings from IDP shelters into private buildings, they continue to be seen as IDP buildings. Their categorization as such impacts the ways in which the residents are imagined by those on the outside. As spaces that were built for other purposes – as hospitals, dormitories, and so forth – the afterlives of these shelters as "durable" housing solutions that exist in a gray space between permanent and temporary, as IDP shelters and private spaces, have considerable effects on residents. The authors discuss the clashing temporalities of the past lives of these structures and their current incarnations. The dwelling spaces themselves, being small and concentrating all activities from eating and sleeping to entertaining into often a single room, also present clashing temporalities for the residents. Through a careful analysis of privatization and homemaking practices, and bringing in this critical dimension of time, the authors deftly offer a critical analysis of the materiality of displacement and the ways in which it affects social lives and the experiences of displacement.

In Chapter 7, titled "Voice through exit: Syrian refugees at the borders of Europe and the struggle to choose where to live," Chiara Denaro draws our attention to how Syrian refugee voices emerged during their migration out of Syria towards Europe. Denaro draws on Albert Hirschman's paradigm of "Exit, voice and loyalty" together with the autonomy of migration theory, subaltern studies, and critical citizenship studies to engage in this analysis. She argues that limited attention is paid to the voices of migrants in transit, but by doing so it is possible to break down the binaries between forced and voluntary migration and this contributes to the recognition of agency and political subjectivity among forced migrants. In her work, she critically interrogates the emergence of voices of refugees who have engaged in protests and turned to digital and social media to document their lives and have their voices and demands heard, revealing the myriad ways in which refugees exercise agency, challenge the structures that seek to contain and push them back, and stake claims to the right to move to where they feel safe. Her work falls into a larger landscape of critical geopolitical work that shows the varied actors involved in the management of the migration and how migrants themselves can shape the geopolitics of migration control. It also calls our attention to *how* we pay attention to voices. Why do we imagine refugees and asylum seekers to be voiceless or speechless? By whom is this voice or speech not heard? In other words, is there an intellectual imperialism at work when we claim that certain people are unable to "speak"? How can we decolonize our understanding of migrants, refugees, and asylum seekers by paying attention to the quotidian ways in which they make their voices heard and by co-producing knowledge (Siddiqui, 2018)?

In the last chapter of this section (Chapter 8), titled "The global refugee camp: coinciding locales of refuge among Sahrawi refugees in North Africa," Kostantina Isidoros draws on her long-term fieldwork among the Sahrawi people living in refugee camps in the Algerian desert to examine the mutual perceptions and social interactions between the Sahrawi people and the humanitarians visiting them. She highlights the intricate interplay of legal, spatial, and political meanings variably attached to categories such as "nomads," "refugees," "citizens," and "statehood" in such perceptions and interactions. In the process, she unsettles dominant assumptions about what and who is "local" and what and who is "global." She also problematizes assumptions about the relative distribution of vulnerability and agentic power in the encounters she observed in the Algerian desert. Indeed, in her chapter, the "global" humanitarians come across as in need of orientation and reassurance as they negotiate the difficult geopolitical terrain of the Algerian desert. Further, her findings show a certain tension traversing the interactions between the Sahrawi people and the humanitarians: the former greet the humanitarians in their camps as socio-spatial formations of statehood-in-waiting, while the latter experience the camps as (probably temporary) harsh spaces in need of humanitarian aid. Ultimately, the chapter proposes and offers an example of how ethnography can be used to study humanitarian interventions as they are experienced on the ground. In doing so, it nicely introduces the third and concluding section of the book.

Scale of intervention

The third section begins with Jonathan Darling's Chapter 9 titled "Out-sourcing refuge: distance, deferral, and immunity in the urban governance of refugees." In this chapter, Darling draws on Esposito's work on immunitary logics to critically examine practices of refugee protection and support generally, but the UK's asylum accommodation system in particular. Darling discusses Esposito's work which develops the interplay between community and immunity. Darling argues that this is central to understanding borders, identity, and difference and responses to refugee reception more generally. Where community is founded on bounding members together, and community is experienced as a risk to the self, immunity operates on a somewhat opposite but complementary logic. As he notes: "immunity enables the individual to defend and retain their self-identity against the exposure of *communitas* and its binds of duty." Immunity involves selective inclusion and as such "presents a distinct relation to otherness, one that seeks to protect and retain self-identity through the selective incorporation, pre-emption, and neutralisation of threats. It is this combination that Esposito (2008) argues makes immunity a fundamental logic behind biopolitical interventions in humanitarianism, the war on terror, and the politics of migration." With this conceptual background in place, Darling goes on to discuss the functioning of the asylum system in the UK. He uses three different ways to expose the immunitary workings of the state: through "practices of distancing, the deferral of responsibility, and the privatization of state functions, each serve to produce immunitary borders within and beyond the territorial limits of the nation-state." He notes how the accommodation system has been privatized and managed by private organizations such as G4S and other subcontractors; how asylum seekers can no longer choose where to live, but rather are put through a central processing system that assigns them housing in different locations. As with other scholars (Gill, 2009), Darling notes how asylum seekers are shifted around breaking social bonds. He discusses how accommodation is provided in locations that have high levels of deprivation. All these processes affect not just the growing marginalization of asylum seekers but also bring into the sharp relief the overlaying of asylum spaces on spaces and populations facing poverty. This presents important social and political questions about the marginalization of subjects. Can we begin to develop a radical critique of neoliberalism and securitization on the one hand and inequality and marginality on the other by bringing together the critical discussions around urban poor and refugees, and asylum seekers? Rather than seeing these groups as conflictual, is it possible to bind them in discourses of solidarity that would provide robust critiques of the state and the state system more generally?

Secondly, in their Chapter 10 titled "Visibilising suffering or stealth humanitarianism? The perils of promoting durable protection in cities of the south," Caroline Kihato and Loren Landau draw our attention to the complexities of protecting refugees and their rights within urban environments. As refugee crises become increasingly urbanized, protecting refugees becomes more complex. Unlike camp settings, urban environments are spatially fragmented and subject to various financial and political changes that are linked to, yet distinct from, those at the scale of the nation state. In cities in the Global South where much of urban displacement takes place, protecting refugees can be highly varied and subject to the whims of local communities and power brokers. Here, refugees share the same kinds of socio-economic struggles as the urban poor; therefore, privileging one over the other can cause tensions and resentments among the local communities. Kihato and Landau point out that in such a condition, insisting on formulaic, rights-based approaches may be counter-productive. Rather, humanitarian organizations are better off working more stealthily with local organizations, including state institutions, to insert protections for refugees into local by-laws. This requires organizations to understand local power dynamics, be willing to be flexible, and work to produce small, incremental changes. This may not be the kind of model that donors seek when funding humanitarian responses, but in an increasingly urban and dynamic world, we perhaps need to abandon earlier models of protection and adopt tactics that tap into the needs and interests of local communities. This is perhaps one of the only ways in which to protect refugees in urban spaces. As such their intervention raises some important questions for academics and practitioners. For example, they draw our attention to invisibilization as a tactic of survival. Indeed, as Palmgren's chapter also shows, being visible as a refugee in an urban environment where rights are limited and/or unevenly enforced may come at great cost – financially and socially. Instead, there may be more acceptance for refugees among local populations if the state simply looks the other way, as Kihato and Landau demonstrate. Further, their work raises questions about rights to the city – how in fact do refugees exercise these if their presence even among the urban poor is so deeply contested? Do we ever reach a moment when the rights of refugees can be demanded in an urban environment where poverty and marginalization are deeply entrenched?

Finally, in Chapter 11, titled "Onward pushes and negotiated refuge: theorizing the fluid national and urban regimes of forced migration in Southeast Asia," Pei Palmgren critically analyzes the complex and informal nature of refugee protection in Southeast Asia. Palmgren specifically looks at Thailand and Malaysia and uses the discussion of Rohingya refugees to illuminate the different ways in which the state colludes with people smugglers and others in clandestinely pushing Rohingya refugees into Malaysia. The crackdown on these practices clearly reveals how deeply involved the Thai state is with these practices. However, it is not just at the level of people smuggling that the state is complicit. Rather, looking at the ambiguous and patchy nature of refugee protection in Southeast Asia, where there is no recognition of refugee status and protection of it either (except non-refoulement), Palmgren reveals how the state is involved in the continuous marginalization and oppression of Rohingya refugees. For example, he shows how urban refugees are constantly extorted by policemen as well as local communities in cities such as Kuala Lumpur and the significant income that goes toward paying these bribes in exchange for not being detained. UNHCR documentation does not hold much authority, if any, in these places. Palmgren thus shows how the legality and enforcement of refugee rights differs at different scales – from the scale of the state to that of the urban. In doing so, he draws our attention to the scalar nature of the law and the need to pay attention to that. Further, his work continues a longer tradition of critical work around the ad hoc nature of law enforcement and the lack of protection and rights that many refugees are subject to in different parts of the world (Campbell, 2006; Coddington, 2018; Sanyal, 2018). These works reveal how the lack of legal frameworks creates socially and economically precarious situations for refugees who are compelled to work in the informal economy for longer hours and lower wages; in other words, their labor is continually exploited. Thus, as Pasquetti and Picker (2017) note, informality becomes a form of confinement. We may ask how thinking about legal ambiguity and ad hoc policing changes our understanding of refugee subjectivity, especially in situations of protracted crises.

Notes

1 While Mignolo (2018: 149) calls for a conceptual movement "past the disciplines" rather than toward interdisciplinarity (which, according to him, "depends on maintaining the disciplines"), as we discuss in this Introduction, interdisciplinarity seems a crucial step toward delinking refugee studies from its still dominant Eurocentric assumptions, thus strengthening cross-regional dialogues about rights, justice, and historical legacies of imperialism and colonialism within its overly fragmented field.
2 With "subjugated knowledges" (e.g., Collins, 1990; Mignolo, 2000), we refer to those types of knowledge produced by and circulating among marginalized groups and places. These knowledges are "enunciations" that are not recognized as legitimate enunciations with global power structures and, as a result, they are often pushed toward the realm of emotionality and away from the presumed lack of emotionality of dominant epistemological perspectives.

References

Agamben, G. [1995] (1998), *Homo Sacer: Sovereign Power and Bare Life* (Stanford: Stanford University Press).

Agier, M. (2011), *Managing the Undesirables: Refugee Camps and Humanitarian Government* (Cambridge: Polity Press).

Arendt, H. (1973), *The Origins of Totalitarianism* (New York: Harcourt Brace Jovanovich).

Bagelman, J.J. (2016), Still waiting: security, temporality, population. In *Sanctuary City: A Suspended State, Mobility & Politics* (London: Palgrave Pivot) pp. 94–104.

Bau, I. (1985), *This Ground is Holy: Church Sanctuary and Central American Refugees* (New York: Paulist Press).

Bhambra, G. (2017), The current crises of Europe: refugees, colonialism, and the limits of cosmopolitanism. *European Law Journal* 23(5): 395–405.

Bloch, A. and G. Dona (eds) (2018), *Forced Migration: Current Issues and Debates* (London: Routledge).

Calhoun, C. (2010), The idea of emergency: humanitarian action and global (dis) order. In Fassin, D. and M. Pandolfi (eds) *Contemporary States of Emergency: The Politics of Military and Humanitarian Interventions* (New York: Zone Books), pp. 29–58.

Campbell, E.H. (2006), Urban refugees in Nairobi: problems of protection, mechanisms of survival, and possibilities for integration. *Journal of Refugee Studies* 19: 396–413.

Chatterji, J. (2011), *The Spoils of Partition: Bengal and India, 1947–1967*, Reissue edition (Cambridge: Cambridge University Press).

Chimni, B.S. (2000), Globalization, humanitarianism and the erosion of refugee protection. *Journal of Refugee Studies* 13: 243–263.

Coddington, K. (2018), Landscapes of refugee protection. *Transactions of the Institute of British Geographers* 43(3): 326–340.

Collins, P.H. (1990), *Black Feminist Thought* (London: Routledge).

Collyer, M. (2016), Geopolitics as a migration governance strategy: European Union bilateral relations with Southern Mediterranean countries. *Journal of Ethnic and Migration Studies* 42(4): 606–624.

Comaroff, J. and J. Comaroff (2012), *Theory from the South: Or, How Euro-America is Evolving toward Africa* (Boulder: Paradigm Publishers).

Coutin, S.B. (2011), The rights of non-citizens. *Annual Review of Law and Social Science* 7: 289–308.

Darling, J. (2010), A city of sanctuary: the relational re-imagining of Sheffield's asylum politics. *Transactions of the Institute of British Geographers* 35: 125–140.

Darling, J. (2009), Becoming bare life: asylum, hospitality, and the politics of encampment. *Environment and Planning D* 27: 649–665.

Fassin, D. (ed.) (2015), *At the Heart of the State: The Moral World of Institutions* (Chicago: Chicago University Press).

Fassin, D. (2013), On resentment and ressentiment: the politics and ethics of moral emotions. *Current Anthropology* 54(3): 249–267.

Fassin, D. (2011), A contribution to the critique of moral reason. *Anthropological Theory* 11: 481–491.

Fassin, D. (2009), Les économies morales revisitées [Revisiting moral economies]. *Annales. Histoire, Sciences Sociales*: 1237–1266.

Feldman, I. (2018), *Life Lived in Relief: Humanitarian Predicaments and Palestinian Refugee Politics* (Berkeley: University of California Press).

Feldman, I. (2015), What is a camp? Legitimate refugee lives in spaces of long-term displacement. *Geoforum* 66: 244–252.

Fiddian-Qasmiyeh, L. and S. Long (eds) (2014), *The Oxford Handbook of Refugee and Forced Migration Studies* (Oxford: Oxford University Press).

Fitzgerald, D. (2019), *Refuge beyond Reach: How Rich Democracies Repel Asylum Seekers* (Oxford: Oxford University Press).

Fitzgerald, S.D. and R. Arar. (2018), The sociology of refugee migration. *Annual Review of Sociology* 44: 387–406.

Fraser, N. and A. Honneth. (2003), *Redistribution or Recognition? A Political-Philosophical Exchange* (London: Verso).

Gieryn, T. (2000), A space for place in sociology. *Annual Review of Sociology* 26: 463–496.

Gill, N. (2009), Longing for stillness: the forced movement of asylum seekers. *MC Journal: A Journal of Media and Culture* 12(1): 10–15.

Go, J. and M. Krause. (2016), *Fielding Transnationalism*. Sociological Review Monograph. (Malden: Wiley-Blackwell).

Goffman E. (1990) [1968], *Asylums: Essays on the Social Situation of Mental Patients and Other Inmates* (London: Bantam Doubleday Publishing Group).

Hyndman, J. (2012), The geopolitics of migration and mobility. *Geopolitics* 17(2): 243–255.

Hyndman, J. (2000), *Managing Displacement: Refugees and the Politics of Humanitarianism* (Minneapolis: University of Minnesota Press).

Hyndman, J. and Giles, W. (2011), Waiting for what? The feminization of asylum in protracted situations. *Gender, Place & Culture* 18: 361–379.

Hyndman, J. and Mountz, A. (2008), Another brick in the wall? Neo-refoulement and the externalization of asylum by Australia and Europe. *Government and Opposition* 43: 249–269.

Kaur, R. (2007), *Since 1947: Partition Narratives among Punjabi Migrants of Delhi* (New Delhi; New York: Oxford University Press).

Kleinman, A., V. Das, and M. Lock. (eds) (1997), *Social Suffering* (Berkeley: University of California Press).

Krause, M. (2014), *The Good Project: Humanitarian Relief NGOs and the Fragmentation of Reason* (Chicago: Chicago University Press).

Landau, L.B. (2018), Displacement and the pursuit of urban protection: forced migration, fluidity and global cities. In Bloch, A. and G. Dona (eds) *Forced Migration: Current Issues and Debates* (London: Routledge), pp. 106–125.

Malkki, L.H. (1996), Speechless emissaries: refugees, humanitarianism, and dehistoricization. *Cultural Anthropology* 11: 377–404.

Malkki, L.H. (1995), *Purity and Exile: Violence, Memory, and National Cosmology among Hutu Refugees in Tanzania* (Chicago: University of Chicago Press).

Martin, L.L. (2012), 'Catch and remove': detention, deterrence, and discipline in US noncitizen family detention practice. *Geopolitics* 17: 312–334.

Massey, D. (2002), Globalization: what does it mean for Geography? *Geography* 87(4): 293–296.

Mayblin, L. (2017), *Asylum After Empire: Colonial Legacies in the Politics of Asylum Seeking* (London: Rowman and Littlefield International).

Mountz, A. (2011), The enforcement archipelago: detention, haunting, and asylum on islands. *Political Geography* 30(3): 118–128.

Mbembe, A. (2003), Necropolitics. *Public Culture* 15(1): 11–40.

Mignolo, W. (2000), *Local Histories/Global Designs: Coloniality, Subaltern Knowledges, and Border Thinking* (Princeton: Princeton University Press).

Mignolo, W. (2018), *On Decoloniality: Concepts, Analytics, Praxis* (Durham, NC: Duke University Press).

Milner, J. and K. Wojnarowicz (2017), Power in the global refugee regime: understanding expressions and experiences of power in global and local contexts. *Refuge: Canada's Journal on Refugees* 33: 7–17.

Mountz, A., K. Coddington, R.T. Catania, and J.M. Loyd (2013), Conceptualizing detention: mobility, containment, bordering, and exclusion. *Progress in Human Geography* 37: 522–541.

Moran, D., J. Turner, and A.K. Schliehe (2018), Conceptualizing the carceral in carceral geography. *Progress in Human Geography* 42(5): 666–686.

Noxolo, P. (2017), Introduction: decolonising geographical knowledge in a colonised and re-colonising postcolonial world. *Area* 49(3): 317–319.

Pasquetti, S. (2019), Experiences of urban militarism: spatial stigma, ruins, and everyday life. *International Journal of Urban and Regional Research* 43(5): 848–869.

Pasquetti, S. (2015a), Negotiating control: camps, cities, and political life. *City* 19: 702–713.

Pasquetti, S. (2015b), Subordination and dispositions: Palestinians' differing sense of justice, politics, and morality. *Theory & Society* 44(1): 1–31.

Pasquetti, S. and Picker, G. (2017), Confined informality: global margins, statecraft, and urban life. *International Sociology* 32: 532–544.

Picker, G. and Pasquetti, S. (2015), Durable camps: the state, the urban, the everyday. *City* 19: 681–688.

Ramadan, A. (2013), Spatialising the refugee camp. *Transactions of the Institute of British Geographers* 38: 65–77.

Said, E. 2001 [2000], *Reflections on Exile and Other Literary and Cultural Essays* (Cambridge, MA: Harvard University Press).

Said, E. 1991 [1983], *The World, the Text, and the Critic* (Cambridge, MA: Harvard University Press).

Sanyal, R. (2018), Managing through ad hoc measures: Syrian refugees and the politics of waiting in Lebanon. *Political Geography* 66: 67–75.

Sanyal, R. (2014), Urbanizing refuge: interrogating spaces of displacement. *International Journal of Urban and Regional Research* 38: 558–572.

Sanyal, R. (2011), Squatting in camps building and insurgency in spaces of refuge. *Urban Studies* 48: 877–890.

Siddiqui, A.I. (2018), Writing with: togethering, difference, and feminist architectural histories of migration [online] https://www.e-flux.com/architecture/structural-instability/208707/writing-with/ [accessed 17 April, 2019].

Torpey J. (2000), *The Invention of the Passport* (Cambridge: Cambridge University Press).

Tsing, A. (2005), *Friction: An Ethnography of Global Connection* (Princeton: Princeton University Press).

Zamindar, V.F.-Y. (2007), *The Long Partition and the Making of Modern South Asia: Refugees, Boundaries, Histories* (New York: Columbia University Press).

Zetter, R. (2018), Conceptualising forced migration: praxis, scholarship and empirics. In Bloch, A. and G. Dona (eds) *Forced Migration: Current Issues and Debates* (London: Routledge), pp. 19–43.

Zetter, R. (1991), Labelling refugees: forming and transforming a bureaucratic identity. *Journal of Refugee Studies* 4: 39–62.

Part I

Experiments of categorizing and control

1

Creating proper subjects: the politics of Hmong refugee resettlement in the United States

Chia Youyee Vang

In March 1986, Kao Xiong anxiously awaited the arrival of his cousin, Ka Neng Xiong, at the Minneapolis-St. Paul International Airport. An International Institute of Minnesota (IIM) bilingual caseworker accompanied him to welcome Ka Neng, Ka Neng's wife La, and their five children. Ninety days after arrival, the parents' employment situation looked grim. In describing the couple's progress toward self-sufficiency, the caseworker noted that Ka Neng was "motivated to take a job, but is concerned that he find [sic] one by which he can feed his entire family." La "will be busy with her children for some time yet," the caseworker added. "I recommend that she get in English classes as soon as possible [so she can eventually take a job]."[1] Ka Neng and La were among the nearly 200,000 Hmong from Laos who fled following the Vietnam War. With no prior migration history to the Western hemisphere, Hmong presence in the United States is intimately tied to their ethnic group's entanglement with US military projects in Southeast Asia in the post-Second World War era. The majority of refugees were transformed from self-sufficient villagers to traumatized, stateless exiles dependent on the assistance of international agencies.

This chapter critiques the ways in which US refugee resettlement law and practices regulate Hmong refugee lives in order to make them the perfect low-wage employee. I demonstrate that state-centered discourses about refugees show little concern with the actual experiences and desires of refugees themselves. Since the international humanitarian regime fashions the modern refugee as a passive and traumatized object of intervention, the ideal refugee needs to conform to this characterization (Gatrell, 2013: 8). Therefore, the ideal refugee is a hard worker that is not only optimistic and grateful but also non-hostile.

Methodology and theoretical framework

As a result of the nature of forced migration and their agrarian background, refugees like the Hmong leave few publicly accessible paper trails. Those who arrived in the United States came with many official documents first created in refugee camps in Thailand by United Nations High Commissioner for Refugees (UNHCR) representatives. Their documented history often began in the refugee camp, a modern site of enumeration, categorization, and assessment by officials and relief workers (Gatrell, 2013: 9). Since most persons in the camps had little or no previous personal identity records, camp registration was frequently their only form of documentation.[2] Recently arrived refugees in the camps were tasked with estimating birth dates for family members and determining who should be included on a family application. As they traveled across the globe, they collected more papers that would be used to determine their eligibility for a plethora of social services. These materials prepared by social service providers comprise the bulk of what is archived and available for scholarly study. Other records that they may have of their journeys across multiple national borders remain either in their own homes, collecting dust in basements, or are tossed into the trash.

To perform what historian Antoinette Burton refers to as a "critical engagement with the past," I examine refugee resettlement records produced by state institutions at the international and national levels and materials created by non-state institutions that administer state policies and programs (Burton, 2005: 21). The available documents not only shape scholarly understanding of conditions, but are also a particular kind of documentation of governmentality. Drawing from Michel Foucault's discussion of "bio-power," anthropologist Aihwa Ong demonstrated in her study of Cambodian refugees that the modern liberal state's "power over life is exercised with the purpose of producing subjects who are healthy and productive" through the state's various technologies of control (Ong, 2003: 8). Government regulations of the refugee body and mind via the multitude of forms specified strategies necessary to transform refugee subjects from displaced victims of war into self-supporting citizens.

Because so much of the archive represents the perspectives of social service providers and camp registration officials, refugee thoughts and feelings about the resettlement process are generally absent. The contents in the case files provide little evidence of refugee agency, but they reveal much about the systems in place to "rescue" and process them. Thus, my reading of the files centers on the different forms of government regulation and subject making. A close examination of the records reveals subtle refugee resistance to government attempts to categorize them into particular subjects and to control their lives via dispersal resettlement policies (Burton, 2005: 7–8). To demonstrate that both subjectivity and agency occurred in the refugee resettlement process, oral histories conducted with former refugees are juxtaposed with data mined from the case records.

This process enables the consideration of refugees not "as helpless victims of forces beyond their control but 'survivors' who create something out of their crisis." (Richmond, 1988: 18). It was precisely their active resistance to dispersal refugee policies that resulted in the establishment of ethnic enclaves in locations such as California, Minnesota, and Wisconsin, a consequence that refugee laws were designed to prevent at the onset of Southeast Asian refugee resettlement in the mid 1970s. For example, refugees were sponsored by individuals and faith-based organizations to small towns and urban cities. Soon after arrival, many moved to join relatives and co-ethics in other locations, often against the wishes of sponsors and resettlement agencies.

In examining resettlement records, I illustrate how state institutions are not neutral but, as anthropologist and sociologist Didier Fassin argued, are imbued with affect, memories, anxieties, and moralities. Professionals representing the state operate in an ideological environment and under regulatory constraints that require them to deal with each case through evaluations and emotions to pass on judgments on what is a true refugee (Fassin et al., 2015: 10). Documents and papers prepared by the agents of the state play a revealing role in how civil servants view refugees. Professionals who implement the policies of the state simultaneously transform or reinvent them (Fassin et al., 2015: 255). Historian Peter Gatrell concluded that "[time] and again, the terms of the conversation are set not by rank and file refugees but by those who speak and act on their behalf and whose programmes dominate the institutional record. No matter how good their intentions, the appropriation of refugee experience is deeply ironic" (Gatrell, 2013: 296). As social anthropologist Yael Navaro-Yashin demonstrated, state practices appear much more ordinary when studied at the scale of the everyday. Articulating affects discharged by institutions, their objects, and practices, she writes, "We can conceive of institutions as having nerves or tempers or, alternatively, as having calming and quieting effects. We can study documents as charged with affect: documents that induce fear; others that inflict confidence; and likewise, those that transmit apathy among those who use them" (Navaro-Yashin, 2012: 33). My examination of the International Institute of Minnesota (IIM) case files allows us to explore non-state practices of governance as resettlement agencies work to create desirable refugee subjects. The records reveal that agencies' implementation of government regulations and surveillance of refugees reflected and reinforced Americans' anxieties about immigration, race, and welfare dependency. More specifically, refugees' acts of subversion/resistance to resettlement agencies' proper subject creation challenged caseworkers' sensibilities and dispositions in the broader context of past imperial entanglements with Southeast Asia and contemporary racial assumptions and anxieties.

Hmong entanglement in Cold War politics

The Hmong are one of the many groups whose entanglement in Cold War politics resulted in their forced migration to the United States and other

Western nations. Tracing their historical roots to southern China, they had migrated in significant numbers to the Indochinese Peninsula in the mid to late 1800s (Michaud, 1997: 119–30; Michaud and Culas, 2004: 61–96). They lived among the many ethnic minorities who occupied the highland areas in present day Vietnam, Laos, and Thailand, and interacted with the ruling regimes when it benefited them (Scott, 2009: 18). Their isolation from the larger societies in which they lived did not make them immune to the greater political and military transformations of the nineteenth and twentieth centuries. The divide and conquer practices instituted by French colonial administrators gave the Hmong in Laos their first experience of the benefits of aligning with an imperial power. Division within their ethnic group intensified as some collaborated with the French while others aligned with nationalists fighting to end colonial domination. This contentious situation further expanded as French colonial rule in Indochina ended in 1954 and US interests in the region increased as part of the growing Cold War rivalry. Although Lao neutrality was declared in 1954 and further solidified in 1962, the people of Laos were pulled into the war as a result of larger US military developments in Vietnam.

Because of its strategic location, both the United States and North Vietnam used Lao territory to stage their military campaigns. The Hmong, who had previously collaborated with the French, took part in US covert operations from 1961 to 1973 against communist forces. Numbering a few hundred in the early 1960s but growing to more than 40,000 by the late 1960s, the Hmong clandestine army supplied and supported by the US Central Intelligence Agency (CIA) faced severe losses. Similar to the predicament of Iraqi and Afghani translators who worked for Western forces, the Hmong who had aligned with Americans faced retribution following US disengagement from Southeast Asia. While the translators were struggling to seek refuge, Hmong were characterized by civilian and military leaders as "America's most loyal allies" for their role in support of the US military, and their resulting suffering due to US enemies recognized them as worth rescuing. Two weeks after the fall of Saigon on April 30, 1975, roughly 2,500 Hmong military officials and their families were airlifted by the CIA to Thailand.[3] The exodus began as a trickle as military elites made what many thought was a temporary escape from the war, and grew in scale and level of desperation as conditions rapidly deteriorated. Fearing for their safety, thousands more sought a way out of Laos on their own. Those who successfully crossed the Mekong River to seek asylum in Thailand would eventually be administered into United Nations-sponsored refugee camps.

State actions and refugee responses

United States policy makers have considered the resettlement of Southeast Asian refugees following the Vietnam War to be one of the largest, most dramatic humanitarian efforts in US history. Sociologist Yến Lê Espiritu has argued that the dominant image both in popular media and in academic studies was of helpless and demoralized refugees who were victims of the Vietnam War in need of care to be provided by Americans. This "rescue and liberation" myth and rhetoric of humanitarianism minimized the horrific impact of US imperialism, and instead positioned and perpetuated the US nation and its warriors as friends and rescuers (Espiritu, 2006: 329–352). This dominant narrative was used to promote public and private collaborations that facilitated the entrance of more than 1.4 million refugees from Cambodia, Laos, and Vietnam to the United States from 1975.[4] However, US refugee policies had never been universalist, as anticommunism became the foundation of American foreign policy during the Cold War and refugees who fled to the West were perceived as "voting with their feet" (Zucker and Zucker, 1996: 28). This "gift of freedom," moreover, did not necessarily provide a safe haven for all refugees. Instead, refugees faced new forms of violence as they sought freedom in the United States and were rendered indebted to empire without end (Nguyen, 2012: 19–20). In other words, refugees feel the need to perpetually be thankful to the US nation for having rescued them from evil communism. It was the requirement of their cooperation with both existing and emergent disciplinary regimes as they sought refuge that placed the refugee in a liminal stage at "'home'[in the United States] and abroad" (Ngô et al., 2012: 671–684). The "different technologies of government" that refugees encountered emphasized the need to transform disadvantaged newcomers into low-wage workers (Ong, 2003: 277).

Although designed under different conditions, refugee laws mirrored larger immigration policies by which immigration officials admitted those who they determined would fit into US society and excluded those they found to be "undesirable and dangerous" to the United States (Gardner, 2005; Lee and Yung, 2010: 31). Decisions to admit refugees were made collaboratively between officials in the country and agency processing representatives abroad. What was different about refugee conditions generally, and Hmong relocation in particular, was the liberal acceptance rate of individuals and families who had limited evidence that they could support themselves once in the United States.

The ways in which Hmong refugees fleeing Laos were treated depended primarily on when they arrived in Thailand. What was initially a small program to respond to the crisis in 1975, involving primarily persons who fled because they had been associated with American involvement during the war, became an expansive effort to address the refugee dilemma. The Indochina Migration and Assistance Act of 1975 allocated funding to the Department of State and the Department of Health, Education, and Welfare to provide special assistance to 130,000 refugees from Cambodia and Vietnam through the end of June 1976.[5] Because of the secretive nature of the war on Lao territory, Laos was not included in this original legislation. On June 21, 1976, the Act was extended to include refugees from Laos, and on October 28, 1977,

Congress amended the law to extend the sunset for when qualifying refugees would receive US assistance through September 30, 1981. The 1977 law also allowed for the creation of a record of residence status that would enable permanent legal residence in the United States. Spouses and children of those who were granted permanent legal residency received the same status.[6]

Hmong who arrived on Thai soil were transported to nearby processing camps. The camps began the refugee subject-making process. Becoming categorized as refugees by the UNHCR enabled them to have access to basic needs support provided by international relief organizations. As stateless people, their rights were intimately dependent on the presence of international relief organizations (Long, 1993: 16). Interestingly, the very organizations that helped them also contributed to the problematic treatment of refugees. For example, Lynellyn Long found in her study of the camp holding the largest Hmong refugee population in Thailand during the 1980s, Ban Vinai, that most refugees merely waited for something to happen. She described the process as dehumanizing, "The international relief community [called] this problem of nothing to do and nowhere to go, 'warehousing'… Such language also [treated] people as commodities to be shipped from place to place. 'Warehousing' [implies] that the commodities are not moving fast enough and the shipments are stalled in the warehouse" (Long, 1993: 93). Relief workers were the first group to have this attitude of unwanted goods toward the refugees. But this attitude soon spread across the complete resettlement process, thereby sustaining the subjectification of refugees as burdens to society.

While relief workers attempted to speed up the process, Hmong refugees resisted by refusing to leave when their applications were approved. Some were conflicted about going to unfamiliar places across the globe. Others hesitated because they had heard how difficult starting a new life in the United States had been for those who left the camps. Still others refused to leave since they had been separated from family members who they hoped would be able to eventually escape and join them in the camp. Spending varied lengths of time in confined camps, most Hmong refugees who decided to resettle in third countries chose to rebuild their lives in the United States. From 1975 to 2006, more than 130,000 Hmong were admitted to the US as refugees (Vang, 2010: 1).[7] In the late 1970s, eleven national voluntary organizations with local affiliations throughout the country assisted with resettling refugees.[8] IIM was one of the American Council of Nationality Services (ACNS) local affiliates. As the national consortium of resettlement agencies, ACNS served as the principal sponsor and local affiliates provided advocacy and support to sponsors and relatives in the United States and abroad.[9]

At the state and local levels, voluntary organizations sought sponsors who would guide refugee integration into local communities. Individuals and congregations around the country answered the call to help rescue refugees fleeing communist takeover of Cambodia, Laos, and Vietnam. In the mid 1970s, refugees could not leave the camps until American sponsors had been identified. Family social science scholar Dan Deztner best described the call to action to assist refugees displaced following the Vietnam War when he wrote, "Postwar feelings of guilt generated a sense of obligation in many Americans to those whose lives had been most directly affected by the decade-long intrusion. There was an unprecedented call for Americans to commit to the financial and social obligations of sponsorship for individuals and families they had never seen before" (Deztner, 2004: 6). Whether sponsors' actions were due to "guilt" or "social obligations," they were carried out only as a result of the institutional factors that facilitated refugee resettlement. President Ford's Inter-Agency Task Force on Indochinese Refugees and the Presidential Advisory Committee on Refugees promoted "an expeditious and coordinated orientation and resettlement of refugees from Southeast Asia." In addition to advocating for resources and backup support at the federal level to assist the activities of the voluntary resettlement agencies, coordination included "[calling] upon all Americans to contribute time, money, and resources."[10]

For the first wave of refugees who arrived in the immediate aftermath of the Vietnam War, sponsors consisted primarily of local church members. By the late 1970s, many former refugees began to serve as co-sponsors for relatives. In addition to completing a "Sponsorship Agreement," these individuals had to demonstrate kinship by filling out an "Affidavit of Relationship." In cases where sponsors and relatives could not provide all expected services, IIM bilingual staff stepped in to assist with things such as registering children for school and helping to complete Social Security card applications. Caseworkers also made home visits to provide basic orientation and to answer questions. These "cultural brokers" were an extension of institutional surveillance to ensure refugees behaved properly.

An important difference between Hmong refugee migrants and some other earlier immigrants to the United States was their household composition. Whereas most labor migrants arrived as young, and often single, adults, the vast majority of Hmong refugees were two-parent households. From 1976 to 1995, 3,367 individuals from 856 Hmong households received support from IIM.[11] Slightly more than three-fourths of the cases included both parents. Single mothers were the second most common type of family. This is partly explained by the fact that many women became widows during the war. Single males made up 8 percent of the total and were primarily either minors or single young men. Few single fathers emigrated and even fewer single women journeyed by themselves. Only 2 percent of arrivals were single women. Of these, the majority were divorced or widowed. While most households were comprised of nuclear families, a number included extended family members making them multi-generation families. Because "the rules for resettlement often seemed arbitrary" and there were no limits on the number of nuclear family members, "refugees who had no surviving nuclear family members resorted to strategies like claiming fake kinship relations with departing refugees" (Ong, 2003: 95). Mai Hang and her mother took advantage of this situation in 1976.[12] Her mother was a widow. Her late father had not been a soldier. She and her mother left Laos because everyone around them fled. When they arrived in the refugee camp, a relative in the Hang clan who had worked in the clandestine army was approved to leave. Her mother begged the relative to claim her as his mother and Mai as his sister. He agreed and added them to his application.[13] Mai revealed that all involved knew it was wrong to not tell the truth to processing authorities, but they were not alone. This was a common practice among refugees, especially families who had been split up. Teenagers who left their parents behind in Laos or whose parents died often had difficulties demonstrating why they feared persecution. One way that they subverted the system was claiming to be a member of an intact nuclear family that afforded them the opportunity to resettle in a third country. Since polygamy was widely practiced, men with multiple wives deceived authorities by applying to resettle with one wife and then claiming that the other wife or wives were sisters who were widows.

Why was household composition important to document and how did it impact the work of resettlement agencies? Relief workers in the camps and IIM employees tried to predict which refugee subjects might experience greater difficulties adapting to life in the host country. More importantly, they needed to demonstrate that they possessed transferable skills to enter the workforce. Thus, they were measured against the heterosexual nuclear family that defined the "norm" for Americans. A female-headed household was regarded as particularly vulnerable economically and most "likely to become public charge." While laws against poverty were historically directed at both men and women arriving at US borders, the application of the phrase "likely to become public charge" was gendered in that it questioned the ability of single and divorced women or widows to support themselves and their families (Gardner, 2005: 88). Consequently, the presence of Asian women and their children raised fears about racial difference and provoked anxieties about poverty and dependency (Gardner, 2005: 176). It also made visible Asian Americans' long legacy of exclusion and inequity. In early history, Asian women, in particular, were regarded as prostitutes, immoral and diseased.[14]

Institutional representatives initially believed that the high percentage of two-parent households would ease the transition of refugees in the host society.[15] What subsequently resulted was a community of refugees where both men and women struggled to find suitable work and a high percentage resorted to public assistance programs for survival because both lacked adequate basic formal education and training. By 1980, more than 60 percent of the US Hmong population lived in poverty, the exact outcome immigration officials had attempted to prevent.[16] Poor Americans, when struggling themselves to make ends meet, often resented the government's support for refugees. When Hmong refugees did not "measure up" to the position of Asians as the model minority, then they confronted a hostile environment that was not supportive of their migration to the United States in the first place.

US immigration laws have historically served as a means to control and/ or deny entry to certain individuals or groups. What was the government's ideal refugee? The processing logic instructed refugees to "speak good English, be employable, be unwilling to accept welfare, and be happy" (Ong, 2003: 60). Being grateful and non-hostile were desirable behaviors. Such requirements were embedded in refugee resettlement policies and practices that required applicants to be labeled in certain ways to show who, or which subjects, could potentially be incorporated into US society. An overarching task in the refugee resettlement process was the construction of an employable refugee subject.[17] Cambodian refugees, as Aihwa Ong found, learned techniques throughout the resettlement process that were supposed to "shape them into autonomous, self-reliant citizen-subjects of freedom" (Ong, 2003: 276). Hmong refugee applicants had to demonstrate not only that they were fleeing persecution, but also that they possessed skills and experiences that would enable them to support themselves once in the host country. A close analysis revealed that most experiences listed on resettlement applications did not correlate with the types of skills necessary for obtaining livable wage jobs in the US.

None of the "occupation and skill" categories on application forms were left blank, indicating that applicants were given no option to mark "other." Occupations recorded were highly gendered. Whereas the female refugee subject was one whose work experience was limited largely to responsibilities in the private sphere, male subjects were described as having engaged in a wide range of professions. In the attempt to create employable refugee subjects, voluntary agency staff listed "farmer/mixed crops" as the work history/skill of 44 percent of female applicants, 43 percent were "sewer/embroiderer," and 12 percent were described as "household worker." A few were referred to as having been students or working in sales. Male applicants were primarily classified as either mixed crops farmers (42 percent) or having military experience (31 percent); 7 percent of men had been students and 6 percent worked in sales.[18] The remaining occupations included health care/nurse, public administration, management, civil servant, village chief, misc./clerical, auto mechanic, machine operating/electrician, taxi driver, teacher, college lecturer, basket weaver, blacksmith, and refugee camp support. Regardless of the actual personal skills listed, to convince voluntary agency staff processing paperwork in camps that they would make good candidates for living in the host country, applicants had to prove that they were either directly involved with US military personnel during the war, or were the spouses and children of someone who had participated in the secret army. Thus, military service was conveniently used as justification for why applicants should be admitted.[19] The importance of military service rendered the Hmong refugee as a "loyal" American subject, which contradicts the contentious history of other Asian immigrants and Asian Americans who had perpetually been suspected of being un-American and disloyal to the US nation. The internment of more than 120,000 Japanese Americans during the Second World War and the treatment of Americans of Middle Eastern descent following the September 11, 2011 terrorist attacks are good examples of this.

It is difficult to determine how roles and skills were assigned to individuals, but as indicated earlier, applicants had to demonstrate that they possessed skills to work after arrival. Therefore, as cultural brokers, bilingual staff assisted applicants in maneuvering through the contested application process. The listing of skills was part of immigration law practices that created "a field of meanings within which self-sufficiency, personal autonomy, and republican citizenship took place" (Gardner, 2005: 89). Institutional records provide only fragmented accounts of clients' lived experiences and reveal more about viewpoints of institutional representatives than about the people they served (Nakamura, 2010: 180). Agency processing staff tried to create subjects that would serve the US state by being employable, healthy, loyal to America, and conforming to proper family and gender roles.

Case notes frequently highlighted refugees' willingness to accept any available employment opportunity. For example, a male refugee was described as "want[ing] any job that feeds [his] family, but [he] would like to become [a] mechanic."[20] The individual had been a mechanic in Laos so his desired job reflected his experience. Sai Lee, a former captain in the clandestine army, arrived in Hawaii in February 1976 and was chosen by a sponsor who owned an apartment building. He remembered his first job, "[The sponsor] had a large apartment building. I believed that my sponsor had brought me to do slave-like work. People on the top floors would throw their trash to an area in the back. My job was to go pick up the trash around the dumpster and place them in the dumpster."[21] After six months, Sai confronted his sponsor about this slave-like job, as Sai referred to it, and sought help from the resettlement agency to find a more suitable position. Angered by Sai's resistance and unappreciative behavior, the sponsor responded with a $1,000 bill for back rent when Sai found another job.[22]

When reviewing the types of work that refugees were believed to have desired, nearly two-thirds were interested in obtaining an assembly job while 19 percent wanted to obtain vocational training prior to entering the labor force. Slightly more than 10 percent would accept "any job requiring little or no English"; 10 percent wanted to pursue employment as janitors and another 10 percent were interested in becoming auto mechanics. "Nurse/ health care employment" and "restaurant worker" were desired by 8 and 5 percent, respectively. The remainder identified professions that included painter, advertising, teacher, machine operator, and bilingual worker.

Significant differences existed between job interests listed for men and those for women. The types of gendered work that Hmong women were thought to have been interested in more closely reflected the work history and skills data gathered in refugee camps. More than two-thirds desired sewing positions while 17 percent were interested in being assembly workers. Refugee women who were identified as farmers, embroiderers, and household workers were indeed limited to jobs that required few English language skills.

The eventual vocational training for refugee women would place emphasis on industrial sewing, cleaning, and electronics assembly rather than clerical work or service employment (Gabaccia, 1994: 124).

When describing the steps necessary for refugee families to move beyond dependence on the Aid to Families with Dependent Children (AFDC) program, caseworkers seemed to be pressured to articulate what would need to happen for heads of household. A representative comment by a caseworker was that "two full-time job for both parents, one person should handle more than one job, or at least one full-time and one part-time" would be required. Another representative case note concluded that the "husband should work more than 40 hours ... Spouse should work full-time." Husbands tended to be viewed as capable of holding more than one job. "One full-time employment for Neng Chou, one part-time employment for wife, or, Neng Chou should handle more than one job," explained a caseworker. Even more excessive expectations were made of refugees, as illustrated by another file that advised "2 full-time employment for both, part-time ESL [English as a Second Language] for husband, tutor at home for wife."[23] It seemed arbitrary and unrealistic to expect these individuals who lacked English language skills, as exemplified by the suggestion of English class and tutoring, to hold two full-time jobs while trying to gain basic survival skills. IIM made ESL classes available to all adults since the ability to speak English was assumed to be the first step in the Americanization process. Lack of English skills was identified as the biggest obstacle refugees needed to overcome, but participation in language learning was influenced by many factors such as gender, age, and the availability of childcare. Caseworkers frequently expressed concerns about refugee resistance to their recommendations to learn English.

Displacement, life in refugee camps, and migration across the world adversely affected the mental health of Hmong refugees. As they rebuilt their lives in the host society, cultural and linguistic change called into question many of the assumptions that allow humans to make sense of the world and to construct their identities (Gabaccia, 1994: 121). How they saw themselves depended largely on the types of interactions they had with others in the business of supporting their adjustment. For refugees who attended ESL classes, teacher evaluations of students' progress provide insights on how refugees were perceived by both mainstream and bilingual/bicultural teachers. Some ESL teachers took on more tasks than just teaching language skills. They also became advocates for their refugee students. On the other hand, teacher comments revealed conflicting, racialized, and gendered assumptions about refugee learning abilities. In many cases, students were described as "slow" learners. Because she could not read at all, her teacher wrote, "Xia [learned] slowly ... This class [tended] to move too fast for her." Since Mai relied on other students to translate for her, she was described as "very conscientious but also very slow [but] she can speak on a survival basis if she has to." Regarding another student's progress, a teacher said, "Vue started out slowly and fell behind; his speaking was stilted. For some reason, he took off. His reading improved, so did his understanding and speech. He almost caught up with the group average by the end of the session. Vue is shy. His responses are slow to arrive." Regarding an older student's struggles, a teacher wrote, "Chang is a very pleasant man who is willing to do whatever is asked of him but his age is a problem with his memory for a new language ... VERY slow learner. Totally dependent on the people next to him. He remembers words, but not which object the word stands for. Doesn't know the alphabet or numbers yet." Frequent contradictory remarks were also made about particular students. For example, a white teacher wrote, "Ger rarely contributes to the discussion. His English is less developed than others. I'm not sure what the problem is here." The bilingual Hmong teacher's notes regarding the same student indicated that "Ger is a pretty quiet student. He learns pretty quick once we are talking in Hmong. His math does improve a little more now."[24]

Social service providers were charged with building refugee capacity to support themselves. Embedded in the "Statement of Understanding" signed by refugees before settling in the US is the agreement that applicants will "accept whatever work may be offered, whether this work [was their] specialty or not." The proper refugee subject is thankful and will accept this "gift" even if it is not something he or she desires. This assumption that refugees would enter the workforce as soon as possible after arrival was reinforced throughout the immediate post arrival period. Sponsors and resettlement agencies often worked diligently to secure jobs for refugees. Caseworkers consistently noted that refugees' prospects for economic success were limited if they were not making progress with their language skills. One of the underlying assumptions was that those involved in ESL classes would be more likely to achieve self-sufficiency. In many instances, caseworkers arbitrarily indicated how long they believed it would take certain refugees to obtain employment, and thus become self-sufficient. Some typical case notes included: "The family will be employed in the next couple of months." "The family adjust well to the living situation [and] will be employed in 18 months." "Studying, [he] will be employed in 12 months." "The husband may have a little more difficulty [finding] a job but hopefully his wife will be getting a job within the next year. This family is doing well. They both are studying hard and they hope to be employed as soon as possible." Caseworkers were under pressure from the government to minimize refugee dependency, which led them to make such hopeful statements.

Reference to work experience prior to settling in the US contributed to the positive perception of a refugee's employability. A caseworker wrote about a male refugee, "Wa Lee is educated and intelligent. He has excellent letters of reference from his jobs in the camp ... Wa Lee should move quickly toward self-sufficiency." Another student's experience of serving as a teacher after having learned some English in the refugee camp added to the expectation that he would be more easily employed. Referring to a female student's experience in Laos, another caseworker wrote, "She knew a little English and she had a lot of experience in nursing in Laos. She [said] she will be working as soon as she can. Hopefully [she] will be getting [a] job soon."

Most refugees who arrived in the mid 1970s did not have family support. Many who arrived later instead had extended family members on which to rely. Having supportive relatives who were making progress toward self-sufficiency was perceived by caseworkers as a positive influence, increasing a refugee's likelihood of becoming self-sufficient. "I think they'll progress quickly because they are learning quickly and [they] have relatives who are good examples for them to learn from," wrote one caseworker. Another discussed the progress one couple made: "They are a little slow in starting, but have good support from relatives. Both Mai and Kou show skill in learning English and they seem to be adjusting well. I think they will do ok. They seem to have good family support and live upstairs from their relatives who have helped them a lot. I think they should become self-sufficient relatively soon." A bilingual caseworker definitely stated, "I believe they will do well because they see their relatives are working and making more money than welfare."

By contrast, new arrivals who lacked relatives as role models were considered to be at a disadvantage. One caseworker noted, "They are not doing very well because their relatives here don't have very much time to help them. They will move to Wisconsin where they have closer relatives." Another wrote, "He will be able to become self-sufficient quickly if he wants to. Unfortunately, his relatives are not helping to motivate him very well." In addition, single parenthood and large families were noted as barriers to employment. One caseworker explained, "She really [had] no idea what to do because only one single mother and too many children and the mother [had] no chance to go to school at all." Another caseworker described the struggles of a large family, "It [was difficult for] the family to decide what to do because they were having too many children. The family cannot speak English and they even don't know how to drive and ride a bus ... So, the [family's] main idea is to [gain English] first. For example, they needed to know how to ride the bus in the area and know more about the community first before they could become employed."[25] These basic but enormous obstacles that Hmong refugees initially confronted contributed to their low socio-economic status. To survive, many resisted social service providers' pressure to work menial jobs and, instead, they enrolled in public welfare programs as an act of resistance to state control.

Conclusion

Hmong refugee migration to the United States occurred against a backdrop of growing anxiety about non-European immigration, unresolved wounds from the Vietnam War, and the impact of the loss of American power. It also rested on the shoulders of a long history of American distrust of Asians and Asian Americans by viewing them as perpetual foreigners regardless of how long they had resided in the United States. The refugee resettlement process was undeniably complex and involved many different actors from the international level to the state, local, and individual levels. Flight and dispersal fractured Hmong lives but, in retrospect, the liberal acceptance rate of Hmong refugees was out of the ordinary because it was based largely on foreign policy interests. American response to the refugees reflected a sense of responsibility and feelings of guilt, along with a genuine humanitarianism, as the memory of American experiences in Southeast Asia merged with its democratic principles. Federal and state governments created the infrastructure required to transport refugees from their countries of first asylum to various locations in the United States, but it was resettlement agencies that were charged with the tasks of transforming refugees into self-supporting residents.

The paper trails left at the archive tell us that camp processing representatives were successful in constructing acceptable refugee subjects to enable their resettlement. In doing so, refugees were expected to follow a set of rules that were developed to quickly transform them into low-wage workers. Documentation of their lives in the case records reveals that migration across the globe affected new arrivals' well-being on multiple levels and many initially "dazed off" as they tried to make sense of their displaced lives in the United States – at the same time that it also makes visible the multiple ways in which they subverted and resisted caseworkers' insistence that they behave properly. Their refusal or inability to enter the workforce demonstrates that even in the most difficult conditions, refugees do exercise some agency.

Notes

1 International Institute of Minnesota Records, General/Multiethnic Collection, Immigration History Research Center, University of Minnesota, Boxes 21–27. Note that all names in case files have been changed to ensure confidentiality.
2 It was also in the camp that most refugees would have a photograph of themselves taken for the first time. Application for resettlement in a third country included a photo of all family members and single shots of each individual.
3 For a detailed overview of the evacuation, see Morrison (1999).
4 It is important to note that closure of the refugee camps under the supervision of the United Nations High Commissioner for Refugees occurred in the mid 1990s. Transnational migration continued to take place as a result of other programs, such as the Amerasian Homecoming Act of 1987 that facilitated the immigration of Vietnamese Amerasian children and their close relatives to the United States, and the 2003 State Department decision to allow 15,000 Hmong refugees from Laos who were living in Thailand to resettle in the US.
5 Indochina Migration and Assistance Act of 1975, May 23, 1975. Public Law 94–23, 94th Congress.

6 Indochina Migration and Assistance Act of 1975. Adjustment of Status of Indochina Refugees and Extension of the Indochina Migration and Refugee Assistance Act of 1975, June 21, 1976. Public Law 95–105, 95th Congress, October 28, 1977.

7 France, Canada, and Australia accepted Hmong refugees but in significantly smaller numbers.

8 The voluntary organizations were the following: American Council for Nationalities Service (ACNS), American Fund for Czechoslovak Refugees (AFCR), Church World Service (CWS), International Rescue Committee (IRC), Hebrew Immigrant Aid and Sheltering Society of New York (HIAS), Lutheran Immigration and Refugee Service (LIRS), Polish American Immigration and Relief Committee (PAIRC), the Tolstoy Foundation (TF), United States Catholic Conference (USCC), World Relief Refugee Service (WRRS), and the Young Men's Christian Association (YMCA).

9 According to a 1982 ACNS letter, it had member agencies throughout the country, including International Institutes in 22 cities (Akron, Boston, Bridgeport, Buffalo, Detroit, Erie, Flint, Gary, Jersey City, Lawrence, Los Angeles, Lowell, Manchester (NH), Milwaukee, Oakland, Providence, St. Louis, St. Paul, San Francisco, San Jose, Toledo, and Youngstown); Nationalities Services Centers in Cleveland and Philadelphia; Immigrants Service League of Travelers Aid in Chicago and Cincinnati; American Civic Association in Binghamton; Affiliates in Albany, Fresno, Honolulu, Santa Rosa, and Washington, DC.

10 "Interagency Task Force on Indochina Refugees (April 27–May 8 1975)," Gerald R. Ford Library and Museum, www.fordlibrarymuseum.gov/library/document/0010/1554449.pdf (accessed December 28, 2019). Task forces to resettle Indochinese refugees were established in a number of states.

11 Author's tabulation of applicant files.

12 Mai Hang interview with author in St. Paul, MN, 2010. Mai Hang is a pseudonym.

13 Mai Hang interview.

14 See Hune and Nomura (2003) and Lee (2015).

15 Shoua Vang, interview with author.

16 The poverty rate for the US Hmong population was 66 percent in 1990. It decreased to 40 percent in 2000 and in 2010 the Hmong American poverty rate was 25 percent.

17 Note that not all files contained information on work history/skills due to the fact that not all families came directly to Minnesota. Data reflects only "heads of households."

18 No information is available to explain what sales work may have entailed.

19 Shoua Vang interview; Sai Lee interview with author, 2006. It should be noted that men claiming to have been soldiers had to prove that they had served by identifying their commanding officers. For years, CIA operative Jerry Daniels worked with processing agency staff to verify military associations.

20 International Institute of Minnesota Records, General/Multiethnic Collection, Immigration History Research Center, University of Minnesota, Box 24.

21 Sai Lee, interview with author, St. Paul, MN, 2005.

22 The initial arrangement was that Sai and his wife would not have to pay rent since he was helping to take care of the property.
23 International Institute of Minnesota Records, General/Multiethnic Collection, Immigration History Research Center, University of Minnesota, Box 28.
24 Teachers and caseworkers signed their names on forms so their identities can be associated with written comments.
25 International Institute of Minnesota Records, General/Multiethnic Collection, Immigration History Research Center, University of Minnesota, Box 25.

References

Burton, A. (ed.) (2005), *Archive Stories: Facts, Fictions, and the Writing of History* (Durham, NC: Duke University Press).

Deztner, D. (2004), *Elder Voices: Southeast Asian Families in the United States* (Walnut Creek: Altamira Press).

Espiritu, Y.L. (2006), The 'We-Win-Even-When-We-Lose' Syndrome: U.S. press coverage of the twenty-fifth anniversary of the 'Fall of Saigon'. *American Quarterly* 58(2): 329–352.

Fassin, D., Y. Bouagga, I. Coutant, J. Eideliman, F. Fernandez, N. Fischer, C. Kobelinsky, C. Makremi, S. Mazouz, and S. Roux (2015), *At the Heart of the State: The Moral World of Institutions* (London: Pluto Press).

Gabaccia, D. (1994), *From the Other Side: Women, Gender, and Immigrant Life in the U.S., 1820–1990* (Bloomington: Indian University Press).

Gardner, M. (2005), *The Qualities of a Citizen: Women, Immigration, and Citizenship, 1870–1965* (Princeton: Princeton University Press).

Gatrell, P. (2013), *The Making of the Modern Refugee* (Oxford: Oxford University Press).

Hune, S. and G.M., Nomura (eds) (2003), *Asian/Pacific American Women: A Historical Anthology* (New York: New York University Press).

Lee, E. (2015), *The Making of Asian America: A History* (New York: Simon & Schuster).

Lee, E. and J. Yung (2010), *Angel Island: Immigrant Gateway to America* (New York: Oxford University Press).

Long, L. (1993), *Ban Vinai: The Refugee Camp* (New York: Columbia University Press).

Michaud, J. (1997), From Southwest China into Upper Indochina: An overview of Hmong (Miao) migrations. *Asia Pacific Viewpoint* 38(2): 119–130.

Michaud, J. and C. Culas (2004), A contribution to the study of Hmong (Miao) migrations and history. In Tapp, N., J. Michaud, C. Culas, and G. Yia Lee (eds) *Hmong/Miao in Asia* (Chiang Mai, Thailand: Silkworm Books).

Morrison, G.L. (1999), *Sky is Falling: An Oral History of the CIA's Evacuation of the Hmong from Laos* (Jefferson: McFarland & Company).

Nakamura, M. (2010), Families Precede Nation and Race?: Marriage, Migration, and Integration of Japanese War Brides after World War II. PhD diss. Minneapolis.

Navaro-Yashin, Y. (2012), *The Make-Believe Space: Affective Geography in a Postwar Polity* (Durham, NC: Duke University Pres).

Ngô, F.I.B., M.T. Nguyen, and M.B. Lam (2012), Guest editors' introduction. *Positions Asia Critique* 20(3): 911–942.

Nguyen, M.T. (2012), *The Gift of Freedom: War, Debt, and Other Refugee Passages* (Durham, NC: Duke University Press).

Ong, A (2003), *Buddha is Hiding: Refugees, Citizenship, the New America* (Berkeley: University of California Press).

Richmond, A. (1988), Sociological theories of international migration: the case of refugees. *Current Sociology* 36(2): 7–25.

Scott, J.C. (2009), *The Art of Not Being Governed: An Anarchist History of Upland Southeast Asia* (New Haven: Yale University Press).

Vang, C.Y. (2010), *Hmong America: Reconstructing Community in Diaspora* (Illinois: University of Illinois Press).

Zucker, N.L. and N.F. Zucker (1996), *Desperate Crossings: Seeking Refuge in America* (London and New York: Routledge).

2

'Niche openings' and compassionate exclusions: the UK's response to children during the refugee crisis

Ala Sirriyeh

In September 2015 one photograph dominated the news and social media. The photograph, by Turkish photo-journalist, Nilüfer Demir, depicted a little boy in a red t-shirt and blue shorts lying face down and still in the surf on a beach in Bodrum, Turkey. Aylan Kurdi, a 3-year-old Syrian refugee child, had drowned with his mother and 5-year-old brother as they attempted to cross the sea with their father to seek sanctuary in Greece. During this spectacle of a child's death, there was an immediate (though temporary) shift in the tone of media, political and public discourse on the so called 'refugee crisis'. There was a noticeably more compassionate discourse around refugees, particularly around the plight of child refugees.

We live in an era in which refugees often face hostile and exclusionary reception conditions in the societies in which they arrive. However, refugee populations are heterogeneous and while the stigmatised identity of 'refugee' often assumes a master status in public debates and policy on asylum, this intersects with discourses that relate to other aspects of the identities of people seeking asylum. Drawing on theoretical insights from work on emotions, I explore how UK government responses to refugee children have been framed and contested based on children's status as moral referents, and through consideration of the ethical demands they place on the nation. This chapter focuses on the case study of the death of Aylan Kurdi in September 2015 and the response of the UK government to child refugees caught up in the Refugee Crisis at this time. While recognising that there is an established precedent of contesting UK government policy towards refugee children based on their status as children, as will be shown in this chapter the refugee crisis and the death of Aylan Kurdi marked a significant rise in attention to, and mobilisation of, a discourse of compassion.

Children and refugees both feature prominently as key populations within debates on rights, recognition and citizenship in the UK (Sirriyeh, 2014). Yet, while refugees are frequently judged as lacking citizenship potential and are rejected through abandonment, confinement or expulsion (Anderson,

2013; Bloch and Schuster, 2005), children are regarded as an investment in the future of the nation, to be moulded into model citizens through protection and guidance (Sirriyeh, 2014). Meanwhile, I argue that a recent shift has taken place from the recognition of the threatened body to the recognition of the suffering body (Fassin, 2011) which has further heightened the status of some refugee children as the ideal 'deserving' refugees.

In this chapter, I consequently suggest that within the wider context of hostility there have been some limited opportunities for inclusion for certain categories of refugees,[1] particularly refugee children, whose identified characteristics fit more favourably within the professed moral and humanitarian values and goals of the receiving societies. This has led to (albeit limited) opportunities for some more progressive policies, which I explore here through the case study of efforts to resettle children caught up in the ongoing refugee crisis. However, I also contend that the discourse of childhood vulnerability can undermine the recognition of children's agency. As Cohen (2001) argued in *States of Denial*, despite the knowledge that suffering is occurring, it is often denied. Suffering is ignored, disavowed or reinterpreted and the appropriate moral responses and intervention are, therefore, withheld. A discourse of childhood vulnerability and claims of 'compassion' are sometimes used in denials of suffering through being presented as justifications for restrictive policies. For example, during the refugee crisis it has been asserted that denying settlement opportunities will reduce incentives for children to make hazardous migration journeys (Stone, 2017). Meanwhile, the suffering of older children has been denied, and they have been excluded when they have struggled to fit this within the narrow parameter of recognition (McKee, 2016). Even if they are initially included, as they age out of childhood in the UK young people have experienced exclusion, but also a *loss* of recognition as they have been stripped of previous rights and inclusions tied to their legal and social status as children (Wade et al., 2012).

This chapter begins with an outline of the theoretical framework, exploring the concept of compassion and how it features within the emotional regime of asylum policy. This is followed by an overview of the UK asylum policy context. I then discuss the response to Aylan Kurdi's death and explore how compassion was expressed for the vulnerable child, leading to some limited opportunities for inclusion. Finally, I examine how, while a discourse of compassion has been used to create 'niche openings' (Nicholls, 2014), seemingly humanising emotions have also been used to justify what are in fact exclusionary and oppressive practices that have further entrenched the exclusion of other refugees.

Compassion as an emotional regime

The UK immigration and asylum regimes have created a hostile environment for undesired migrants and refugees (Anderson, 2013; Bloch and Schuster,

2005). However, as Nicholls (2014: 25) has argued (writing in the US context), even in the most hostile immigration contexts there are 'internal contradictions' that produce 'cracks and fissures that can serve as narrow niche-openings for some immigrants'. Nicholls observes that during the 1990s and 2000s, the US government increasingly policed and sanctioned undocumented immigrants, leading to a significant rise in detentions and deportations. Nevertheless, Nicholls (2014) found that despite these conditions, 'niche openings' – that is narrow, highly conditional and limited terms of inclusions – emerged for some undocumented young people during the 2000s because they and their allies could present the young people's characteristics and behaviour (innocence, assimilation and productivity) as being aligned with US cultural, political and economic values and interests.

In this chapter, I suggest that Nicholl's (2014) concept of 'niche openings' can be utilised to describe the limited and conditional terms of inclusion that have been extended to some refugee children in the UK. I argue that these niche openings have been produced in a context in which asylum has been rearticulated as an act of compassion towards passive and vulnerable victims, instead of a right which they are entitled to claim. I explore the structure of compassion as an emotional regime (Hochschild, 2002) in UK government policy discourse on asylum, I consider how this has enabled niche openings, and I reflect on the impacts of this on policy and practice towards refugee children during the refugee crisis.

In Aristotelian terms, compassion is, 'a painful emotion directed at another person's misfortune or suffering' (Nussbaum, 1996: 31). As Nussbaum (1996) explains, 'it requires and rests on three beliefs: (1) the belief that the suffering is serious rather than trivial; (2) the belief that the suffering was not caused primarily by the person's own culpable actions; and (3) the belief that the pitier's own possibilities are similar to those of the sufferer'. Nussbaum (2013) contends that the third criteria is not simply similar possibilities, but actually *eudaimonistic judgement.* She observes (2013: 11) that we are more likely to feel deep emotions, such as compassion, in relation to people or events which 'we are somehow connected to through our imagining of a valuable life', and to people who are in our 'circle of concern'. I argue that the re-articulation of asylum through the frame of compassion has meant that many people seeking asylum have been denied sanctuary because they have not been recognised as deserving subjects of compassion in this highly conditional framing of the emotion. Niche openings have arisen for child refugees whose characteristics position them as worthy recipients of compassion. Yet even these 'openings' for children are limited, while compassion has also been used to justify what were in effect exclusionary and oppressive practices towards refugee children during the refugee crisis, as mentioned earlier.

Refugees have been regarded as a moral touchstone, used to interrogate the ethical status of nation-states (Cohen, 2006). However, as immigration and asylum have become increasingly politicised, the moral category of 'refugee' has been contested and fragmented into the sub-categories of *genuine refugees* who are deemed to have legitimate claims for asylum, and *bogus asylum seekers* whose claims are disputed (Sales, 2002). Fassin (2011) described a similar trajectory in France. Writing about the de-legitimisation of people seeking asylum in France during the late 1990s and early 2000s, he documented how legitimacy was instead conferred on those who could present a case for leave to remain based on the evidence of their *suffering* body (as opposed to their *threatened* body). The growing culture of disbelief meant that the threatened body, associated with political asylum, was now seen as suspect and conflated with the discredited economic migrant, and there was a decline in the number of people granted asylum in France. However, in the same period there was a rise in the number of people granted humanitarian leave to remain through the invocation of the 'illness clause' of the 1998 Conditions of Entry and Residence of Foreigners legislation. Fassin (2005: 371) used the concept of 'biolegitimacy' to describe the shift in which the suffering physical body became the paramount basis for legitimacy, recognition and rights, asserting that the right to life was 'being displaced from the political sphere to that of compassion'.

In the UK, a similar shift has taken place from the recognition of the threatened body to the recognition of the suffering body. In the policy case study discussed by Fassin (2011), the recognition of the suffering body was performed outside of the asylum system (through the illness clause legislation). However, recent developments in the UK in the context of the refugee crisis indicate this shift in legitimacy has taken place within the frame of asylum, where the attribute of 'vulnerability' has become central to the framing of legitimacy within the asylum system. This has led to a transformation of a rights-based discourse on asylum into a discourse of compassion, in which asylum is framed in government policy discourse as a 'generous' and 'compassionate' humanitarian act, rather than a moral and legal obligation.

I suggest that the refugee child, or the assumed characteristics and circumstances of the refugee child, have become understood as the characteristics of the 'genuine' refugee in this re-articulation of asylum. Hochschild (2002: 118) describes an emotional regime as 'a set of taken-for-granted feeling rules (rules about how we imagine we should feel) which are connected to framing rules (rules about the way we think we should see and think)'. The feeling and framing rules that have developed around childhood intersect with contemporary discourse about refugees to construct refugee children as worthy subjects of compassion. Framing rules are social norms that govern what we should feel, to whom, and about what; for example, this could include the belief that children are weak, have limited agency and are, therefore, innocent and vulnerable. Meanwhile, given the development of British child welfare policy norms, described later, there is a moral framing rule that the UK is a nation-state that promotes and protects the welfare of children. Bearing in mind these framings of children's characteristics and condition, and the identity and characteristics of the UK as a nation-state, the British government and peoples might be expected to feel and express care and compassion towards children, including refugee children.

Asylum policy and refugee children in the UK

In recent decades, some refugees have arrived in the UK through organised resettlement schemes (Collyer et al., 2017). However, most travel independently and apply for asylum on their arrival in the UK. In the 1990s, the number of people arriving independently increased, reaching a peak of 84,000 applications in 2002 (Sirriyeh, 2013a). This prompted concerns about the asylum process and was a catalyst for a series of restrictive measures instituted through legislative and policy changes, as discussed further below. The number of asylum applications has decreased since then, although it began rising again in 2011. In 2015, it rose by 31 percent in comparison to 2014 (Refugee Council 2016a). In 2015, 32,733 adults submitted asylum claims (Refugee Council 2016a) and 5,202 children were dependents on adult asylum claims (Refugee Council 2016b).

In addition to children who arrive as dependents, other children claim asylum in the UK as unaccompanied minors. In 2015, 3,253 unaccompanied minors claimed asylum. Although, during the refugee crisis, the focus was on Syrian refugees, Syrians constituted only the seventh largest number of claims among unaccompanied children (169 Syrian children in 2015) (Refugee Council, 2016b). Most children seeking asylum in the UK are granted a temporary leave to remain and must apply for further leave to remain when they are 17.5 years old, facing the risk of refusal and deportation as they reach adulthood (Wade et al., 2012).

The UK declined to take part in the United Nations High Commissioner for Refugees (UNHCR) resettlement programme for Syrian refugees, opting to contribute aid for the relief effort in the Middle East rather than resettling refugees in the UK (Kingsley, 2016). In January 2014, there was a shift in this response, following considerable pressure from the UNHCR, charities and politicians across party lines in the UK (McGuiness, 2017). On 29 January 2014, Theresa May (then Home Secretary) announced the introduction of the Syrian Vulnerable Persons Resettlement Programme (SVPRP) to resettle the 'most vulnerable refugees' directly from camps in the Middle East. According to May, those who would be prioritised as the 'most vulnerable' were 'survivors of torture and violence, and women and children at risk or in need of medical care'; by June 2015, just 216 people had been resettled through the SVPRP (McGuiness, 2017). On 7 September 2015, following renewed pressure to expand the SVPRP in the aftermath of Aylan Kurdi's death, Prime Minister Cameron announced that the programme would be expanded to resettle up to 20,000 refugees over the course of that Parliament. Over half of the people resettled through this scheme were children (Home

Office, 2016). In April 2016, a 'children at risk' scheme was introduced to resettle vulnerable children and their families from the Middle East and North Africa (MENA) region (Home Office, 2016). In February 2016, Lord Dubs introduced an amendment to the Immigration Bill 2016 to bring up to 3,000 unaccompanied children living in camps in Calais, Greece and Italy to the UK. After a period of intensive campaigning for what became known as the 'Dubs Amendment', it was passed in May 2016. However, in February 2017, the closure of this programme was announced after only 350 children had been resettled, despite claims from local councils that they had the capacity to offer more places (Stone, 2017).

Immigration and asylum policy has been a high-profile topic of political and public debate for a long time in the UK. However, in recent years it has assumed a centre-stage position because of the politicisation of migration in local and global politics (Castles and Miller, 2003). Significant attention was focused on the increased numbers of people who sought asylum in the UK from the 1990s to the early 2000s. Although numbers have declined significantly in recent years, the ongoing global refugee crisis, and debates on the role to be played by the UK and Europe during a period of austerity and as the UK voted for – and prepares to – exit the European Union, have meant that refugee policy has become a high-profile issue once again.

As immigration and asylum have become increasing politicised, the moral category of 'refugee' has been contested and fragmented into the sub-categories of genuine refugees and bogus asylum seekers, as discussed earlier. Throughout the past two decades a series of immigration and asylum legislation has introduced restrictions and conditionalities through policies such as: the introduction of the dispersal system for housing support for asylum seekers; payment though vouchers; restrictions on the right to work; limitations on the right to appeal asylum decisions; and a requirement for landlords to check immigration status (Lewis et al., 2014). These conditionalities are designed to make life increasingly difficult for people seeking asylum in the UK and those who remain after their applications have been refused, to deter them from seeking to remain in the UK. People seeking asylum have reported that they experience a culture of disbelief in the UK asylum system in which their testimonies are mistrusted and disputed and every effort is made to discourage them from remaining (Hynes, 2011). This produces and reinforces a distinction between refugees and asylum seekers and a hierarchy of deservingness.

The development of this notion of the figure of the 'genuine' deserving refugee, in conjunction with social and historical understandings of childhood, has led to debates on contemporary responses to child refugees in the UK centring on the emotional regime of compassion. In the remainder of this chapter, I examine the UK's response to the ongoing refugee crisis, and explore how the feeling and framing rules that have developed about children, and refugee children in particular, mean that *some* refugee children fit the criteria of compassion outlined by Nussbaum (1996). I argue that this discourse of compassion has often been mobilised in support of contradictory policies, depending on differing understandings of the notion of compassion and differing understandings of what a compassionate outcome looks like. This has created both 'niche openings' (Nicholls, 2014), but also some exclusionary and oppressive outcomes.

Saving and protecting the innocent child

Refugee children enter a relationship with the state based on their identity as refugees, but also based on their identity as 'children'. The UN Convention on the Rights of the Child (CRC) 1989 enshrined the universal rights of the child (Article 2) and stated duties to protect children (Article 4). Article 3 of the CRC declares the 'best interests' of children must be the primary concern in making decisions that affect them.

The precarious status of asylum-seeking children has been a key area of contention in asylum debates in the UK, while the growth of a children's rights discourse has simultaneously enabled campaigns to centre on the welfare of children in asylum policy (Sirriyeh, 2014). The Children Act 2004 established a duty on state agencies in the UK to safeguard and promote the welfare of children, drawing on notions of children as inherently vulnerable. However, this duty excluded children in immigration detention centres since, although the UK ratified the CRC in 1991, until 2008 it held a reservation on Article 22 – which requires states to ensure that refugee children receive appropriate protection and humanitarian assistance (Sirriyeh, 2014). After the UK withdrew this reservation, Section 55 of the Border, Citizenship and Immigration Act 2009 placed a duty on the UK Border Agency to have regard for children's safety and welfare during their duties.

Since the Victorian era, charity campaigns in the UK have focused on the plight of 'children without a childhood' (Piper, 1999) and the notion of 'child saving' whereby these children are rescued and restored to proper childhood; the Victorian era also focused on the deserving poor more generally. Children in these campaigns were portrayed as physically frail, vulnerable and without a voice (Piper, 1999). Children on the move in the public world of adults, such as street children, needed to be returned to the private and sedentary world of the domestic sphere, where they could be cared for. In the contemporary era, young refugee children, such as Aylan Kurdi, mobile and out of place, are regarded as today's 'children without a childhood'. Their fragility and dependence on others place them at risk of serious suffering or harm and, therefore, in need of protection.

Refugee children as subjects of compassion

In 2014 and 2015, there was an unprecedented escalation in the numbers of people travelling to Europe as they fled the Syrian civil war, political instability in Libya and persecution and economic hardship in other parts of the world (Kingsley, 2016). As the horror of deaths in the Mediterranean Sea garnered media and public attention in the spring and summer of 2015, the response of the EU was deemed to be deeply inadequate and was critiqued as exacerbating the crisis and lacking in compassion (Eleftheriou-Smith, 2015). The UK government had declined to take part in proposed EU resettlement programmes and advocated reducing the scope of search and rescue operations in the Mediterranean, ostensibly to dissuade people from making treacherous journeys across the sea to Europe (Crawley et al., 2017; Kingsley, 2016).

However, the publication and circulation of the photographs of Aylan Kurdi on 2 September 2015 led to an immediate shift in media, political and public discourse (European Journalism Observatory, 2015). The photographs of Aylan circulated rapidly around the world. British tabloid newspapers, which had been renowned for their hostile headlines on migration and refugees, now lamented the horrific fate of 'tragic Aylan' and (temporarily) engaged in more sympathetic reporting on the plight of the people journeying to Europe; these people were now more likely to be referred to as 'refugees' rather than 'migrants' (Goodman et al., 2017). Under pressure to adjust to a shift in public sentiment, on 7 September, Prime Minister David Cameron declared that 'the whole country has been deeply moved by the heart-breaking images that we have seen over the past few days' (HC deb 7 September 2015, c23). He announced that the SVPRP would be expanded and would resettle 4,000 Syrians each year until 2020 (HC deb 7 September 2015, c24).

What was it about the photographs of Aylan that induced such sentiments of compassion? I suggest that this occurred because the images of Aylan were encountered and narrated in ways that engaged with feeling and framing rules about childhood and British national identity. These mapped onto the framework and criteria for compassion outlined by Nussbaum (2013); these are that suffering should be serious, the person suffering was not at fault and that the person suffering is in our circle of concern.

Aylan's age and his status as a *young* child was central in the commentary on the images and his death. Although he was 3 years old he was often described in the British media as a 'toddler' (a term usually used to describe younger children) and through adjectives such as 'tiny', 'little' or 'small' (Hall and Macfarlan, 2015). As Warner (2015: 7) has observed, 'in the hierarchy of innocence, children are *the* moral referent'. An invocation of childhood innocence was also seen in previous cracks in the hostile immigration regime, such as in the 2010 announcement by the Coalition government that they would 'end' child immigration detention. In announcing the end of child detention, the Deputy Prime Minister at the time, Nick Clegg, stated that detention was 'something no innocent child should ever have to endure' and that 'there is no greater test of civilized society than how it treats its young children' (Deputy Prime Minister's Office, 2010).

As a very young child, Aylan was identifiable as a relatable human face, but had not yet taken on the more troubling and contentious characteristics attached to refugees in some media reporting. Similar in composition to contemporary aid appeals, the photographs of Aylan showed him 'cast adrift' (Manzo, 2008: 642) from his family; either alone on the beach, or in the arms of a stranger (the Turkish police officer), he was depicted as having suffered in a dangerous environment and having been in need of protection. Unlike those who had survived the journey to Europe, his body was still and lifeless and he demanded nothing. Lacking agency, he was faultless. In the debates in Parliament, people who remained in the Middle Eastern camps, especially children, were contrasted with those who had already achieved relative 'safety' in Europe. Former Defence Secretary, Liam Fox, declared that, 'if we are genuinely to help refugees, this cannot simply be about helping the fittest, the fastest and those most able to get to western Europe. We must help those who are left behind in the camps, who are sometimes the most vulnerable' (HC deb 7 September 2015, c34). In other words, the 'left behind', who like Aylan had not reached Europe, were the ideal subjects of compassion.

The response of compassion towards Aylan also emanated out of eudai-monistic judgement. Although Nussbaum (2013) argues that being able to imagine similar possibilities for oneself is not essential for feeling compassion, she accepts that this can aid eudemonistic judgement. This was noticeable in the response to Aylan's images. Commentators, including MPs and journal-ists, frequently drew on their experiences as parents, or imagined how they might feel as a parent if Aylan was their child (Phillips, 2015). Unlike more graphic photographs of death seen during the refugee crisis, including dead children in dishevelled clothing floating in the sea, although we are aware that a great tragedy has occurred, Aylan's image was peaceful. His clothing was intact, and he appeared as if he was sleeping. In commentary on Twitter, Aylan was frequently likened to a sleeping child and people remarked that his posture was like that of their own children when they slept. As Labour MP, Yvette Cooper, observed, the photographs had moved people because they were 'the image of a three-year-old on a beach, a picture that should have been full of life and joy and instead was a tragedy' (HC deb 8 Sep 2015, c245). The image of the small child on the beach or asleep was familiar and relatable; through their everyday experiences of playing with their children on holiday beaches or putting their children to bed, people could conceivably picture themselves in this scene. Death was even more horrific and shocking because it was out of place in this familiar and usually happy setting. Scottish National Party MP, Alison Thewliss (HC deb 8 Sep 2015, c492), said that after seeing the images she, 'held my own children tighter that night as they slept in their beds'; indeed, #CouldBeMyChild, was one of the popular hashtags used to comment on the photograph (El-Enany, 2016).

However, eudemonistic judgement also went beyond the imagining of similar possibilities. A compassionate response towards Aylan, and by extension other refugee children, fitted within the existing celebratory narrative of pride in the morality of the British nation-state and its peoples. Moreover, a response of compassion not only aligned within this celebratory national narrative but was also understood as necessary for undoing the shame brought on the nation by the government's inadequate responses to the refugee crisis thus far. As the Liberal Democrat MP, Alistair Carmichael, stated (HC deb 8 September 2015, c284), 'the question it brings to my mind is how the people of Britain will be seen on the world stage. That is what is at stake here. It is not a question of numbers, but of our standing in the world.'

In the months following the publication of Aylan's photographs, reference continued to be made to the UK's history of welcoming refugees and, particularly, to mass displacement during the Second World War and the Kindertransports whereby Jewish refugee children had been rescued and resettled in the UK. In his amendment to the Immigration Bill 2016 (to include the resettlement of unaccompanied minors who had arrived in Europe), Lord Dubs referred to the UK's history of providing sanctuary to refugee children through the Kindertransports, through which he himself had arrived in the UK. He described the figure of the vulnerable, innocent refugee child at risk of serious harm and living in miserable conditions in camps in Europe, and he contrasted this with the celebrated sophistication and humanitarianism of Europe, highlighting the discrepancy between the celebrated values of the region and the potentially shameful proof that the region had fallen short of these professed standards. He reminded Parliament that it had recently been Holocaust Memorial Day, and of the gratitude expressed by former Kindertransport refugee children to the UK and what these refugee children had gone on to achieve. He also reminded MPs of the UK's professed status as a moral leader, stating that, 'in 1938–39, most countries refused to help, and it was only the United Kingdom that allowed the children entry. We were alone, and we set an example that other countries did not follow.' His speech attempted to invoke compassion for the fate of these children through appealing to both the emotions of pride and shame by articulating this (contested) interpretation of national history that proclaimed the UK as an exemplar nation-state that had always welcomed refugees, and by drawing on the narrative of 'child saving' elaborated on earlier. The Dubs Amendment was passed in May 2016.

Compassion and exclusion

It is most commonly argued that immigration and asylum policy discourse draws on, and mobilises, hostile or 'negative' emotions such as hate, fear or anxiety (Jones et al., 2017). However, seemingly humanising emotions can also be used to justify what are in fact exclusionary and oppressive practices (Berlant, 2004). While campaigners who advocated an expansion of refugee resettlement in the wake of Aylan's death drew heavily on a discourse of compassion, compassion was also referenced by those seeking to justify the refusal of the resettlement of refugees who had reached Europe. Justifying the UK's resettlement from camps in the Middle East rather than from Europe, David Cameron asserted that this would save lives because it would 'not encourage more people to make this perilous journey' (HC deb 7 September 2015, c39). This was a continuation of the logic for scaling back rescue operations at sea on the basis that more people would attempt these dangerous journeys and thus risk their lives if they thought they were likely to be rescued (Kingsley, 2016). Meanwhile, although those advocating the resettlement of unaccompanied children who had arrived Europe argued that this would protect them from human trafficking, those opposed to this measure suggested conversely that it would increase the risk of human trafficking. For example, in a question to the Prime Minister in the House of Commons debate on 7 September, Conservative MP Gareth Johnson asked whether resettlement from Europe did not give 'a green light to people smugglers and encourages exploitation?' referring to the government's 'good track record' on tackling modern slavery and trafficking (HC deb 7 September 2015, c63). In February 2017, it was announced that the Dubs resettlement programme would end, after settling just 350 children. In announcing the closure, the Home Secretary Amber Rudd said that the programme had created a pull factor and that children were returning to the demolished camps in Calais in the hope that they would be resettled in the UK (Stone, 2017). She stated that 'the Government has always been clear that we do not want to incentivise perilous journeys to Europe particularly by the most vulnerable children' (Stone, 2017).

Nicholls (2014) observes that while niche openings may present within a wider context of hostility, these are narrow and highly conditional, meaning that only a few people can fit through these cracks and many others are excluded. Refugee and migrant rights campaigners in the UK have frequently emphasised that migrant and refugee children should be treated as 'children first' in accordance with their rights enshrined in the UN CRC (Sirriyeh, 2014). However, many of these children are older children and teenagers, and they often find that contradictory discourses around their identities as refugees and children come into tension, often leading to their expulsion from the protection of childhood. In October 2016, the first groups of children and young people arrived in the UK from Calais under the Dublin III regulations to be reunited with their relatives in the UK; those who were to be resettled under the Dubs Amendment were still waiting to be relocated. British newspapers published photographs of the young people (all of whom were teenage boys) as they arrived in Croydon (London) and speculated about their age. For example, the *Daily Mail* published the headline 'The first Calais "*children*" arrive in Britain: Migrants *who claim to be* aged 14 to 17 are reunited with their families in the UK as French prepare to demolish Jungle camp' [my italics] (Linning and Curtis, 2016). The quotation marks around the word 'children' suggested it was a contested status, while the phrase 'claim to be' implied disbelief. Similarly, the *Daily Star* also used quotation marks around the term 'kids' in their headline and stated that they were 'supposedly', aged 14–17 years old, again suggesting an element of disbelief (McKee, 2016). The subheading of the article reiterated this suspicion stating that, 'THE first "*child*" migrants fleeing the Calais Jungle camp were given asylum in Britain yesterday – *with many looking older than their years*' (McKee, 2016).

Responding to these headlines, the Conservative MP David Davies observed that they 'don't look like children' and stated, 'I hope that British hospitality is not being abused', controversially suggesting that their teeth should be examined to determine their ages (Withnall, 2016). This was the latest incident in a long running culture of disbelief around the age claims of teenage refugees (Wade et al., 2012). Age determination has assumed an important place in social work assessments in the UK since it has implications both for determining eligibility for support from children's services and for young people's subsequent placement pathways. In 2010, I interviewed refugee young people during a study about their experiences of foster care provision in England (Sirriyeh, 2013b). Some young people reported that they were received with an air of watchfulness and suspicion and that their ages had been disputed by the Home Office, social workers or foster carers as they were deemed to be acting older than their claimed age or their physical appearance was not deemed to tally with this age.

In *States of Denial*, Cohen (2001) argued that despite their knowledge that suffering is taking place, people often deny it through ignoring, disavowing or reinterpreting what is taking place, and withholding the appropriate moral responses of compassion and intervention. In seeking to explain how denial was legitimated, Cohen (2001) asserted that there were three possibilities as to what was being denied. Through 'literal denial' people asserted that something did not happen or was not true; through 'interpretive denial' they claimed that what had happened was actually something else, and not what it appeared to be; or, finally, through 'implicatory denial' the psychological, political or moral implications were denied or minimised. Compassionate responses appear to have been withheld from many older refugee children, and especially teenage boys, due to 'interpretative denial'. On the cusp of adulthood and fast-tracked into adulthood by the hardships and challenges they have faced, many teenage refugee young boys lose the protective cloak of 'vulnerability' and become the subject of the concerns that are often attached to adult male migrants and refugees. The young people in Calais were responded to not as innocent children, but through the frame of 'militarised masculinities' (Allsopp, 2015). They were strong and exhibited agency in having undertaken the arduous journey to Europe and through placing demands on the UK. Writing in the *Daily Star*, McKee (2016) stated that, 'despite looking considerably older than the teenage cutoff point, the "children" are *demanding* asylum and saying they come from war-torn countries' [my italics]. Not only were these children 'demanding' asylum, the quotation marks implied that they may not be 'children' at all. They were, therefore, seen through the familiar frame of 'bogus' asylum seeker, not only trying to deceive British people, but, in this case, also pushing in and taking the places of younger innocent children. These boys (or young men) fitted the description that Theresa May gave of refugees and migrants in Calais in her speech to the Conservative Party conference as Home Secretary in 2015. She described them as the fittest and strongest people who had made it to Europe and 'who sometimes manipulate it [the UK asylum system], for their own ends at the expense of the more vulnerable', and she observed that, 'three quarters of asylum seekers in Britain are men and the vast majority are in their twenties' (Independent, 2015).

Age not only affects young people gaining entry to the UK and support from children's services, but also how they are treated in transitions out of care. At the age of 18, and even earlier for many at the age of 16, refugee young people face sharp and fast-track transitions to independent living (Wade et al., 2012). At 18, given that most of these young people have not been granted refugee status (see earlier), they face the prospect of being refused asylum and risk deportation as they are no longer protected from this outcome by their status as children. In 2014, 245 former unaccompanied minors were served with Removal Directions (Brokenshire, 2015).

Conclusion

Viewed as lacking agency and out of place in the public realm, children often struggle to be recognised as political actors and so as persecuted people. However, as the figure of the 'genuine refugee' becomes increasingly characterised as vulnerable, and asylum is reframed as compassion for the suffering body, rather than obligation to the threatened body, refugee children have become the figure of the refugee par excellence, as seen in the response to the death of Aylan Kurdi. Indeed 'vulnerability' and passiveness, characteristics associated with the image of the refugee child, have become the predominant characteristics associated with the 'genuine' refugee, and there has been a move overall from recognition of the 'threatened body' to recognition of the 'suffering body', or the inherently vulnerable body. This has led to niche openings for some refugee children who have been able to gain some access to recognition and support as asylum has been reframed through the emotional regime of compassion. However, a discourse of compassion has also been used to justify exclusionary and oppressive responses to children, while the highly conditional and narrow criteria for compassion has also reinforced the further exclusion of those people who are unable to meet these terms.

To date, research on emotions and asylum has understandably focused predominantly on hostile emotions expressed towards people seeking asylum and the fear and distress that they experience. However, as has been shown in this chapter, there are moments of interruption to this dominant discourse on asylum. Meanwhile, rather than simply calling for greater compassion, a case has been made here for engaging critically with compassion in asylum discourse, policy and practice to examine how and when it can interrupt and on what terms, recognising also the ways in which it has been appropriated and mobilised to enforce violence and exclusion.

Notes

1 Unless otherwise specified, I use the term 'refugee' as an overarching term to refer to people who are at any stage of the asylum application process.

References

Allsopp, J. (2015), The refugee crisis: demilitarising masculinities. *Open Democracy* (17 September 2015), www.opendemocracy.net/5050/jennifer-allsopp/refugee-crisis-demilitarising-masculinities [accessed 1 January 2020].

Anderson, B. (2013), *Us and Them? The Dangerous Politics of Immigration Control* (Oxford: Oxford University Press).

Berlant, L. (2004), Compassion (and withholding). In *Compassion: The Culture and Politics of an Emotion* (New York: Routledge, 2004), pp. 1–15.

Bloch, A. and L. Schuster (2005), At the extremes of exclusion: deportation, detention and dispersal. *Ethnic and Racial Studies* 28(3): 491–512.

Brokenshire, J. (2015), Asylum: Children: Written Question – 16866 (18 November 2015) [online] www.parliament.uk/business/publications/written-questions-answers-statements/written-question/Commons/2015–11–18/16866/ [accessed 1 January 2020].

Castles, S. and M. Miller (2003), *The Age of Migration: International Movements in the Modern World* (3rd Edition) (Basingstoke: Palgrave Macmillan).

Cohen, S. (2006), *Deportation is Freedom! The Orwellian World of Immigration Controls* (London: Jessica Kingsley Publishers).

Cohen, S. (2001), *States of Denial: Knowing about Atrocities and Suffering* (Cambridge: Polity Press).

Collyer, M, R. Brown, L. Morrice and L. Tip (2017), Putting refugees at the centre of resettlement in the UK. *Forced Migration Review* 54: 16–19.

Crawley, H., F. Duvell, K. Jones, S. McMahon and N. Sigona (2017), *Unravelling Europe's 'Migration Crisis'* (Bristol: Policy Press).

Deputy Prime Minister's Office (2010), Deputy Prime Minister's speech on child detention (16 December, 2010) [online] https://www.gov.uk/government/speeches/deputy-prime-ministers-speech-on-child-detention [accessed 1 January 2020].

Eleftheriou-Smith, L. (2015), Bishops slam Cameron's refugee crisis response and urge him to take in 50,000 Syrians. *Independent* (18 October 2015) [online] www.independent.co.uk/news/uk/home-news/bishops-slam-camerons-increasingly-inadequate-response-to-refugee-crisis-and-urge-him-to-take-in-a6698546.html [accessed 1 January 2020].

El-Enany, N. (2016), Aylan Kurdi: the human refugee. *Law and Critique* 27: 13–15.

European Journalism Observatory (2015), Research: How Europe's newspapers reported the migration crisis [online] en.ejo.ch/research/research-how-europes-newspapers-reported-the-migration-crisis [accessed 1 January 2020].

Fassin, D. (2011), *Humanitarian Reason: A Moral History of the Present* (Oakland: University of California Press).

Fassin, D. (2005), Compassion and repression: the moral economy of immigration policies in France. *Cultural Anthropology* 20(3): 362–387.

Goodman, S., A. Sirriyeh and S. McMahon (2017), The evolving (re)categorisations of refugees throughout the refugee/migrant crisis. Special issue: The European Union and the refugee crisis: identities, challenges and responses, *Journal of Community and Applied Social Psychology*, DOI: 10.1002casp.2302.

Hall, J. and T. Macfarlan (2015), Humanity washed ashore: Outpouring of grief continues for Syrian toddler Aylan, three, after images of his dead body on a Turkish shoreline shocked the world. *Daily Mail* (4 September 2015) [online] www.dailymail.co.uk/news/article-3222829/Outpouring-grief-continues-images-Syrian-toddler-Aylan-Kurdi-s-dead-body-Turkey.html [accessed 1 January 2020].

Hochschild, A. (2002), Emotion management in the age of global terrorism. *Soundings* 20: 1–10.

Home Office (2016), New scheme launched to resettle children at risk [online] www.gov.uk/government/news/new-scheme-launched-to-resettle-children-at-risk [accessed 1 January 2020].

House of Commons Debate (2015), Refugee crisis in Europe (8 September 2015) [online] www.publications.parliament.uk/pa/cm201516/cmhansrd/cm150908/debtext/150908–0002.htm [accessed 1 January 2020].

House of Commons Debate (2015), Syria: refugees and counter-terrorism (7 September 2015) [online] www.publications.parliament.uk/pa/cm201516/cmhansrd/cm150907/debtext/150907–0001.htm [accessed 1 January 2020].

Hynes, P. (2011), *The Dispersal and Social Exclusion of Asylum Seekers: Between Liminality and Belonging* (Bristol: Policy Press, 2011).

Jones, H., Y. Gunaratnam, G. Bhattacharyya, S. Dhaliwal, K. Forkert, E. Jackson, R. Saltus and W. Davies (2017), *Go Home? The Politics of Immigration Controversies* (Manchester: Manchester University Press).

Kingsley, P. (2016), *The New Odyssey: The Story of Europe's Refugee Crisis* (London: Guardian Faber Publishing).

Lewis, H., P. Dwyer, S. Hodkinson and L. Waite (2014) *Precarious Lives: Forced Labour Exploitation and Asylum* (Bristol: Policy Press).

Linning, S. and J. Curtis (2016), Britain: Migrants who claim to be aged 14 to 17 are reunited with their families in the UK as French prepare to demolish Jungle camp. *Daily Mail* (17 October 2016) [online] www.dailymail.co.uk/news/article-3843900/First-migrant-children-arrive-UK-Calais-French-prepare-raze-Jungle-camp-ground.html#ixzz4apRC0zv0 [accessed 1 January 2020].

Manzo, K. (2008), Imaging humanitarianism: NGO identity and the iconography of childhood. *Antipode* 40(4): 632–657.

Independent (2015), Theresa May's speech to the Conservative Party Conference – in full. *Independent* (6 October 2015) [online] http://www.independent.co.uk/

news/uk/politics/theresa-may-s-speech-to-the-conservative-party-conference-in-full-a6681901.html [accessed 1 January 2020].

McGuinness, T. (2017), The UK Response to the Syrian Refugee Crisis. House of Commons Library – Briefing Paper No. 06085 (16 February 2017) [online] researchbriefings.files.parliament.uk/documents/SN06805/SN06805.pdf [accessed 1 January 2020].

McKee, R. (2016), First Calais "kids" arrive: Migrant asylum seekers supposedly aged 14–17 arrive in UK. *Daily Star* (17 October 2016) [online] www.dailystar.co.uk/news/latest-news/554455/Calais-kids-aged-14–17-arrive-inUK-look-older-expected [accessed 1 January 2020].

Nicholls, W. (2014), From political opportunities to niche-openings: the dilemmas of mobilizing for immigrant rights in inhospitable environments. *Theory and Society* 43: 23–49.

Nussbaum, M. (2013), *Political Emotions: Why Love Matters for Justice* (Cambridge, MA: Harvard University Press).

Nussbaum, M. (1996), Compassion: the basic social emotion. *Social Philosophy and Policy* 13(1): 27–58.

Phillips, A. (2015), After Aylan Al-Kurdi's tragedy we must let the refugees in and learn from them. *Mirror* (8 September 2015) [online] www.mirror.co.uk/news/uk-news/after-aylan-al-kurdis-tragedy-6407578 [accessed 1 January 2020].

Piper, C. (1999), Moral campaigns for children's welfare in the nineteenth century. In King, M. (ed.) *Moral Agendas for Children's Welfare* (London: Routledge), pp. 33–52.

Refugee Council (2016a), Asylum statistics annual trends [online] www.refugeecouncil.org.uk/assets/0003/9435/Asylum_Statistics_Annual_Trends_December_2016.pdf [accessed 1 January 2020].

Refugee Council (2016b), Children in the asylum system – December 2016 [online] www.refugeecouncil.org.uk/assets/0003/9438/Children_in_the_Asylum_System_December_2016.pdf [accessed 1 January 2020].

Sales, R. (2002), The deserving and the undeserving? Refugees, asylum seekers and welfare in Britain. *Critical Social Policy* 22(3): 456–478.

Sirriyeh, A. (2014), Sanctuary or sanctions: children, social worth and social control in the UK asylum process. In Harrison, M. and T. Sanders (eds) *Social Policies and Social Control: New Perspectives on the Not-so- Big Society* (Bristol: The Policy Press), pp. 71–86.

Sirriyeh, A. (2013a), *Inhabiting Borders, Routes Home: Youth, Gender, Asylum* (Oxford: Routledge).

Sirriyeh, A. (2013b), Hosting strangers: hospitality and family practices in fostering unaccompanied refugee young people. *Child and Family Social Work* 18(1): 5–14.

Stone, J. (2017), Ministers say child refugee scheme they are closing early "incentivises" children to become refugees. *Independent* (9 February 2017) [online] www.independent.co.uk/news/uk/politics/child-refugees-dubs-amendment-amber-rudd-calais-camps-a7570981.html [accessed 1 January 2020].

Wade, J., A. Sirriyeh, R. Kohli and J. Simmonds (2012), *Fostering Unaccompanied Refugee and Asylum Seeking Young People: Creating Family Life across a 'World of Difference'* (London: BAAF).

Warner, J. (2015), *The Emotional Politics of Social Work and Child Protection* (Bristol: Policy Press).

Withnall, A. (2016), Dentists condemn MPs calls for child refugees from Calais to have teeth checked. *Independent* (19 October 2016) [online] www.independent.co.uk/news/uk/home-news/david-davies-dentists-condemn-mp-call-for-calais-refugees-to-have-teeth-checked-a7368841.html [accessed 1 January 2020].

3

The banality of displacement: re-reading Hannah Arendt to instil critical thought in the Colombian refugee crisis[1]

Ulrich Oslender

The violence of labelling

While much attention in conversations on the contemporary global refugee crisis is placed on the Middle East, Africa and Asia (and increasingly on Europe as a receiving host region), it is the South American nation of Colombia that has one of the highest numbers of internal refugees worldwide. Since 1985, over six million people have been internally displaced; that is, more than 10 percent of Colombians have at some point in their lives been forced to flee their homes as a result of violence (CODHES, 2014; IDMC, 2014). Different from many other refugee crises in the world that put certain countries temporarily on the map as 'displacement hotspots', the crisis in Colombia has been evolving at a slower, yet creepingly consistent pace. This trend is less characterised by spectacular displacements resulting from large-scale bombing and military campaigns – such as in Syria, Sudan, Iraq, etc. – but by the smaller scale, yet unceasing removal of people from their lands. Displacement has become such a persistent feature in society that Colombians seemingly have got used to it and its manifold manifestations: women and children begging at street intersections; boys balancing machetes on their fingertips at traffic lights to attract drivers' attention and an occasional coin or bill.

One may argue that a normalisation process has set in that is accompanied by a standardising vocabulary in the media, government circles and non-governmental organisation (NGO) reports, where refugees are labelled 'IDPs' (internally displaced persons). While some organisations may work towards obtaining such a legal definition of IDP – for example, in order to access certain government services or United Nations High Commissioner for Refugees (UNHCR) aid set aside for people identified as such – others feel there is an increasing tension between a disembodied, legalist label and a more embodied approach that recognises the impact of political violence and the political agency of the displaced. Colombian photo-journalist Jesús Abad

Colorado's 2006 exhibition titled 'Memory, Place, and Displacement' (shown at the Museum of Anthropology at the University of British Columbia in Vancouver, Canada), for example, is an angry reaction to these labelling processes and disembodied representations of violence and terror. As he comments in the foreword to the exhibition's catalogue:

> The victims wander about marked by the label of the displaced and the exiled; the excluded and the refugees. They are trivialized in reports and statistics from different governments that minimize the numbers and dispute them with the Non-Governmental Organizations in articles and soundbites in the mainstream media ... Men and women from *mestizo* communities, blacks and indigenous people from all over the country, are not anonymous beings. They have a face and a name ... They still hope, still long for, still desire, this war to end. They want that monster called violence not to continue grabbing their lands, their lives and dignity. (Abad Colorado, 2007: 3)

In this chapter, I want to reflect on why such a concrete embodiment so often gets lost in debates over the armed conflict in Colombia. For this, I introduce the idea of the 'banality of displacement'. With this notion – drawing on Hannah Arendt's suggestive ideas regarding the 'banality of evil' – I want to capture two distinct but related processes. First, the normalisation of violence over time and the steady uprooting of rural communities in Colombia make 'forced displacement' appear as a mundane, banal social fact. The emergence of the IDP as a social category accounted for in government and NGO statistics attests to this development. National governments devise complex strategies to count their internally displaced population, with official figures often passionately contested by NGOs. In particular, I examine a longstanding statistical dispute in Colombia and the ways in which the internally displaced have been identified, counted and categorised.

Second, I draw on the writings of Hannah Arendt and her take on 'banality', which goes beyond the term's common associations of 'normalcy', 'routine' or 'mundane'. Instead, she stresses 'thoughtlessness' – or a generalised breakdown in critical thinking – as a mechanism through which evil is enacted. Such an approach to the displacement discourse, I argue, is useful as it allows us to focus on the *processes* that produce displacement as a normalised phenomenon. These processes include the production of thoughtless attitudes (e.g., in government or NGO circles) – or an 'attitudinal thoughtlessness' – towards a situation that seemingly requires pragmatic, immediate solutions, while often sacrificing – willingly or not – a deeper, more complex understanding of the situation at hand. In this context, 'thoughtlessness' does not mean that no thought is invested – quite the contrary – but, as Arendt might say, just not the right kind of thought; truly critical thinking has often been absent from these debates. In other words, 'the banality of displacement' is not merely an observable fact (a normalised phenomenon in society), but is actively produced (in discourse).

To illustrate this banality at play and to show how attitudinal thoughtlessness is produced, I want to focus on two interrelated aspects. First, I examine the administrative and statistical history of 'IDP management' in Colombia, and in particular the disputes over displacement statistics that have caused significant tension between government agencies and NGOs. By dissecting the ways in which the counting of the internally displaced takes place, I demonstrate the overall effect that these quarrels over statistics produce in presenting the displaced persons as mere numbers. This, I argue, has come at the expense of a more complex characterisation of the internally displaced population. Examining the case of Afro-Colombian communities, I show how what I call a 'colour-blind' approach to displacement has meant that, despite this group's recognition as an ethnic minority in the 1991 constitution, for years no data was collected regarding the ethnic composition of the displaced population. I provocatively ask a simple question: How can we explain the fact that census data on Afro-Colombians has been collected systematically since 1993, but until 2005 no distinction was made in the ethnic make-up of IDPs in Colombia? We simply do not know how many of the displaced were Afro-Colombians, although it is claimed (in the popular imagination and by several academics) that black groups have been affected disproportionately compared to the rest of the population. As I show – aiming to extend Arendt's reflections on banality – a breakdown in critical thinking can be observed that seemingly failed to even consider this question. By exposing this thoughtlessness, the banality of displacement approach can help instil critical thought to counter the normalisation of the phenomenon of displacement.

In the final section, therefore, I discuss some of the ways in which the banality of displacement has been contested more recently, both from civil society through the work of social movements, NGOs and artists, and by Colombia's Constitutional Court, which has challenged the government over its handling of the national displacement crisis through a number of interventions and orders.

Arendt and the banality of evil

During 1961–62, the Jewish philosopher Hannah Arendt witnessed the proceedings against ex-*Obersturmbannführer* Adolf Eichmann, who was put on trial in Jerusalem under Israel's Nazis and Nazi Collaborator Punishment Law of 1950 for his role in the Holocaust. Arendt published her observations in a series of articles in *The New Yorker* between February and March 1963. In May 1963, these appeared in book form as *Eichmann in Jerusalem: A Report on the Banality of Evil*, an enquiry into why and how a law-abiding 'ordinary citizen', who at first was in charge of the forced emigration of Jews from Nazi Germany, would later oversee their transportation to the extermination ghettos. In her opinion, 'it was of great political interest to know how long it takes an average person to overcome his innate repugnance toward crime, and what exactly happens to him once he has reached that point' (Arendt, 1977: 93).

Arendt was heavily critiqued for what many saw as her trivialising the Holocaust. The controversy arose partly with the subtitle of the book: a report on the banality of evil. In fact, the expression 'banality of evil' only appears once in the book, right towards the end, when Arendt (1977: 252) summarises the horror of the Holocaust as the 'fearsome, word-and-thought-defying *banality of evil*'. Following the controversy, she justified the notion in an afterword to a later edition:

> for when I speak of the banality of evil, I do so only on the strictly factual level, pointing to a phenomenon which stared one in the face at the trial. Eichmann was not ... stupid. It was sheer thoughtlessness – something by no means identical with stupidity – that predisposed him to become one of the greatest criminals of that period. And if this is 'banal' ... that is still far from calling it commonplace ... That such remoteness from reality and such thoughtlessness can wreak more havoc than all the evil instincts taken together ... that was, in fact, the lesson one could learn in Jerusalem. But it was a lesson, neither an explanation of the phenomenon nor a theory about it. (Arendt, 1977: 287–288)

What Arendt was concerned about was in fact to understand this 'strange interdependence of thoughtlessness and evil' (Arendt, 1977: 288). It is this aspect of banality – the thoughtlessness, or lack of critical thought – that I want to engage with when thinking through the discourse of displacement in Colombia.[2] The positive purchase we get from thinking with Arendt's ideas is this: rather than simply using 'banal' interchangeably with 'mundane', 'commonplace' or 'routine', a focus on the breakdown in critical thinking offers at least two advantages. First, it helps us see that banality is not just something that is 'simply there', a mundane presence, but instead that it is actively produced. Second, it enables us to imagine ways of subverting this banality. By exposing the lack of critical thought that underlies the displacement discourse and its 'remoteness from reality', we can call for a re-thinking of a given situation, instilling fresh and critical thought.

Banality and attitudinal thoughtlessness

The 'strange interdependence of thoughtlessness and evil' that Arendt (1977: 288) wanted to capture in the notion of banality is revealed in the Colombian context in three principal ways. First, there is the thoughtlessness of the individual committing an act of violence. We may consider the paramilitary fighter, for example, who hacks his victims to death with a machete, plays football with their heads or rapes a *campesino* woman in front of her husband. As María Victoria Uribe (2004) has shown, the collective torture and assassination of unarmed and defenceless people has become a recurrent cultural practice in Colombia, infused by the semantics of political terror. The individual paramilitary hereby takes part in an orchestrated act of gruesome violence that does not require his capacity for thinking. The thoughtlessness of the individual is in fact necessary for the smooth operation of the logic of terror as a communicative strategy.

Second, I argue that a lack of critical thought has permeated the institutional level. Laws are adopted in response to escalating numbers of *campesinos* fleeing the countryside and filling up the urban spaces. New administrative bodies are created to deal with the ever-increasing phenomenon. I do not suggest that individuals in these institutions do not think, or are not committed to improving this situation – far from it. Yet, displacement is banal in that it has become accepted as part of the social fabric that simply has to be dealt with. It is often not problematised as such. This 'institutional thoughtlessness' may in itself be seen as an act of violence, which, as I show below, has led to the statistical invisibilisation of Afro-Colombians as an ethnically differentiated displaced population.

Third, thoughtlessness gives way to a significant ontological change. The people who are forced to flee their homes and leave everything behind to save their lives are no longer *campesinos*. On arrival in the cities of refuge, they are transformed into *desplazados* (the displaced). Not only have their bodies been (re)moved from one place to be inserted into another, but their very being has been changed in the process. Their new status is that of an 'internally displaced person', or, conveniently abbreviated for statistical purposes, 'IDP'. They form part of a standardised vocabulary that includes statistics, expert discourses, national policies and legislations. As Abad Colorado (2007: 3) denounces in the quote above, they 'wander about marked by the label of the displaced and the exiled; the excluded and the refugees. They are trivialized in reports and statistics from different governments that minimize the numbers and dispute them with the Non-Governmental Organizations in articles and soundbites in the mainstream media.'

Of course, one may argue that the category of IDP certainly works against the invisibility of displacement. And as I mentioned above, social organisations may well be keen to be recognised as representing IDPs, as aid and social services are attached to such a legal recognition. Individuals may also feel empowered 'thanks to their displacement' in often unexpected ways (see Cárdenas, 2018). Yet what the critique of the categorisation as 'displaced' points to is the loss of complexity that this ontological change entails. Formerly *campesinos*, fisherfolks, black, indigenous or *mestizo*; these very diverse people are now all subsumed into this one category of IDP and treated as the same. I want to illustrate what this loss of complexity may lead to by first examining a statistical dispute in Colombia between NGOs and government bodies in the counting of the displaced to then explore the specific case of Afro-Colombians and how for decades their ethnic specificity has been overlooked – with very tangible results for this population group.

War over numbers: counting the displaced

There are two major bodies that produce statistics on internal forced displacement in Colombia today: the government agency Unit for Integrated Support and Reparation for Victims – UARIV (*Unidad para la Atención y Reparación Integral a las Víctimas*), and the non-governmental Consultancy for Human Rights and Displacement – CODHES.[3] While the latter has operated since 1992, the former is the latest in a number of newly created governmental agencies charged with accounting for the phenomenon of forced displacement. This makes it hard at times to keep track of how government data is gathered and processed. The discrepancies found in respective statistics are largely due to the different methodologies employed in gathering and evaluating data on displacement. It is important to explain these differences here, as countless government bodies, NGOs, UN agencies and academics draw on these quite different data sets to make their point.

Unit for Integrated Support and Reparation for Victims (UARIV)

UARIV is the government body in charge today of dealing with all aspects related to internal forced displacement. It is the result of a number of institutional changes and diverse legislations. Even though forced migrations have occurred throughout Colombian history, it was not until 1995 that the government formally acknowledged the problem and adopted a policy towards it. CONPES (*El Consejo Nacional de Política Económica y Social*) document 2804 outlines government responsibilities for protecting those who are forced to flee their homes as a result of political violence (DNP, 1995). This first official policy statement drew on data provided by the Episcopal Conference the previous year, which forced the government to take a stance on this issue. It was subsequently developed into Law 387 of 1997, the principal legislation for the 'assistance, protection, consolidation, and socio-economic stabilization of the people internally displaced by violence in the Republic of Colombia'.

The processing of displacement data has gone through different phases. The first basic data collection between 1995 and 1999 was administered by the Ministry of the Interior and Justice. In July 1997, an electronic database was established to systemise information. In March 1999, the government agency *Red de Solidaridad Social* (Social Solidarity Network, RSS) was charged with coordinating data collection with policies providing assistance to the displaced population. As a statistical tool for these ends, RSS launched in April 2001 the informational data base SUR (*Sistema Único de Registro*). For the first time, a standard format was adopted for the collection of information on the displaced population, including name, age, gender and marital status. It is noteworthy that it did not consider the displaced's ethnicity, an omission I elaborate upon below. Further modifications of governmental programmes occurred in July 2005, when the presidential agency *Acción Social* was created to replace RSS, and in June 2006, when the SUR data system was replaced by the more elaborate online information system SIPOD (*Sistema de Información de Población Desplazada*).

For someone to be considered an 'IDP' and to receive emergency assistance (such as food and clothing) and continued support (such as housing, schooling and health care), s/he is required to submit a formal declaration with a government institution. Failing to do so, the claimant neither receives any support nor appears in the official displacement register. This has been one of the principal critiques of government statistics: they leave out all those who are either afraid to register as displaced (be it for fear of reprisals or stigmatisation), who do not have the required identification documents on them when intending to register (ID papers may get lost when fleeing violence) or who are not even aware of their rights. Once the displaced person has successfully registered, the submitted declaration is evaluated by government officials. Should the latter believe that it was not made in good faith, the displaced person's application is refused. In a recent analysis, CODHES (2011) estimates that 34 percent of IDPs are not officially registered, and that 25 percent of applications for IDP status are turned down. As a result, government accumulated figures were for a long time far below those given by NGOs that hold a broader, more inclusive definition of displacement.

Consultancy for Human Rights and Displacement (CODHES)

Established as a non-profit organisation in 1992, CODHES is the principal NGO that deals with all aspects of forced displacement in Colombia. Since 1995, it has operated the information system SISDHES (*Sistema de Información sobre Desplazamiento Forzado y Derechos Humanos*), which produces estimates of the numbers of displaced by consulting a range of sources, including organisations of displaced persons, human rights NGOs, local authorities, UN agencies and media outlets. Between 1995 and 1998, these data were gathered and displayed by province. Since 1999, they have been available per municipality, providing more finely combed statistics. CODHES rejects the idea that a displaced person has to successfully register in order to be considered as IDP. Thus, since 1998, the NGO also conducts annual socio-demographic surveys to provide qualitative data on the condition of the internally displaced, examining the causes of forced migration, the routes via which the displaced flee their homes and the characteristics of the zones of expulsion and arrival.

For data prior to 1995, CODHES applies the estimate presented by the 1994 Episcopal Conference report, according to which forced displacement had affected 720,000 people between 1985 and 1994. These figures do not show up in government reports – as the Colombian government formally acknowledged the existence of internal displacement only in 1995 – and contribute to the discrepancy between NGO reports and government statistics when accumulated data are compared. Moreover, government data are highly fluid, in that people have up to one year to register as displaced. The data for any particular year are thus retrospectively adjusted up to four years later due to possible delays in evaluating declarations and the processing of data. Figures presented by *Acción Social* in 2011, for example, put the total accumulated number of registered IDPs in Colombia at 3,875,987, whereas CODHES (2011) accumulated estimates come in at a total of 5,281,360, a significant discrepancy of around 1.4 million people.

Why (better) numbers matter: contesting the colour-blind discourse of displacement

In 2004, I spent three months in Colombia carrying out fieldwork to examine the ways in which the Afro-Colombian population had been affected by forced displacement. Previously – in the late 1990s – I had conducted research into the place-based mobilisation strategies of the social movement of black communities over land claims in the Pacific coast region (Oslender, 2004, 2016b). The situation on the ground had shifted dramatically since then. Instead of securing their legally guaranteed collective land titles in the Pacific river basins, many of these communities were forcefully driven off their lands by armed groups. The proportion of Afro-Colombians among the displaced population has since increased significantly, to the extent that they are said to constitute more than one third of all internally displaced persons in Colombia (IDMC, 2014; Ng'weno, 2007: 174, 189).

Yet, in 2004, it was impossible to come by any reliable data on the ethnic composition of the displaced population. This seemed surprising, given the fact that Colombia had adopted a new constitution in 1991 that was to significantly reshape the relations between the nation and its Afro-descendant population, which was for the first time officially acknowledged as a distinct cultural group, as *comunidades negras*, or 'black communities'. The constitution marked the beginning of the 'ethnicization of blackness' in Colombia (Restrepo, 2004). 'Blackness' became a state-regulated discourse, a field of struggle, a structure of alterity (see also Escobar, 2008; Paschel, 2010, 2016; Wade, 1993, 2002). More specifically, Law 70 had been passed in 1993 'to establish mechanisms for protecting the cultural identity and rights of the Black Communities of Colombia as an ethnic group' (Chapter 1, Article 1). This law further specified the right to communal land ownership for rural black communities in the Pacific coast region, which began to be implemented in 1996 and has since led to more than five million hectares of tropical rainforest lands being titled collectively (Offen, 2003; Oslender, 2004, 2016b). In other words, significant legislation had been passed in Colombia since 1991 that acknowledges the existence of Afro-Colombians as a differentiated cultural group within the nation-state. A national census in 1993 included a question on ethnicity, and even though the resulting data were deeply flawed due to the ambiguous nature of the census question, it set an important precedent of counting the national population in terms of ethnicity.[4] Yet, when the Colombian government finally passed legislation on forced displacement in 1997 (Law 387), no provisions to actually count Afro-Colombians among the displaced were made.

This failure to address the ethnic differentiation of the displacement phenomenon appeared to me truly 'word-and-thought defying', to borrow Arendt's (1977: 252) phrase of astonishment. I think it is too easy to blame it solely on institutional structures of racism, as many observers would do. Much has been written on this structural racial discrimination that continues to exist in Colombia and that hides behind the official inclusionary discourse of *mestizaje* (Paschel, 2016; Wade, 1993). Yet, I do not believe this alone can explain the absence of ethnicity in official displacement discourse. Interviews I conducted in 2004 with both government officials and NGO workers revealed that state institutions and CODHES were so caught up in their 'war over numbers' (described above) that they simply did not ask more complex questions about the displaced population. Individuals in these institutions were so overwhelmed by the sheer amount of people that arrived destitute in the cities to seek refuge from the war in the countryside and required emergency assistance that issues regarding people's identity, including ethnicity, were not considered. As one RSS worker told me in an interview: '*no se nos ocurrió*' – it didn't occur to us.

It is precisely this lack of critical thought that I want to capture with the notion of banality of displacement. It is not that no thought went into the counting procedures; far from it. My above discussion shows that it clearly did; just not the right kind of (critical) thought. The displaced persons remained mere numbers. There was no place for their identity in the counting mechanisms. My proposal for capturing this absence with the notion of banality is not an explanation of the phenomenon of forced displacement per se. Rather it is an expression of a truly astonishing fact that stared one in the face and for which there just was no easy explanation. I find critical reflection over this sense of astonishment far more interesting and telling than short-hand explanations that point to the supposed explanatory powers of general racial discrimination. To cite Arendt, for when I speak of the banality of displacement, 'I do so only on the strictly factual level, pointing to a phenomenon which stared one in the face ... It was sheer thoughtlessness ... But it was a lesson, neither an explanation of the phenomenon nor a theory about it' (Arendt, 1977: 287–288).

To illustrate this sense of astonishment from an Afro-Colombian perspective, I quote from an interview that I conducted with an activist from the Process of Black Communities (PCN), one of the principal Afro-Colombian grassroots organisations. She had been forced to flee her home in the southern Pacific coastal town of Tumaco three years earlier, when paramilitary groups threatened

her because of her community work. Sitting with me in a busy cafeteria in
the centre of Bogotá one December afternoon in 2004, she explained:

> The State has not come up with the necessary policies to attend to the
> displaced population. For example, since I have been here [in Bogotá], for
> three years now, we at PCN keep stressing the need for a differentiated
> attention to the problem. That is, in this country there are displaced from
> indigenous communities, there are Afro-Colombian displaced, there are
> displaced *campesinos* and displaced *mestizos*. So we said that one has to
> differentiate between this very varied displaced population, so that at least
> one has an idea of how many people of a certain ethnic group have been
> displaced. And also what kind of help do these people need in accordance
> to their ethnic and cultural characteristics. That doesn't exist in Colombia
> at the moment. Even though we have insisted on this for some time. We
> have led campaigns. We have talked to government officials. This simply
> hasn't happened yet. We organised an observation mission here in Colombia,
> for example, and one of the recommendations for the Colombian State
> that came out of it was for the need to set up differentiated assistance
> programs according to the differing needs of the ethnic groups. But today
> you see this form from the Social Security Network [RSS] and you don't
> find this differentiation anywhere. There are no questions that would establish
> this difference. No register exists in Colombia that would tell you how
> many Afro-Colombian displaced there are … The little that does exist, and
> it is little, is data handled by NGOs, such as CODHES. They have some
> statistics, the Network [RSS] has other statistics, and other NGOs have
> yet again other statistics. So when you sit down to write a report you have
> to struggle with all these different numbers, because there is no real statistics.
> One always talks about rough estimates, but there are no clear statistics,
> because in Colombia we just don't register things.

This rather long quote reveals the deep sense of frustration that Afro-Colombian
activists experience in their attempt to receive official acknowledgement for
the differentiated ways in which they as an ethnic group are affected by the
armed conflict. One of the elemental differences that ethnicity makes to the
experience of forced displacement relates to patterns of everyday food
consumption. Most displaced Afro-Colombians come from the tropical
rainforest areas of the Pacific coast lowlands, where their staple diet is based
on plantains and fish. On arriving in the cities of refuge, such as the capital
Bogotá, which lies at 2,600 metres altitude, they are provided with food
assistance consisting of mostly beans and meat, which many of the displaced
find hard getting used to, let alone take a liking to. As the above quoted PCN
activist remembers her own displacement from the Pacific coast:

> For me it was very difficult. When I arrived in Bogotá I got terribly sick,
> because the climate here is very cold and I come from a hot climate on

the coast. The food here is based on meat, chicken, beans. When over there we have fish, crab, langoustines, all types of seafood. So it is completely different, the food. The atmosphere here is also different. People show less solidarity, they are quiet, you live in a building and people hardly greet you. When there in your village you know everybody, you walk along the streets, greet the whole world, everybody knows you ... So the context changes dramatically. It becomes very difficult.

Food aid in the first three months usually consists of the staples rice, beans, lentils and cooking oil – *una forma de alimentar que a la gente le enferma*: 'a way of eating that makes us sick'. This simple bureaucratic fact of undifferentiated food aid reveals the lack of critical thought invested in the assistance programme that ignores cultural differences in the displaced population. It is one of the first things on the minds of the displaced themselves, however, as radically changing food patterns not only affect their digestion negatively but also constitute a further break away from their cultural identity, intensifying the experience of uprootedness and abandonment. Afro-Colombian activists often evoke this example of enforced changes in food consumption to illustrate the need for a differentially structured governmental response to the displacement drama. Doing so, they insert critical thought into an 'institutional thoughtlessness' that borders on a criminal laissez-faire approach. It is by pointing out the seemingly obvious that banality can be challenged and, eventually, broken.

Breaking banality

In *The Will to Knowledge* Michel Foucault (1998: 101) reflects on the potential for subverting dominant discourse: 'We must make allowance for the complex and unstable process whereby discourse can be both an instrument and an effect of power, but also a hindrance, a stumbling-block, a point of resistance and a starting point for an opposing strategy.' In 2004, Colombia's Constitutional Court took on such a role of providing a 'starting point for an opposing strategy'. Issuing a ground-breaking ruling – known as T-025 – the Court affirmed that the state of affairs for IDPs in Colombia was 'unconstitutional'. Among other aspects, this ruling points out that 'the registration process is not adequate for the identification of specific needs of the displaced who belong to groups of a major level of vulnerability, such as ethnic groups'.

Since then the Constitutional Court has issued several orders making specific demands of the national government to rectify this situation. In particular, Decree 005 of 2009 has become a crucial reference point for NGOs and Afro-Colombian activists. In this decree, the Court lamented the fact that 'the policy of attention for the displaced population has not adopted a differentiated approach that would value sufficiently the specific needs of displaced Afro-Colombians', despite the fact that the Constitution had declared black communities 'subjects worthy of special constitutional protection' (Corte

Constitucional, 2009). It also denounced the fact that 'numerous doubts exist regarding official displacement figures of the Afro-Colombian population' and lambasted the unreliable statistics of 'the information systems ... that have failed to include Afro-Colombians as victims of forced displacement'. In the words of a CODHES worker: 'It was the Constitutional Court via its follow-up rulings, especially Decree 005, that from the institutionalism of the state played a fundamental role not only in the visibilisation of displaced Afro-Colombians in official registers, but also in advancing in the effective protection of their rights' (email communication with S.L., 15 May 2014).

After years of denouncing the lack of ethnic differentiation, Afro-Colombian activists found an ally in the State's judiciary. The Court's intervention does not only lay bare its diverging views from the government – and thereby expose the fragmentation of the state – it also exposes the banality of the official displacement discourse and how it has been produced over time through an attitudinal thoughtlessness regarding the ethnic variable in displacement statistics and policies. It is here where we see the positive purchase of extending Arendt's notion of banality as a condition that has been actively produced over time, and not something that is merely mundane or ordinary. The Court's Decree 005 of 2009 is a watershed in the breaking of this banality.

One important result of the Court's intervention is the adoption of Law 1448 of 2011, also known as the Victims' Law (*Ley de Víctimas y Restitución de Tierras*). It was passed with the aim of expanding government assistance and reparations to all eligible victims of the armed conflict, including IDPs. According to CODHES (2013: 6), it constitutes a 'radical change in state policies with respect to the [country's] conflict and its victims'. Among others, Law 1448 created yet another body in charge of registering the displaced population. As of 2012, the Unit for Integrated Support and Reparation for Victims UARIV (*Unidad para la Atención y Reparación Integral a las Víctimas*) replaced the government agency *Acción Social* and created the new RUV register (*Registro Único de Víctimas*), replacing the previous SIPOD system.[5] This new register reviewed previous state statistics on displacement and adjusted them retrospectively. It now agrees with NGO statistics that 6.3 million Colombians have been internally displaced since 1985; that is, more than one in ten Colombians have at some point in their lives been forced to flee their homes as a result of violence.

Government figures now also show data on the ethnic distribution of the displaced population. However, it appears, that here the 'war over numbers' continues. The latest government figures suggest that 10 percent of all displaced are Afro-Colombians, whereas a 2010 national verification commission administered by CODHES put this figure at 22.5 percent (*Comisión de Seguimiento a la Política Pública sobre Desplazamiento Forzado* 2012: 153–154). Other NGOs estimate it to be as high as 37 percent (Sanchez, 2012: 7). While precise figures are still up for debate, there is no doubt that Afro-Colombian displacement has finally become formally acknowledged. For black activists, these new and 'better' numbers are important, in that they

serve as a tool in denouncing the state's lack of attention given to the particularities of the Afro-Colombian experience of displacement and in demanding
the fulfilment of their rights to be protected as a distinct cultural group, as
anchored in Colombia's constitution. Clearly, accounting for the ethnic variable
in displacement statistics has inserted a hitherto lacking critical sensibility to
the displacement discourse and removed one aspect of that discourse's banality,
namely its ethnic invisibilisation.

Conclusions

I began this chapter with reflections on an embodiment of violence and war
in Colombia by photo-journalist Jesús Abad Colorado. Exhibitions such as
his are a radically different way of talking about displacement in Colombia
that put the individual experience in the frame and on the map, countering
the disembodied representations found in statistics and in the bureaucratic
categorisation of the individual as an 'IDP'. His photography is one way of
challenging what I call the 'banality of displacement'. With this notion I want
to capture not only the normalisation of violence over time, which has made
forced displacement appear as a mundane, commonplace social fact in
Colombia, but also the attitudinal thoughtlessness, or lack of critical thought
invested, which has produced this normalisation. Through a prolonged reflection
on this thoughtlessness, as revealed in statistical struggles between NGOs
and government agencies, I have attempted to recover an aspect of Hannah
Arendt's reflections on banality that often gets lost in the literature. Rather
than simply juxtaposing 'banal' with 'mundane' or 'routine', recovering the
notion of thoughtlessness that Arendt was so intrigued about opens possibilities
to examine the ways this banality is actively produced. The 'war over numbers'
between NGOs and government agencies in Colombia is a reflection of a
generalised pattern of a breakdown in critical thinking as a mechanism through
which normalisation is enacted. Such an approach to banality, I argue, beyond
merely exposing thoughtlessness per se, can help re-insert critical thought
to counter the normalisation of the phenomenon of displacement.

As I have shown, the last decade has been witness to a number of important
interventions in the redirecting of the displacement discourse in Colombia.
It is not just artists like Abad Colorado and ethnic social movements that
have confronted its bureaucratic banality. The country's Constitutional Court,
through its numerous rulings and challenges to the central government, has
proved a crucial ally in the mobilisation of an opposing strategy to redirect the
discourse. As Foucault (1998: 101) states, discourse can also be 'a hindrance,
a stumbling-block, a point of resistance and a starting point for an opposing
strategy'. Capturing this changing discourse through the notion of banality
is not a way of explaining displacement per se or creating a theory about it.
Rather it is a way of grasping the 'word-and-thought-defying' speechlessness
that this discourse generates in us at times. In this sense it is hoped that the

reflections on banality offered here can usefully be deployed to illuminate other scenarios beyond the Colombian case examined here.

Notes

1 This chapter is a revised version of arguments first presented in the journal *Political Geography* (Oslender, 2016a).
2 It is worth noting that the French sociologist Daniel Pécaut (1999) has described the ways in which the violence in Colombia has become trivialised in public perception as 'banality of violence'. He suggests that the relative lack of public outcry against political violence in Colombia can be explained through processes of normalisation, in which violence is perceived to always have been present. However, Pécaut does not engage Arendt's work on the banality of evil.
3 Most data can be found online. CODHES has monitored forced displacement since 1992: www.codhes.org. For UARIV, see: http://rni.unidadvictimas.gov.co/. A good source of data and analysis is the Geneva-based Internal Displacement Monitoring Centre IDMC: www.internal-displacement.org. Websites last consulted 8 December 2017.
4 The 1993 census found only 1.5 percent of respondents belonging to a 'black community', while the latest census of 2005 estimates Afro-Colombians to constitute 10.5 percent of the national population (DANE, 2006). These considerable differences can partly be explained by issues of black self-identification in a dominant context of whitening (Wade, 1993). Most observers consider Afro-Colombians to make up 26 percent of the national population (Ng'weno, 2007: 102; Wade, 2002: 6).
5 Displacement data are now available at UARIV's *Red Nacional de Información* RNI: http://rni.unidadvictimas.gov.co/?q=v-reportes. SIPOD was still used for displacement data prior to 2012.

References

Abad Colorado, J. (2007), Memory, Place, and Displacement: A Journey by Jesús Abad Colorado. (UBC Museum of Anthropology, Vancouver).
Arendt, H. (1977) [1963], *Eichmann in Jerusalem: A Report on the Banality of Evil* (Harmondsworth: Penguin Books).
Cárdenas, R. (2018), 'Thanks to my forced displacement': blackness and the politics of Colombia's war victims. *Latin American & Caribbean Ethnic Studies* 3(1): 72–93. DOI: 10.1080/17442222.2018.1416893.
CODHES (2014), El desplazamiento forzado y la imperiosa necesidad de la paz: Informe de desplazamiento 2013 (Bogotá: CODHES).
CODHES (2013), La crisis humanitaria en Colombia persiste: el Pacífico en disputa. Informe de desplazamiento forzado en 2012, Documentos CODHES 26 (Bogotá: CODHES).

CODHES (2011), Codhes Informa: De la seguridad a la prosperidad democrática en medio del conflicto, Boletín, Número 78, Bogotá, 19 September 2011.

Comisión de Seguimiento a la Política Pública sobre Desplazamiento Forzado (2012), El reto ante la tragedia humanitaria del desplazamiento forzado: superar la exclusión de la población desplazada. Vol.11 (Bogotá: CODHES).

Corte Constitucional (2009), AUTO N° 005 de 2009, Referencia: Protección de los derechos fundamentales de la población afrodescendiente víctima del desplazamiento forzado, en el marco del estado de cosas inconstitucional declarado en la sentencia T-025 de 2004, Sala Segunda de Revisión, Bogotá, 26 January 2009.

DANE (Departamento Administrativo Nacional de Estadísticas) (2006), Colombia, una nación multicultural: su diversidad étnica (Bogotá: DANE).

DNP (Departamento Nacional de Planeación) (1995), Programa nacional de atención integral a la población desplazada por la violencia, Documento CONPES 2804 del 13 de septiembre (Bogotá: Departamento Nacional de Planeación).

Escobar, A. (2008), *Territories of Difference: Place, Movements, Life, Redes* (Durham, NC: Duke University Press).

Foucault, M. (1998) [1976], *The Will to Knowledge: The History of Sexuality*, Volume one (London: Penguin Books).

IDMC (Internal Displacement Monitoring Centre) (2007), Internal displacement: global overview of trends and developments in 2006 (Geneva: Norwegian Refugee Council).

IDMC, Colombia (2014), Displacement continues despite hopes for peace (Geneva: Norwegian Refugee Council).

Ng'weno, B. (2007), *Turf Wars: Territory and Citizenship in the Contemporary State* (Stanford: Stanford University Press).

Offen, K. (2003), The territorial turn: making black territories in Pacific Colombia. *Journal of Latin American Geography* 2(1): 43–73.

Oslender, U. (2016a), The banality of displacement: discourse and thoughtlessness in the internal refugee crisis in Colombia. *Political Geography* 50: 10–19.

Oslender, U. (2016b), *The Geographies of Social Movements: Afro-Colombian Mobilization and the Aquatic Space* (Durham, NC: Duke University Press).

Oslender, U. (2004), Fleshing out the geographies of social movements: black communities on the Colombian Pacific coast and the aquatic space. *Political Geography* 23(8): 957–985.

Paschel, T. (2010), The right to difference: explaining Colombia's shift from color blindness to the Law of Black Communities. *American Journal of Sociology* 116(3): 729–769.

Paschel, T. (2016), *Becoming Black Political Subjects: Movements and Ethno-racial Rights in Colombia and Brazil* (Princeton: Princeton University Press).

Pécaut, D. (1999), From the banality of violence to real terror: the case of Colombia. In Koonings, K. and D. Kruijt (eds) *Societies of Fear: The Legacy of Civil War, Violence and Terror in Latin America* (London: Zed Books) pp. 141–167.

Restrepo, E. (2004), Ethnicization of blackness in Colombia: toward de-racializing theoretical and political imagination. *Cultural Studies* 18(5): 698–753.

Sanchez, G. (2012), Stopping irreparable harm: acting on Colombia's Afro-Colombian and indigenous communities protection crisis NOREF Report (Norwegian Peacebuilding Resource Center, Oslo) June 2012.

Uribe, M.V. (2004), Dismembering and expelling: semantics of political terror in Colombia. *Public Culture* 16(1): 79–95.

Wade, P. (2002), Introduction: the Colombian Pacific in perspective. *Journal of Latin American Anthropology* 7(2): 2–33.

Wade, P. (1993), *Blackness and Race Mixture: The Dynamics of Racial Identity in Colombia* (London: Johns Hopkins University Press).

4

Refugees welcome? The politics of repatriation and return in a global era of security

Case study: The Rohingya in Bangladesh

Tazreena Sajjad

The violence that erupted on 25 August 2017 in the Rakhine State in Myanmar led to an exodus of Rohingya refugees to Bangladesh. By mid 2018, the total number of *Rohingyas* in the southern district of Cox's Bazaar in the Chittagong Division was over 919,000, although this is still a conservative estimate (ICSG, 2018). More likely, today Bangladesh hosts over a million Rohingyas. Called the fastest growing refugee crisis since the Rwandan genocide, the 2017 arrivals underscore the plight of a people too often forgotten in the international system. This is not, however, the first exodus of the Rohingyas to Bangladesh – the country has been their host since the 1970s, when successive waves arrived during the intensification of violence against the people of the Rakhine State by the government of Myanmar (GoM).

Unlike many Western and some non-Western countries, which have focused on fortification of borders and auxiliary security measures to deter the irregular migrant writ large, Bangladesh, while not a state party to the 1951 Refugee Convention, has been largely hospitable to the arrival of successive waves of Rohingya refugees. However, government policies and shortage of resources have made conditions extremely difficult for the Rohingyas over the years. The most recent arrivals have overstretched the country's capacity to offer shelter, creating a large-scale humanitarian crisis on the ground. Furthermore, an increasing reluctance to serve as a long-term host, and ongoing security concerns about political and financial support for militarised insurgents by domestic right-wing parties and external actors, have led Bangladesh to demand that the GoM take back the new arrivals. On 23 November 2017, the two countries signed a deal to facilitate the return of thousands of Rohingyas and on 31 May 2018 the UN and Myanmar reached a deal for their repatriation. Neither of these arrangements included input from the Rohingya. The most recent repatriation efforts encouraged by the government of Bangladesh (GoB) in November 2018 were ultimately stalled because the Rohingyas refused to repatriate voluntarily, underscoring that, as in the past, there is little change in the socio-political context in Myanmar, which continues to perpetuate systematic government-sanctioned discrimination and violence against this beleaguered group.

Beyond the obvious criticisms of the ongoing efforts to systematically return Rohingyas to Myanmar, refugee repatriation programmes writ large raise compelling questions about the extent to which they are a durable solution to a complex situation. First, what do emerging patterns of cyclical refugee repatriation reveal about its politics and dynamics? Second, do such policies of many host states and UNHCR practices signal a significant shift in the transnational dimension of refuge and, if so, how? And third, what can we learn about the interplay between state and transnational dimensions of refuge if we situate the Rohingya case within the broader context of how refugees have been securitized in the international system?

While repatriation programmes to turbulent contexts are not new, this trend has accelerated since the 1990s. In fact, growing practices of 'voluntary' and 'safe and dignified' returns, 'coerced and forced' returns and 'cash-for-return' are conducted under conditions of duress, such that the line between deportations and repatriation in some contexts is increasingly becoming blurred. These shifts, which at times include support from the United Nations High Commissioner for Refugees (UNHCR), underscore several realities: (i) the precedence consistently placed on the interests of donor countries over those of the displaced; (ii) the pervasive climate of anti-refugee and anti-immigrant sentiment acutely manifest in the West, and picking up traction in the Global South long exhausted from carrying the largest share of the global refugee burden; (iii) the cyclical nature of repatriation processes given the protracted nature of today's conflicts, as in the case of the Rohingya, where populations are returned to the same context multiple times without any substantive change to the socio-political circumstances that forced them to flee in the first place; and (iv) the privileging of the containment model and the 'hard' security concerns of the Global North, while ignoring the economic, social *and* security concerns of the Global South (e.g., see Hathaway et al., 1997).

In using the Rohingyas as a case study to critically examine the narrowing of the transnational space for sanctuary within the broader context of the securitisation of the refugee, this chapter finds that repatriation programmes are ultimately not a solution to a refugee crisis, but are a *temporary* fix for donor and host states. Second, such a prioritisation establishes a positive relationship between the temporality of refuge and framing the 'Outsider' as a social, medical, political and cultural challenge in general, and a security threat in particular, generating what may be defined as the temporality–security nexus. Third, this framing, which has been deeply entrenched in the psyche and institutionalised arrangements in the West, is diffusing into host countries in the Global South. Simultaneously, by ignoring a more comprehensive approach to displacement, which would take into account structural inequities in the international system, state policies and the UNHCR, functioning within the temporality–security model have constituted a *threat* to refugees. Such a dynamic is not occurring in a vacuum – it is a response to the changes in the international system and 9/11, which have demanded a security-oriented approach to the 'Other', thereby systematically undermining traditional humanitarian norms. Ultimately, the dominance of the security paradigm in the international refugee protection regime means that while the Global South's adoption of the security-oriented approach toward the refugee is singularly blamed for forced returns, the *indifference* of the Global North to burden-sharing, and their role in the global diffusion of security norms, is overlooked.

Along the temporality–security continuum: repatriation as a viable solution

Consistence and change in the repatriation model

Refugees are an anomaly in a well-established international system, since they are violently pushed out of the normal state–citizen contract and forced to seek protection outside of their own border (Haddad, 2008; Harrell-Bond, 1995). Their mere presence invokes states' moral obligations to international norms, underscoring what Malkki has argued: a different form of entanglement in a context where the state and international bureaucracies characterise the national order of things by a territorialised polity and an identifiable people (Malkki, 1995). Consequently, the idea of 'return' is vital to the normalisation of state business.

The guiding principles of refugee protection have shifted significantly since the Second World War. Post 1945, based on the European experience, appeals were made to states based on the value of the freedom of movement, and the need for permanent resettlement in the host country, stressing the economic benefits refugees would bring to the labour force, their contributions to market demands and the opportunity to 'decongest' the continent through favourable distribution of a displaced population to 'overseas democracies' (Harrell-Bond, 1995). The Eurocentric nature of the focus meant there was little to no recognition of refugees in the 'Third World' and their right to protection.

During the 1970s, the principle of *non-refoulement* codified in Article 33 of the 1951 Refugee Convention, and repatriation as one of the three durable solutions, was embraced by the UNHCR in a global context where displacement was largely seen as a 'Third World' problem following national liberation struggles in Africa and Asia. This was compounded by the severe limitation of the possibility of obtaining asylum in the Global North (Zolberg et al., 1989).

By the 1980s, the international system was less receptive to refugees. The increasing concern that they were a source of destabilisation of the international order, and an unwillingness to recognise the degree to which global inequalities were generating severe economic, environmental and civil turbulence and displacement, contributed to this rising trend (Hathaway and Foster, 2014). The Global South, already struggling with significant economic disparities and structural adjustment programmes, in addition to carrying a disproportionate number of displaced populations, was less willing to host refugees indefinitely (Hathaway and Foster, 2014). Donors started exhibiting 'compassion fatigue', paving the way for the UNHCR to aggressively promote voluntary repatriation, even in contexts where conflicts had not ended (Harrell-Bond, 1989; Webber, 2011). On a geopolitical level, Chimni observed, the end of the Cold War also meant that 'the refugee no longer possessed ideological or geopolitical value, [resulting in] … a series of restrictive measures which constitute … the non-entree regime' (Chimni, 1998: 351). In short, since the 1980s, Barnett argues (2001a) that the UNHCR, which aimed to encourage humanitarianism without necessarily expanding humanitarian space, 'tried to avoid offending sovereignty-sensitive governments by asking for "safety and dignity" and not a marked improvement in human rights' (Barnett and Finnemore, 2004: 101). Consequently, its pragmatic humanitarian agenda shaped by pressures from donor and host countries began to erode the traditional protection guarantees given to refugees, instigating a prominent system of deterrence and containment at the expense of refugee rights (Barnett, 2001).

By the 1990s, powerful countries became more deliberate about deterring the entry of asylum seekers at their borders. In fact, increasingly regarding refugees as an issue of 'high politics', dominant states tightened their immigration policies and motivated a more powerful UN Security Council to implement 'humanitarian measures' to limit their flows, including policies of containment within camps (Roberts, 1998: 388). Simultaneously, the image of the refugee that emerged was radically different – from being 'white, male and anti-communist' to indistinctive large masses in the 'Third World' and a threat to resources and security. This 'myth of difference' became critical in warehousing refugees far from Western shores and with UNHCR assistance (Chimni, 1998: 351). Furthermore, as these refugees opted to go home rather than being in camps, there was a greater interest in repatriation, *non-refoulement* and cessation clauses (Hathaway, 1997). In fact, return was framed as a human right such that 'voluntary repatriation [became] the basic or primordial solution' (Coles, 1991: 68). Correspondingly, the 1990s became known as the 'decade of repatriation' with the UNHCR developing new terms to classify these movements, such as 'safe return' and 'imposed return', which in practice did not require consent of refugees and constituted, in essence, involuntary or forced repatriation. The UNHCR also laid out a framework which included declaring which countries were ready for refugee returns, withdrawing services from populations readied for repatriation, invoking cessation clauses of the 1951 Refuge Convention to make repatriation obligatory and cooperating with countries engaged in forced repatriation. In short, it emphasised refugee protection within a statist security paradigm and the promotion of voluntary repatriation as the most humane solution (Chimni, 1998; Goodwin-Gill, 1999).The Rohingya repatriation programmes in the 1970s and 1990s should be understood within the context of these broader geopolitical changes. Such shifts indicated that the transnational space for refuge was shrinking dramatically, and the UNHCR was less focused on addressing the needs of people in crisis and more aimed at eradicating a sore issue for (Western) states (Costello, 2016). These dynamics continue to set the stage for the current developments surrounding the Rohingya crisis (and others) today. Last, but not least, 9/11 provided a watershed moment in consolidating the idea that refugees constitute a security threat to the body polity of the state. Indeed, the recent terror attacks in the West in particular have served to heighten a *security mentality* preoccupied with sovereignty, identity, borders and terrorism; their conflation with migration now justifies denial of entry to, and speedy repatriation of, the forcibly displaced.

The securitisation of refugees and implications for repatriation

The securitisation of migration presupposes that the existence and management of specific issues as security problems is a result of an intersubjective process, such that they enable policy-makers to adopt any means they deem appropriate to suppress the threat (Balzacq et al., 2014). Migration, already nestled within embedded assumptions of 'Otherness', has been a suitable candidate for the securitisation phenomenon dovetailing with its criminalisation where 'all the discourses, facts and practices made by the police, judicial authorities …local governments, media, and a part of the population … hold immigrants/aliens responsible for a large share of criminal offences' (Palidda, 2011: 23). Since 9/11, according to a 2016 Pew Research study (Wike et al., 2016), the understanding that the refugee and the migrant from the 'Third World' have ties to terrorist organisations has had significant traction. The consequences of such assumptions in the West have resulted in the adoption of 'hard security' measures, including the construction of border walls and fences, deployment of drones and armed personnel, arrangements with third countries for migrant deterrence, establishment of offshore detentions, asylum processing sites, denial of asylum claims, labelling of individuals in ways that de-legitimises their claims and, as Parkin (2013) argues, increasing numbers of deportations of those classified as being in the 'risk' category to volatile contexts.

There is a dearth of literature systematically examining how and to what extent countries in the Global South have responded to the global discourse of, and policy measures stemming from, the securitisation of migration. What is possible to discern is that there has been a recent rise in building walls and fences and, when financially possible, the use of surveillance mechanisms in the 'non-Western' world with technical assistance from Western countries. For instance, since the mid 1980s India has built an 8-foot high double-walled barbed-wire fence, which is electrified in some parts, to seal most of its border with Bangladesh, together with the stationing of border patrols to prevent the entry of Bangladeshi migrants anxious to visit relatives or seek a livelihood (Banerjee, 2010; Brown, 2010; Jones, 2012). This has been in conjunction with a steady securitisation of undocumented Nepali and Bangladeshi migrants within its borders, with the latter in particular being framed as a 'national security threat' responsible for sheltering subversive activities (Joseph, 2006). Elsewhere, wall-building projects include Algeria's 100-km fence along its Moroccan border; its plan to build another on its border with Libya; and Tunisia's ongoing construction of a wall along the Libyan border with assistance from Germany and the US. The discussion of Trump's wall in the US has not gone unnoticed in Central and South America, where Ecuador has constructed a 'Trump-styled' wall on its border with Peru and where there are now demands for walls against Guatemalans, Haitians and Cubans, Peruvians and Bolivians (Desidera, 2017).

Outside of such deterrence measures, refugee repatriations are increasingly taking place in several non-Western contexts, at times involving UNHCR-initiated cash payments to encourage people to 'go back', even to contexts which are extremely volatile. Many, if not all, of these returns clearly underscore the security argument – that refugees have not only overstayed their welcome, but are increasingly a source of security concern for the host country, as in the case of Afghan refugees in Pakistan, Somali refugees in Kenya and Nigerian refugees in Cameroon. In each of these instances, there is evidence of widespread police and/or military abuse, extortion and intimidation, and threats of deportation where even the UNHCR has cut back food rations to incentivise return – even when refugees have expressed deep concerns about repatriation (Human Rights Watch, 2000; MSF 2002; USCR 1995). While the GoB did not use force to repatriate Rohingyas – although it has deployed the military to maintain 'order' – in the attempted 2018 repatriation process, refugees have repeatedly underscored their fear and anxiety about the dangers that wait them if they are forced to return (Wright and Saeed, 2018).

The dominant practice of lowering the standard for 'safe returns' and financial incentivisation is increasingly being observed in Western contexts including in Sweden, Denmark, France, Italy and Greece to contexts as problematic as Afghanistan, Iraq and Somalia. Germany, where the number of deportations to Afghanistan have doubled in recent years, has launched a new programme 'Your Country, Your Future Now!' where families who volunteer to leave receive up to €3,000 to encourage return (Paravicini, 2017). This pattern of paying refugees to leave is now being replicated in contexts such as Ghana, Kenya, Tanzania and Israel.

Several scholars have described such financialisation of return policies as manifestations of forced deportations, arguing that compelling refugees to repatriate is wrong (Carens, 1987; Fekete 2005; Gibney, 2004). In and of itself, providing financial incentives for voluntary return need not be problematic if returns are informed, respectful, reversible and voluntary, and when the payments involve no use of force (Gerver, 2017). In fact, the facilitation of voluntary return has been institutionalised through the Assisted Voluntary Return and Reintegration (AVRR) programme run by the International Organization for Migration (IOM) for those who wish to return voluntarily to their countries of origin. However, it is possible to argue that IOM's programmes that are geared toward voluntary returns ultimately serve the interests of nation-states and focus on control rather than protecting the needs of migrants (see, for example, Ashutosh and Mountz, 2010). Further-more, there is no empirical research that suggests that the AVRR programme alone has been instrumental in the decision-making process of migrants returning to their country of origin. This suggests that external factors, including an inhospitable political climate, lack of economic opportunities, challenges to family reunification and an ongoing uncertain future, play significant roles in influencing the decision to return, despite the fact that many face serious challenges, including deadly violence, upon repatriation. This casts doubt on the extent to which such returns are 'voluntary' and sustainable. While there is no similar financial model that has been operationalised for the Rohingya, past patterns of repatriation and current pressures to return underscore that the unchanging situation in Myanmar will continue to violate their basic rights to protection. Subsequently, any measures to promote repatriation will serve the interests of primarily Bangladesh, but just as importantly of donor states who may be deploying similar measures of coerced returns to asylum seekers within their own borders.

The Rohingya: a never-ending crisis of an invisible people

On 25 August 2017, the Arakan Rohingya Salvation Army (ARSA) allegedly attacked more than 30 police posts in northern Rakhine (BBC News, 2018). In response, the government mounted a scorched-earth campaign supported by local Buddhist mobs, resulting in the destruction of hundreds of Rohingya villages, the indiscriminate killing of civilians and the commission of systematic acts of rape and sexual violence (Edroos, 2018). In the first month of attacks, at least 6,700 Rohingyas were killed with 656,000 people crossing into Bangladesh, 380,480 of whom were children (Human Rights Watch, 2018). The recent violence has been called an act of ethnic cleansing and the UN human rights chief stated that elements of genocide cannot be ruled out in the current situation (Westcott and Koran, 2018).

The violent developments in 2017 were not the first time that the Rohingya were forced to flee. Long denied citizenship based on the argument that they were 'illegal Bengalis', the Rohingya first arrived in Bangladesh in the late 1970s following an oppressive campaign to drive them out of Myanmar. By May 1978, more than 200,000 Rohingya had fled to Bangladesh (Smith, 1999). The first round of repatriation began with UN assistance, although it was not until the GoB restricted food rations that large numbers of Rohingyas began the journey 'home' (Smith, 1999). By the end of 1979, more than 180,000 Rohingyas had been repatriated (UNHCR, 2000).

The second Rohingya repatriation (1991–92), where over 250,000 Rohingyas fled Myanmar due to large-scale forced labour, rape and systematic religious persecution, was criticised for being overwhelmingly 'forced'. Findings from individual refugee interviews revealed that only approximately 30 percent of the Rohingya were willing to return (Lambrecht, 1995). By 1994, the UNHCR had instituted a mass repatriation programme through which thousands of Rohingyas were returned to Myanmar each week, in what was widely assessed to be 'less than optimum conditions' (Human Rights Watch, 2000). The GoM announcement that it would not accept refugees beyond 15 August led to an expedition of the repatriation process between 1993 and 1997 resulting in approximately 230,000 Rohingyas being returned. On 15 November 1998, the repatriation programme was restarted, but under strict conditions – that the GoM could verify residence, that only complete families would be accepted, that the number of returnees would be limited to 50 a week, and the authorities would be allowed to confirm each refugee's willingness to return (Human Rights Watch, 1996). The stringency of these conditions meant that repatriation was often impossible, even for those who wanted to return to Arakan.

As conditions in the Bangladesh camps deteriorated, camp officials and the UNHCR were accused of employing coercive tactics during the registration process and also violating the principle of *non-refoulement* (Abrar, n.d.; Human Rights Watch, 2000). The official repatriation process ended in 2005 with the UNHCR acknowledging that it was not a viable solution.

An anatomy of challenges: structural pressures and security concerns

Bangladesh's recent response to Rohingya entry has been largely laudable. At the height of the crisis, in a message of solidarity PM Sheikh Hasina had declared:

> We have the ability to feed 160 million people of Bangladesh and we have enough food security to feed the 700,000 refugees … we have let the Rohingya in on humanitarian grounds and I ask the people of this country to help ease their suffering in whatever way they can. (*Dhaka Tribune*, 2017)

Contrasting the leadership of Su Kyi, who has denied the genocide or the presence of the Rohingya with Bangladesh's PM, a *Newsweek* article stated that 'Hasina has shown greater compassion than many leaders from larger and richer countries' (Dhume, 2017). It is critical to recognise that the plight of the Rohingyas is reminiscent of Bangladesh's painful history of genocide during the country's own violent independence struggle from Pakistan, which resulted in 10 million Bengalis seeking refuge in India while millions more were internally displaced. The cancellation of the most recent repatriation programme in November 2018 because the Rohingya refused to repatriate underscores two parallel realities: that while the GoB is eager for the Rohingya to return to Myanmar, it is responsive to external pressure, Rohingya demands to be allowed to stay and – unlike other contexts – unwilling (as of yet) to use force to return refugees to Myanmar.

The constraints on Bangladesh as a host country while the Rohingya crisis continues are critical to understanding why the welcome is fast waning despite the ongoing sympathy among Bangladeshis for their plight. At one level, food and fuel prices in the areas where the camps are concentrated are rising; there are alarming levels of sexual violence and human trafficking targeting women and girls; a shortage of work opportunities for locals; and fear of a health epidemic spreading to the local population. At another, the Rohingya have been framed as a security threat to Bangladesh's internal stability. In recent years, such concerns have created a rich context for some politicians to shape public perception about the Rohingya camps and their ties to crime and terrorism. For instance, the Awami League government has perceived political organisations among the Rohingya as a security risk because of their leaders' longstanding relationship with the fundamentalist Bangladesh *Jamaat-e-Islami* (JI), which has a strong foothold in the Chittagong area adjacent to Rakhine, and because they are allegedly an ally of main opposition party, the *Bangladesh Nationalist Party* (BNP) (Lintner, 2017). Furthermore, Bangladesh has consistently expressed concerns about the more radical break-away faction of the *Rohingya Patriotic Front* (RPF) and the *Rohingya Solidarity Organisation* (RSO), which historically enjoyed support from international extremist networks in Pakistan, Afghanistan and Malaysia (Lintner, 2001). The presence of an insurgent group inside Bangladesh's borders has also been a source of contention between Bangladesh and Myanmar since the 1990s, prompting the Burmese government to launch a massive counter-offensive to 'clear up' the border area in 1991. According to *The Daily Star* (Islam, 2004) an underground illegal small arms trade through which smugglers allegedly evade arrest using information supplied by refugees, and the fact that Myanmar has long been known as a 'narco-state' and a route for a thriving underground weapons market, have meant that some political figures have consistently argued that the Rohingya constitute a security threat to Bangladesh (Rahman, 2010). In a 2017 *Business Insider* interview, the Foreign Minister claimed that 'Myanmar "intruders" … have become a national security concern for Bangladesh', echoing India's stance on the Rohingya, shaped by its diplomatic relationship with GoM, internal security concerns, a deep-seated reluctance to admit a (largely) Muslim population and other geopolitical concerns (Upadhyay, 2017; Yhome, 2018).

While the GoB has not taken measures like some European countries or India to restrict Rohingya access, Bangladesh border guards denied entry to several thousand Rohingyas in 2016 and 2017. Other policies have included banning marriages between Bangladeshi and Rohingyas (BBC, 2018), restricting mobility within the camps (UNHCR, 2007) and a 2018 effort to relocate Rohingyas to Bhasan Char,[1] a remote 'floating' island which has very little basic infrastructure (*Dhaka Tribune*, 2018). The 2018 UN–Myanmar deal, together with the earlier agreement between Bangladesh and Myanmar on repatriation, does not offer assurances to the Rohingyas about citizenship status, freedom of movement or religion or protection from persecution upon their return. This current push for a speedy repatriation of the Rohingya is not, however, unique in the international system, but rather is unfolding within a broader context of ongoing host country exhaustion, framing the 'refugee' as a national security threat, and a diffusion of the security norms of countries in the Global South, underscoring the temporality–security nexus.

Diffusing norms of securitisation and repatriation to the Global South: on the learning curve

While sovereignty continues to be the most sacred tenet of the international system, states are interdependent and often conditioned by the behaviour of others. Several international typologies, such as the distinction between 'Beveridgean' and 'Bismarckian' welfare states, suggest that a common blueprint is the primary source of several national policies (Gilardi, 2012). The now established consensus that dependence is an integral part of the international system leads to the argument that diffusion is its consequence. Diffusion is not the only means through which states duplicate behaviour; coercion also plays an important role, as may be observed when nation-states under different forms of pressure adopt international norms (Weyland, 2007). Existing research in norm diffusion or diffusion through coercion has particularly paid attention to sovereignty, free trade, collective security, human rights and women's rights to explain how multiple states in the international system adopt, or are forced to adopt, frameworks of recognition and protection for issues that do not fall under traditional understandings of security. Furthermore, scholars have identified multiple pathways through which norms are absorbed into domestic policy: through the influence of norms on the beliefs and values of a state actor (Nadelmann, 1990; Nye and Keohane, 1987; Young, 1989); the tenets becoming enmeshed in a country's domestic political processes as a consequence of standard operating procedures of bureaucratic agencies (Young, 1989); when government officials and societal actors invoke an international norm even if they are unpopular (McElroy, 1992); or as a consequence of institutionalising legal norms into national laws. In addition, the domestic structural context and the salience of the norm in question play vital roles in influencing the absorption of an international rule or norm into policy (Cortell, 1996).

   Given that certain practices, even if unpopular among segments of domestic population and international actors, create the permissive environment for practice – for example, use of violations of human rights norms in the name of security – it is important to consider whether and to what extent the current trend of securitising migration and practices such as forcible repatriation is emerging as common practice prioritising the political expedience of the state *at the expense of* the refugee. Correspondingly, practices such as building fortifications against irregular immigrants, militarised pushbacks and coerced and forced returns should come under significant scrutiny to unpack the politics and power that is facilitating such a normative shift. There is a critical meeting point of the discourse and values of dominant states regarding the migrant writ large, with the ongoing challenging ground realities of the countries in the Global South, exacerbated by the discontents of globalisation – environmental pressures, overpopulation, rising nationalism growing economic disparities – that are creating the permissive grounds for the temporality–security nexus, where expulsion in the name of repatriation becomes a pragmatic solution to forced displacement.

The securitisation of the UNHCR and the ongoing neglect of the security concerns of the Global South

A discussion of security and securitisation is incomplete without making the following observations. First, the role of the UNHCR in the dynamics of refugee securitisation must be examined critically. This points toward two possible conclusions: that the agency remains at the mercy of state interests and practices and is in fact less effective than before in influencing state response to the displaced; or, a beleaguered UNHCR is falling in line with state practices and legitimising them. To the extent that the UNHCR is involved in coerced returns, it is important to interrogate the implications of the securitisation discourse within the agency. Over the last several decades, the UNHCR has come under significant criticism for bowing to state interests, particularly of the donor states on which it is largely dependent for funding, such that traditional humanitarianism and legal rights and responsibilities have been compromised (Chimni, 1998). Hammerstad argues that there has been a notable shift within the agency with regard to the security question, as the UNHCR has consistently attempted to strike a balance between responding to donor interests and its own mandate for refugee protection (Hammerstad, 2000). Yet, its usage of 'security' remains largely ambivalent: at one level, it invokes the broader conceptualisation of the term to refer to notions of human security which focus on the individual; on another, its approach is more oriented toward responding to refugee flows as a threat. Likewise many of its policies of prevention, repatriation and containment, which have ranged from 'warehousing' refugees, to ensuring IDPs remain located inside their country of origin, to ensuring early returns of displaced populations to highly uncertain futures including through controlling food rations – as has been the case in past Rohingya repatriation efforts.

Second, underscoring the ongoing question of security is the reality that such concerns of non-Western states are never considered to be as important as those of the Global North. In coverage of repatriation from non-Western states, there is condemnation expressed about such policies and how they are implemented. Yet there is very little attention paid to their ongoing resource constraints and the complex security issues that arise from long-term encampments. Irrefutably, Kenya, Pakistan, Lebanon and others have notable security questions stemming from cross-border incursions and militarising refugee camps that sometimes result in contexts of long-term displacement (see, for instance, Lischer, 2005). Certainly, such realities with regard to the Rohingya in Bangladesh have created the grounds for framing the long-term refugee as a security threat and legitimising speedy repatriation. It is imperative to emphasise that host countries, even those that are not party to the Refugee Convention – such as Bangladesh, cannot violate the principle of *non-refoulement*. However, examining their behaviour in isolation from the broader global securitised context and marginalisation of their security concerns allows blame to be attributed without deeper recognition of the permissive environment created by powerful states for disregarding refugee rights.

Making the link: fewer sanctuaries, more returns in an era of securitisation of migration

The following conclusions emerge in the context of this examination. First, repatriation as the most durable solution to a refugee crisis is the product of a long history of complex negotiations that have always privileged state concerns, particularly those of the Global North. Second, shifts in expanding the conditions under which repatriation is carried out are not new –there is a history of people being returned to less than ideal conditions. What has changed drastically, particularly since 9/11, is the extent to which the international system has been willing to acquiesce to the lowering of standards for return, such that coerced repatriation, at times with the assistance of the UNHCR, and with financial incentivisation, has become more acceptable, even when the risk to returnees is extremely high. Third, the UNHCR's ongoing securitisation since the late 1990s has meant that it functions rather ambivalently, caught between the need to satisfy its donors, which places a heavily securitised framework through which displaced populations are viewed, and its own responsibility to protect the displaced. None of these shifts are taking place in a political or ideological vacuum. Rather, they have been shaped by the ongoing efforts in the West to securitise the refugee and develop an institutionalised system that sees the 'Other' as a criminal and security threat, the diffusion of these norms into the Global South – long weary of carrying the largest share of the refugee burden, and an ongoing lack of recognition of their legitimate security concerns brought on by large-scale refugee flows. The confluence of each of these dynamics resulting in the temporality–security nexus means that repatriation is no longer sustainable

– it has become a temporary fix for states, and the expansion of ways to return refugees implies that the line between deportation and refugee repatriation is starting to blur.

On the one hand, when considering the Rohingya case within the broader history, what is striking is Bangladesh's general 'open-door' policy toward the Rohingya, at least in terms of allowing them entry, and, second, its response to not forcing repatriation in the face of international criticism and as a consequence of Rohingya resistance to being returned. Arguably, in a global political climate which engenders pathways to militarised fortifications and forcible returns with UNHCR and IOM compliance in some instances and 'cash-for-return' policies, the country's humanitarian response certainly defies the 'new normal'. Simultaneously, it is imperative to critique the GoB's pressure on the Rohingya to return in the absence of GoM's commitment to changing the conditions on the ground that would facilitate return. Such a critique cannot ignore the fact that countries like Bangladesh, Pakistan, Kenya and others cannot alone shoulder the responsibility for complex humanitarian crises. By pointing fingers at immediate host countries, the more complex picture of the failure of the Global North to adequately address questions of refugee securitisation, equitable burden-sharing, their own treatment of displaced populations at their borders and the security concerns of the Global South too often gets overlooked. A durable solution for displaced people demands a revisiting of the questions of whose security is prioritised in the interest of whom and the implications of a security-oriented approach which is contributing to cycles of displacement and return.

Ultimately, it is important to echo Hathaway's concern – is 'mandated repatriation simply a euphemism for refoulement?' (Hathaway et al., 1997: 154). Currently, state actions and organisations such as the UNHCR and IOM, which seem to function within the temporality–security model, constitute a threat to refugees. Without a critical examination of how the security frame is being generated, reproduced and legitimised through state discourse and practices to respond to refugees, the Global South will continue to be responsible for both carrying the refugee burden and the blame for systematic abuse of the displaced, while ensuring the Global North remains underexamined as a critical player in the status quo.

Notes

1 *Chars* are tracts of land or sand bars that emerge as islands but are not generally permanent in nature.

References

Abrar, C.R. (n.d.), Repatriation of Rohingya refugees [online] http://www.burmalibrary.org/docs/Abrar-repatriation.htm [accessed 15 January 2018].

Ashutosh, I. and Mountz, A. (2010), Migration management for the benefit of whom? interrogating the work of the International Organization for Migration. *Citizenship Studies* 15(1): 21–38.

Banerjee, B. (2010), The Great Wall of India [online] Slate. https:// slate.com/technology/2010/12/india-is-fencing-off-its-border-with-bangladesh-what-will-that-mean-for-millions-of-potential-climate-refugees.html [accessed 11 June 2018].

BBC News. (2018), Rakhine: What sparked latest violence? [online] http:// www.bbc.com/news/world-asia-41082689 [accessed 15 January 2018].

Balzacq, T., S. Guzzini, M.C. Williams, O. Wæver and H. Patomäki (2014), What kind of theory – if any – is securitization? *International Relations* 29(1): 97–102.

Barnett, M. (2001), Humanitarianism with a sovereign face: UNHCR in the global undertow. *The International Migration Review* 35(1): 244–277.

Barnett, M. and M. Finnemore (2004), *Rules for the World: International Organizations in Global Politics* (Ithaca: Cornell University Press).

Brown, W. (2010), *Walled States, Waning Sovereignty* (Brooklyn: Zone Books).

The Business Insider (2017), Rohingya Muslims may be threat to Bangladesh's security: Foreign minister [online] https://www.business-standard.com/article/news-ani/rohingya-muslims-may-be-threat-to-bangladesh-s-security-foreign-minister-117061600587_1.html [accessed 18 January 2018].

Carens, J. (1987), Aliens and citizens: The case for open borders. *Review of Politics* 49(2): 251–273.

Chimni, B.S. (1998), The geopolitics of refugee studies: a view from the south. *Journal of Refugee Studies* 11(4): 350–374.

Coles, G.J.L. (1991), Refugees and human rights. *Bulletin of Human Rights* 1: 63–74.

Cortell, A.P. (1996), How do international institutions matter? The domestic impact of international norms and rules. *International Studies Quarterly* 40(4): 451–478.

Costello, C. (2016), Safe country? Says who? *International Journal of Refugee Law* 28(4): 601–622.

Desidera, B. (2017), The many walls of Latin America: from the border between Mexico and Guatemala to Macri's Argentina. SIR [online] https://agensir.it/mondo/2017/02/24/the-many-walls-of-latin-america-from-the-border-between-mexico-and-guatemala-to-macris-argentina/ [accessed 21 December 2018].

Dhaka Tribune (2018), Rohingya relocation to Bhashan Char to begin from October [online] https://www.dhakatribune.com/bangladesh/nation/2018/09/18/rohingya-relocation-to-bhashan-char-to-begin-from-october [accessed 11 November 2018].

Dhaka Tribune (2017), If we can feed 160m, we can also feed 700,000 Rohingya refugees [online] http://www.dhakatribune.com/bangladesh/2017/09/12/bangladesh-can-feed-700000-rohingya-refugees/ [accessed 15 January 2018].

Dhume, S. (2017), Forget Aung San Suu Kyi. This is the real heroine of the Rohingya crisis. Newsweek [online] http://www.newsweek.com/forget-aung-san-suu-kyi-real-heroine-rohingya-crisis-674452 [accessed 15 January 2018].

Edroos, F. (2018), ARSA: Who are the Arakan Rohingya Salvation Army? [online] Al-Jazeera.com. http://www.aljazeera.com/news/2017/09/myanmar-arakan-rohingya-salvation-army-170912060700394.html [accessed 15 January 2018].

Fekete, L. (2005), The deportation machine: Europe, asylum and human rights. *Race and Class* 47(1): 64–78.

Gerver, M. (2017), Paying refugees to leave. *Political Science* 65(3): 631–645.

Gibney, M. (2004), *The Ethics and Politics of Asylum* (Cambridge: Cambridge University Press).

Gilardi, F. (2012), Transnational diffusion: Norms, ideas, and policies. In Carlsnaes, W., T. Risse and B. Simmons (eds) *Handbook of International Relations* (Thousand Oaks: Sage Publications), pp. 453–477.

Goodwin-Gill, G (1999), 'Refugee identity and protections fading prospect,' in Nicholson, F. and P. Twomey (eds) *Refugee Rights and Reality* (Cambridge: Cambridge University Press), pp. 220–552.

Haddad, E. (2008), *The Refugee in International Society: Between Sovereigns* (Cambridge: Cambridge University Press) (Cambridge Studies in International Relations). doi: 10.1017/CBO9780511491351.

Hammerstad, A. (2000), Whose security? UNHCR, refugee protection and state security. *Security Dialogue* 31(4): 391–403.

Harrell-Bond, B. (1995), Refugees in the international system: the evolution of solutions. Refugee Studies Centre [online] https://www.rsc.ox.ac.uk/publications/refugees-and-the-international-system-the-evolution-of-solutions [accessed 16 January 2018]

Harrell-Bond, B. (1989), Repatriation under what conditions is it the most desirable solution for Refugees? An agenda for research. *African Studies Review* 32(1): 41–69. [online] http://www.aljazeera.com/news/2018/01/deadline-looms-afghan-refugees-pakistan-180131072420673.html [accessed 10 February 2018].

Hathaway, J.C. and M. Foster (2014), *The Law of Refugee Status*, 2nd edn (Cambridge: Cambridge University Press).

Hathaway, J.C. (1997), The meaning of repatriation. *International Journal of Refugee Law* 9(4): 551–558.

Hathaway, J.C., A. Acharya and D. Dewitt (1997), *Reconceiving International Refugee Law* (The Hague: Martinus Nijhoff Publishers).

Human Rights Watch (2000), Burmese refugees in Bangladesh: still no durable solution [online] https://www.hrw.org/reports/2000/burma/burm005–01.htm [accessed 15 January 2018].

Human Rights Watch (2018), Burma: Landmines deadly for fleeing Rohingya: military lays internationally banned weapon [online] https://www.hrw.org/news/2017/09/23/burma-landmines-deadly-fleeing-rohingya [accessed 15 January 2018].

Human Rights Watch (1996), The Rohingya muslims: ending a cycle of exodus? [online] https://www.hrw.org/report/1996/09/01/rohingya-muslims-ending-cycle-exodus [accessed 15 January 2018].

ICSG (2018), Situation Report: Rohingya Refugee Crisis [online] https://www.humanitarianresponse.info/sites/www.humanitarianresponse.info/files/documents/files/iscg_situation_report_19_july_2018.pdf [accessed 16 November 2018].

Islam, M. (2004), Bandarban border 'open' to arms smugglers. *The Daily Star* [online] http://archive.thedailystar.net/2004/12/04/d4120401033.htm [accessed 20 January 2018].

Jones, R. (2012), *Border Walls: Security and the War on Terror in the United States, India, and Israel* (New York: Zed Books).

Joseph, J. (2006), Securitization of illegal migration of Bangladeshis to India. *Institute of Defence and Strategic Studies* [online] https://www.rsis.edu.sg/wp-content/uploads/rsis-pubs/WP100.pdf [accessed 11 November 2018].

Lambrecht, C. (1995), *The Return of the Rohingya Refugees to Burma: Voluntary Repatriation or Refoulement?* (Washington, DC: US Committee for Refugees).

Lintner, B. (2017), Mishandling the Rohingya crisis may open new frontier for terrorism. Yale Global Online [online]. https://yaleglobal.yale.edu/content/mishandling-rohingya-crisis-may-open-new-frontier-terrorism [accessed 20 January 2018].

Lintner, B. (2001), Bangladesh extremist Islamist consolidation, South Asia Terrorism Portal (SATP), Vol 14, Article 1 [online] https://www.satp.org/satporgtp/publication/faultlines/volume14/Article1.htm [accessed 11 November 2018].

Lischer, S.K. (2005), *Dangerous Sanctuaries: Refugee Camps, Civil War, and the Dilemmas of Humanitarian Aid* (Ithaca: Cornell University).

Malkki, L. (1995), Refugees and exile: from "refugee studies" to the national order of things. *Annual Review of Anthropology* 24(1): 495–523.

McElroy, R.W. (1992), *Morality and American Foreign Policy* (Princeton: Princeton University Press).

MSF (Medecins Sans Frontières) (2002), 10 years for the Rohingya refugees in Bangladesh: past, present and future [online] https://doctorswithoutborders.org/sites/default/files/2018-08/rohingya_report_2002.pdf [accessed 12 December 2019].

Nadelmann, E.A. (1990), Global prohibition regimes: the evolution of norms in international society. *International Organization*, 44(4): 479–526.

Nye, J. and R.O. Keohane (1987), Power and interdependence revisited. *International Organization* 41(4): 725–753.

Palidda, S. (2011), A review of the principal European Countries. In *Racial Criminalization of Migrants in the 21st Century* (Farnham: Ashgate), pp. 23–30.

Paravicini, G. (2017), Germany offers refugees benefits in kind to return home. Politico [online] https://www.politico.eu/article/germany-offers-refugees-benefits-in-kind-to-return-home/ [accessed 18 January 2018].

Parkin, J. (2013), The criminalisation of migration in Europe: a state-of-the-art of the academic literature and research. *CEPS* No. 61 [online] https://www.ceps.eu/system/files/Criminalisation%20of%20Migration%20in%20Europe%20J%20Parkin%20FIDUCIA%20final.pdf [accessed December 1, 2018].

Rahman, U. (2010), The Rohingya refugee: A security dilemma for Bangladesh. *Journal of Immigrant and Refugee Studies* 8(2): 233–339.

Roberts, A. (1998) Implementation of the laws of war in late-twentieth-century conflicts. In Schmitt, M.N. and L.C. Green (eds) *The Law of Armed Conflict: Into the Next* (Newport: Naval War College), pp. 359–388.

Smith, M. (1999), *Burma: Insurgency and the Politics of Ethnicity* (London and New Jersey: Zed Books).

UNHCR (2007), Bangladesh: analysis of gaps in the protection of Rohingya refugees [online] https://www.unhcr.org/en-us/46fa1af32.pdf [accessed 21 December 2018].

UNHCR (2007), UNHCR sign deal on voluntary return of Afghans [online] http://www.unhcr.org/468bb4542.html [accessed 18 January 2018].

UNHCR (2000), The state of the world's refugees 2000: fifty years of humanitarian action 'rupture in Asia' [online] http://www.unhcr.org/3ebf9bb8e.html [accessed 16 January 2018].

Upadhyay, S. (2017), The future of India's do-nothing policy toward the Rohingya. *The Diplomat* [online] https://thediplomat.com/2017/12/the-future-of-indias-do-nothing-policy-toward-the-rohingya/ [accessed 10 November 2018].

US Committee for Refugees (USCR) (1995), Return of the Rohingya refugees to Burma: voluntary repatriation or refoulement? [online] https://refugees.org/wp-content/uploads/2019/02/The-Return-of-the-Rohingya-Refugees-to-Burma_Voluntary-Repatriation-or-Refoulement_March-1995_Curt-Lambrecht.pdf [accessed 12 December 2019].

Webber, F. (2011), How voluntary are voluntary returns? *Race and Class* 52(4): 98–107.

Westcott, B. and L. Koran (2018), Tillerson: Myanmar clearly 'ethnic cleansing' the Rohingya CNN [online] https://www.cnn.com/2017/11/22/politics/tillerson-myanmar-ethnic-cleansing/index.html [accessed 15 January 2018].

Weyland, K. (2007), *Bounded Rationality and Policy Diffusion: Social Sector Reform in Latin America* (Princeton: Princeton University Press).

Wike, R., B. Stokes and K. Simmons (2016), Europeans fear wave of refugees will mean more terrorism, fewer jobs. *Pew Research Center* [online] http://www.pewglobal.org/2016/07/11/europeans-fear-wave-of-refugees-will-mean-more-terrorism-fewer-jobs/ [accessed 20 January 2018].

Wright, R. and S. Saeed (2018), 'We will not go': Rohingya fear repatriation to Myanmar. CNN International [online] https://www.cnn.com/2018/01/23/asia/bangladesh-rohingya-repatriation-fears-intl/index.html [accessed 11 June 2018].

Yhome, K. (2018), Examining India's stance on the Rohingya crisis. ORF Issue Brief, No. 247. [online] https://www.orfonline.org/wp-content/uploads/2018/07/ORF_IssueBrief_247_Rohingya_FinalForUpload.pdf [accessed 10 November 2018].

Young, O.R. (1989), The politics of international regime formation: managing natural resources and the environment. *International Organization* 43(3): 349–375.

Zolberg, A., A. Auhrke and S. Aguayo. (1989), *Escape from Violence: Conflict and Refugee Crisis in the Developing World* (New York: Oxford University Press).

Part II

Inhabiting displacement and crafting futures

5

At sea: maritime Palestine displaced

Diana Allan

We have been in the boat for three hours and it is still dark. Only a hint of yellow marks the horizon separating sea and sky. Away from the grinding waves of Jal el Bahar on Tyre's coast – quite literally, a "sea terrace" – the silence is striking. Barely a word has passed between father and son since we set out from port. The slap of water on wood and the clink of a gerry-rigged lightbulb for night fishing (now off) are the only sounds. Both work patiently and methodically, their movements supple and quick. They gesture to each other occasionally, knowing when and where to move, in a dance of list and balance. A swell rocks the small boat, which heaves and creaks before settling back into a comfortable horizontal. Abu Hani, on the bow, braces his legs and feels the deck with his feet, moving them further apart to steady himself – the boat's surface is rough, the paint gritted with sand. Hasan also stiffens, absorbing the rocking motion. All the while he continues to reel in a long net that floats out into the darkness and the white wake behind the boat. Later, he tells me he feels most alive at sea because constant change demands alertness in body and mind – a contrast to the deadening stasis of camp life. "I know the sea from above and below," he says.

These silent rituals constitute embodied ways of knowing for Abu Hani and Hasan, Palestinian fishermen who for decades have worked off the coast of South Lebanon. Their actions are tuned to a protean environment, to its surges and cycles; they reflect a rhythmic understanding of winds and tides, of shifting terrain above and below the water line, of the feeding pastures and seasonal migrations of fish. This knowledge is charged; it enacts history and relation to place through routines, habits and techniques that assert a right to livelihood. Particular ways of arranging nets, threading and baiting hooks, or making weights (by pouring molten lead into sand), reflect years of experience that have enabled specialized skills to be performed with dexterity and ease. The Ibrahim family's history – their attachment to their home in an unofficial Palestinian beach camp in south Lebanon, and to their work as fishermen – is connected to another history, that of the 1948 displacement, in particular to one of its lesser-known chapters. With the Israel–Palestine conflict understood to be over territory, it is unsurprising that the Nakba – the term used by Palestinians to describe the 1948 expulsion, literally "the catastrophe" – itself is remembered and represented, iconically, as a flight by land. But it was also a flight by sea, a dispersal between shores by boat, a tracing of watery webs across the Mediterranean, or the "White Sea" as it is known to Arabs. Those webs remained taut and supple in voices and bodies, in the kinetics of maritime diasporic life, even as they faded from the canonical texts of historical memory.

The enclaves of Palestinian fisher families along the coast of Lebanon and Syria today, most often in neighborhoods close to ports, reveal historic ties between maritime communities across the Levant. Patterns of coastal refuge reveal pre-state pasts when fishermen, traders, and seaman moved freely along the Mediterranean littoral. Under the Ottoman administration of Greater Syria prior to 1917, the coast from Latakia in Syria, to Jaffa in Palestine formed a single administrative unit. Networks of fishing, commerce, and smuggling – and the communities they sustained – knitted together coastal cities and villages, making fluid social and spatial configurations. They also established trajectories of mobility that determined the routes taken by many Palestinians who fled by boat in 1948. While peasant farmers were re-establishing village and clan networks in camps (Peteet, 1995; Sayigh, 1979), fishermen regrouped around ports, intermingling with their host community. Even today, the old cities of Sidon and Tyre are inhabited by Palestinian fisher families from Acre and Haifa respectively; fishermen from Jaffa mainly relocated to Beirut, many settling close to the Ouzai Port.

Scholarship on Palestinian refugees in Lebanon (and elsewhere) has focused almost exclusively on the camps; these have been both historically central (as the seat of the revolution during the PLO's heyday) and visually iconic (in their marginalization, congestion, and neglect, a metonymic image of the Palestinian condition). But flight by sea set fisher families apart from camp communities, often in what came to be known as "informal gatherings." It is a striking fact that in the vast body of literature on the Palestinian displacement the experiences of fishermen, and the maritime more generally, remains largely invisible. The iconic topography of the Nakba is landlocked, calling to mind scenes of overloaded trucks, barefoot children pushing carts filled with household belongings, and chaotic scenes of people fleeing en masse. The figure of the Palestinian refugee appears rigorously terrestrial. His synecdoche – in both scholarship and nationalist discourse – is the *fellahi* peasant farmer fleeing on foot with little more than the clothes on his back. As Edward Said (1999) observed, this familiar set of images of the 1948 expulsion constructs a vision of primitive helplessness. It depicts a people who appear nomadic, without resources, technology, or prospects, whose landless victimhood seems inevitable. The "othering" of Palestinians also effectively sets the stage for colonial redemption in the form of a civilizing,

European modernity. The fisherman leaving by boat introduces a different set of associations.

As Alexis Wick (2016) has shown, the very idea of the maritime has long been associated with a progressive, European modernity. Arab and Ottoman cultures, by contrast, have been conceptualized as regressive, land-oriented, and agricultural. In modern, professionalized historiography, this terra-centrism has reinforced nationalist politics and geography, often placing the sea outside of – even at odds with – state-centric logics (Wick, 2016: 9). Rediker suggests how this permeates down to the semiotic level, in the naturalized opposition of "legible land" and "signless sea," deepening the sense that "only the landed spaces of the earth's surface are real" (cited in Bassi, 2016: 75). The maritime is understood to be geographically and conceptually marginal, marking the periphery.[1] In the Palestinian context, this has been compounded by the history of British and Israeli colonial dispossession. While 1948 marks the loss of Palestine as a territorial entity, it is also the year that Palestinians – with the exception of those in Gaza – lost the sea. One might read this loss of coast and maritime connectivity as a synecdoche for Israel's relentless disloca-tion of Palestinian land and life that continues to this day. In the context of entrenched colonial occupation, it is understandable that land remains the iconic centerpiece of Palestinian culture and political struggle, and that scholarship should follow suit. However, these scholarly biases and omissions have produced lacunae not only in our knowledge of Palestinian littoral life before and after the Nakba, but also in the complex geographies of exile routed through the sea. The neglect of Palestinian fisher histories in Lebanon – the forms of mobility and material coping strategies at sea, the economic ties and solidarities brokered with host communities – has inadvertently contributed to the stereotype of Palestinian refugees as encamped, immobile, humanitarian subjects (Feldman, 2012).

Two contradictory – though equally disparaging – images of Palestinian coastal life prevail in mainstream discourse and scholarship (Ben-Yehoyada, 2013; Dictaphone Group 2017; Tamari, 2008).[2] The first presents pre-1948 coastal villages as insular, poor, and tangential to the wealth and power of a landed, agrarian interior; the second views them as dangerously fluid and subject to an unsettling, incipient cosmopolitanism. Salim Tamari, in his book *Mountain against the Sea* (2008), argues that villages built on the shore almost never faced the sea. Instead their gaze – and implicitly their aspirations – were oriented inland (Tamari, 2008: 31). "The saying '*al-bahar ghaddar*' (the sea is treacherous) was not only a reflection of popular (in this case, peasant) attitudes toward the uncertainties of nature," writes Tamari, "but also … unpredictable social forms … on the coastal plains" (Tamari, 2008: 24). Tamari regards coastal life as marginal to the formation of a Palestinian nationalist imaginary because it lies outside networks of patronage that are bound to territorial administrative structures. The basic social unit of Palestinian culture is unequivocally understood to be the family farm. If the *fellahi* peasant farmer has been pivotal to narratives of homeland, coastal communities occupy a kind of "structural blind spot" (Wigen, 2007: 5). By extension, refugees from coastal communities, who claim ties to particular waters and to histories of mobility and labor at sea, are narratively marginalized in nationalist discourse, where territorial and statist orders are privileged (Malkki, 1992). Prompted by Tamari's claim, I once asked Umm Ahmed, an elderly refugee from Zib now living in El Buss camp, whether Zib's houses faced inland. She was incredulous: "Why would we not face the sea? Our house was on the beach. The sea is beautiful – it was our life!" Then, as if to underscore the irrelevance of the question, she added – "Is Acre afraid of the sound of the sea?! (*Hawf Akka min al-sawt al-bahar?*)"

My own interest in Palestinian fishermen and coastal dwellers, both in Palestine and in Lebanon, has been fostered both by ongoing work with the Nakba Archive and by two films I made with Palestinian fishermen in Lebanon.[3] In the interviews recorded for the archive, I was often struck by how elderly fishermen recalled their lives before the displacement – through detailed description of working lives at sea. For many, "Palestine" was recollected as a constellation of material practices, as much as an iconic place. When asked if he had ever visited the border with Palestine in his boat during his years in exile, Said Otruk – a fisherman from Acre – responded emphatically: "I don't have the right nets to fish there" (Allan, 2018a). Such a trip would be pointless. The presence of maritime borders seemed less an obstacle than the lack of nets for the fishes one might find there. I heard this again and again in interviews with fishermen: a tendency to recall Palestine – to conceptualize its coastal villages and towns – through genealogies of labor at sea. The poet Ezra Pound coined the word "periplum" to suggest a seafarer's geography ("not as land looks on a map/but as sea bord seen by men sailing"). The fishermen I know navigate Palestine by mnemonic periplum, not by statist cartography but by corporeal coordinates, a dance of list and balance.[4]

This chapter is a tentative attempt to reclaim and reconnect experiences of exodus, labor, and resistance at sea – cross-cutting past and present – through a body of water, where fishing is both subject and method. What might forgotten Palestinian histories of maritime displacement yield? If we follow fishermen like Abu Mustafa Ataya – Umm Ahmed's father – where do they take us? UNRWA's family files from 1950 turn up 287 names that list sea-related occupations – "sailor," "seaman," "stevedore," "fisherman," and the anachronistic "A1 sailor" (the "*rayes al-bahar*," or boat captain). Did refugees who came by boat continue to live on the coast and work as fishermen in Lebanon? What obstacles did they face? Did any attempt a return by boat? How do their narratives of flight invite a reimagining of the now familiar history and geography of 1948? As the Mediterranean again becomes visible as a space of mass migration in the wake of the Arab uprisings, these earlier trajectories of exodus by boat form part of a migratory *longue durée* in the region. The technologies of containment, boundary-making, and border control now deployed by EU states to restrict migrant mobility in the central Mediterranean (Stierl, 2017) find their precursors in Israel's evolving maritime policy of securitization and territorialization, as colonial occupation extends into the sea. In Gaza, where the sea now figures as a "fourth wall" in a brutal, decade-long blockade, fishermen are at the forefront of the struggle to contest ever-more restrictive maritime borders. Their continued labor at sea – often in the face of gunfire, arrest, and the seizure of boats and equipment – represents a form of counter-governmentality and the assertion of the right to livelihood and mobility.

"This is how we left ..."

On May 14, 1948, just days before the end of the British Mandate in Palestine, the Jewish Haganah's Carmeli Brigade attacked the Palestinian coastal village of Zib, located some 14 kilometers north of Acre, just south of Ras al-Naqura, which marks the border with Lebanon. The attack was carried out by sea, by a contingent of Jewish fighters (some of whom washed up on the beaches of the neighboring village of Es-Sumeriya, unable to fight due to seasickness). In interviews recorded by Nafez Nazzal in the camps in Lebanon in the 1970s, refugees described how Zionist forces, arriving by boat and wearing red and white *kuffiyehs*, were initially mistaken for Arab reinforcements (Nazzal, 1978: 55). In the face of heavy mortar fire from the boats, Zib's small militia disbanded and villagers fled. Many escaped in fishing boats docked in the small harbor and sought refuge in Lebanon. Umm Ahmed recalled these events, and the steady flow of boats transporting Jewish immigrants in the preceding months:

> For some time Jews from Europe had been coming by boat to nearby beaches. My uncle's orchards went down to the shore, and they secretly entered this way and went to Nahariya [a Jewish coastal settlement about 3 km away]. It was well organized. They came by ship, and were transported by small boats from these ships to the shore. We'd sometimes find their clothes floating on the water ... They were wretched, like *nawar* [Dom people] ... When the Jews attacked us they also came by boat ... People who had boats fled by sea – the water was crowded with boats. Those without boats went to El-Mazra'a and Mansouri [in the Northern Galilee]. Others, like us, went Qlaileh, near Tyre. My father's two boats were filled with our neighbors. This is how we left ...

Like other narratives of flight by sea I have heard, Umm Ahmed's figures as an ellipsis bracketed by the moment of departure and arrival – a sudden shift from one world into another. While the (largely illicit) immigration of Jews by sea forms part of the Zionist narrative, heroicized in texts like Leon Uris's Zionist epic, *Exodus* (1958), the sea has not figured in Palestinian nationalist iconography, nor representations of the Nakba. Remarkably few photographs or narratives document flight by sea.[5] Experiences like Umm

Ahmed's – she and her family were forced into their fishing boats, in a dramatic inversion of the proverbial Arab threat to throw Jews into the sea – have gone unrecorded.

Accounts of passage by boat feel qualitatively different from accounts of displacement overland. The sea often figures as a liminal, unfathomable space of transition, or the indistinct backdrop to land – a natural border to be passed through and over. Unlike accounts of protracted journeys overland – as refugees were forced from one village to another, before being pushed over the border into Lebanon – the temporality of journeys by boat is brutally foreshortened – truncated, like a door that abruptly opens and closes, separating home from exile. The familiar narrative tropes and geographic coordinates that chart arduous journeys on foot (the villages visited, the landmarks passed, the struggles of people encountered en route), which give shape to a collective imaginary of societal destruction, are largely absent in narratives of flight by sea which appear hermetic: "this is how we left." Said Otruk's recollection of leaving Acre by ship, in April 1948, is equally spare: "Where do you want to go? someone asked us. To Beirut I replied." Otruk's description of that voyage is reduced to a single, repeated sentence: "And we got on the boat." He goes on to recall how he transported people in his fishing boat to Greek passenger ships anchored outside Acre's shallow harbor that had been chartered by the Lebanese government to provide passage for refugees. "Destinies were made in my boat. People were deciding whether to go to Hama, Beirut or Alexandria."

"When the medium itself is fluid and moving, what is a meaningful measure of distance?", asks maritime historian Karen Wigen (2007: 12). How did the material and visceral effects of flight by sea shape the experiences of refugees and their narrative rendering? Boat travel produces its own registers for describing space and time. Prepositions reflect the particular way bodies move and are moved at sea, suggesting a relationship that is transitional and passive. One tends to move "on" land but "by" sea, where mobility is enabled both by boats and the movement of the sea itself. If accounts of flight overland implicitly inscribe a state-centric cartography of borders – mapped by the movement of bodies across them – journeys by sea seem to erode them, highlighting their fluidity. Narratives of flight by sea also tend to cohere around descriptions of things people carried with them. "I came with only a small stove. We had two, a new one and an old one," Umm Ahmed told me. "I thought, I'd leave the new one at home for safekeeping, I imagined it might be lost or damaged." Like pointer stars, salvaged possessions – a Primus stove, pots, fishing nets, a child's pet dog, and so on – orient and emplot narratives, and enable speakers to discursively navigate open waters that elude description.

Similarly, accounts of babies born and lost at sea, like objects saved from oblivion, also recur in stories of flight by boat. Resembling myth and almost never first-person, they symbolize social and moral dissolution and form the narrative tissue connecting individual experience to a collective history of loss and rupture. "There were many people ... one woman gave birth on board, so they called the boy Bahar [sea]," recalled Umm Jamal, when I interviewed her in Shatila in 2004. "They were shooting at us from the port ... the bullets fell on our heads like stars" (Allan, 2007: 263). Or the story of the mother who threw her baby overboard, mistaking it for a cushion (along with its variant, the mother who, beside herself, grabs a pillow and leaves the baby). While these memes offer little historical explanation, like the accounts of children and the infirm abandoned along the roadside, they vividly capture the incomprehensible horror of forced flight. They act as narrative anchors and stand in for the social and geographic locators that typically chart trajectories on foot. They also denote the social and material worlds left behind, lost wealth, and the onset of poverty.

Border crossings

Umm Ahmed is the daughter of Zib's Mukhtar, Ahmed Hussein Ataya (Abu Mustafa). When I first met her in El Buss camp in 2010, she was in her 80s. Wrapped in a thick blanket on a bed in the center of the living room, she appeared regal. Her stories were polished. She described the rhythm of coastal life, which was structured around daily visits from a fishmonger who came from Akka. "Every day he brought us ice to refrigerate the fish, and would take away the day's catch. Sometimes he waited for hours for the men to return from sea." Like other women in her family, her days were spent on the beach weaving and fixing nets, and cleaning fish:

> All my family worked at sea – it's in our blood. My father knew the best places to fish West of Ras al-Naqura ... Until now, fishermen still call this place "Abu Mustafa's Sea" ... We carried the fish on big platters on our heads ... Neighbors would congratulate my father and encourage our efforts: *Oh fish! Your bones have injured me! Oh angel you are blessing us ('adthmak jurhani ya samak! Mana'm allayna ya mallak)* ...

In his capacity as village headman, Abu Mustafa had not only managed a jail in their house, but was also responsible for issuing sea permits for the British Mandate, and oversaw twelve boats belonging to the Taha, Ramadan, Ondus, and Chaker families harbored in the port. "We *were* the port," Umm Ahmed told me, drawing an imaginary map on her blanket to underscore the proximity of their house to the sea. "It was a seaport not made by men – boats passed through a natural opening. That's why it was called "Al-Shok" [passageway]." Her son sitting with us produced a photograph of his grandfather's house, now the Museum of Akhziv (the settlement built over Zib's ruins in 1949). "Hippies," he told me, had turned the village into a nature reserve and re-named it – not without irony – "The free and independent republic of al-Zib."

While land borders with Israel were soon sealed, Lebanon's maritime borders remained unmarked and largely unmanned until 1983, when Legislative Decree No. 138 concerning Territorial Waters and Sea Areas was finally passed.[6] For fishermen like Abu Mustafa, who came to Lebanon in their boats, permeable sea borders enabled a continuity of labor practices in exile. If Otruk was reticent to return by sea, others were less so. Like peasant farmers who returned to harvest crops during their first years in Lebanon, I encountered refugees who continued to fish in the same waters off the coast of Palestine, complicating narratives of 1948 as a definitive rupture. Otruk, Abu Mustafa, and others who left by boat relocated to port cities where they had social and economic networks. "We went to Tyre because my father knew many people there through trade," recalled Umm Ahmed, noting how before 1948 her father had traveled to Tyre, Sidon, and Tripoli to trade, buy goods, and smuggle arms during the Great Revolt (1936–39). "He used to go north with full pockets and an empty boat, and returned with flour, sugar and dynamite." After 1948, Abu Mustafa continued to work with his brothers and former partners from Zib from the Taha, Chaker, and Ramadan families, sharing boats and equipment and returning to familiar fishing grounds. When their situation improved, each family member worked alone.

These genealogies of labor and exchange at sea continue to animate social memory and practice among Palestinian fishing families in Lebanon today. Palestinian fishermen are often quick to remind me that it was they who introduced many of the purse-seining techniques used in Lebanon today, in particular the *"mobattan," "brushta,"* and *"jaroofi"* nets. (The diffusion of fishing technologies from Palestine is something that Lebanese fisherman also acknowledge.) Mahmoud, a fisherman in his late 50s from the Zebawi family, also hailing from Zib, recounted how his father had taught him to fish – "we all of us have this skill, we all fish." The family had collectively fished for years off Zib and the Israeli coastal town of Nahariya. "The waters from Nahariya up to the border with Lebanon were empty for many years. Few Jews fished then" – wryly adding that they had come to Palestine to build a state, not to fish. Those who went back took risks, but were richly rewarded.

In 1958, during one of these illicit fishing trips, Mahmoud's father was arrested by the Israeli navy for "crossing regional borders" and sentenced to two months in Atlit jail. Mahmoud recounted with pride the exchange between his father and the Israeli judge:

He told the judge the Israeli officer had followed him into Lebanese waters, and thus had sworn a false oath on the Torah. "How do you know that you were in Lebanese waters when you were arrested?" the judge asked. "I am from this region," he replied. "I have journeyed from Zib to Naqura [which marks the border] hundreds of times; I know the taste of those waters … We have fished there for generations. Is it logical this Polish man knows more than me? You have sentenced me and seized the boat that many families live from." The judge told him the boat would be returned. A few weeks after my father was released, the Red Cross told the Lebanese police that his boat was at Naqura and that he must collect it.

What emerges from this exchange is the fluid and contested nature of sea borders and an embedded understanding of rights, emanating not from a newly imposed political order but from established ways of working. Maritime borders figure as an abstraction to be discursively navigated, and belonging to place as inseparable from routines of work. Where one fished continued to be guided by local knowledge and customary practice, rather than maritime borders that remained largely notional. A statist cartography had not yet taken hold and spatial imaginaries were mobile, informed by habit and the fugitive paths of migrating fish. The socio-economic topographies of lived experience trump ethnonationalist ones and material aspirations are understood to be inseparable from political ones. Everyday strategies for navigating Israeli colonial power are made manifest in routines of maintenance.

Tempted as we might be to view this encounter in terms of resistance to Israeli colonial authority and the legitimacy of newly minted borders, the conversation isn't really framed this way. The story is about the right to livelihood and specific forms of work practiced over generations, and its cultural substrate is one in which state imaginaries have yet to wrest control of individual experience and practice. The attachment to particular fishing grounds is rooted less in nationalist feeling than in the intimate rhythms of work, to practices that maintain life and make it meaningful. The "taste" of the water is a synecdoche, the phenomenological sediment from a fluid body of knowledge, rights, and rituals. This is not to overstate the distinction between a "non-modern" and modern (Western) liberal tradition of rights, but to recognize that in practice rights claims emerge from highly localized histories and practices deriving as much from a "structure of feeling" as from a civil code (Subramanian, 2009: 19).

When the Zebawi family subsequently moved to Kuwait in the 1960s, they took their boat with them – a logistical feat that involved transporting it overland on a six-wheel truck. Thirty years later the boat returned with them to Tyre. Now unseaworthy, it is docked in the port. Mahmoud's mother recalled the fateful day in 1947 when her husband went to Acre to buy it, just months before they fled to Lebanon. "That day he took my gold and we fought." For the Zebawis the boat is talismanic – bought with wedding gold in Palestine, made the means of escape during the Nakba, impounded by Israel in 1958, returned to Lebanon by the ICRC, and transported to and from the Gulf – and integral to this family's history. It is a symbol of dispossession and displacement but also the means by which this family has maintained ties with Zib and sustained life in exile. Despite his mother's protestations, Mahmoud followed his father to sea. "My mother believes a seaman eats one day and starves for ten." "No," she corrected, "A seaman doesn't eat – there is no stability. A fisherman may have 5 days of good weather and 25 days at home without work." While poor oversight of the fishing industry, pollution, and aggressive overfishing have made it an unsustainable source of livelihood for Palestinians and Lebanese fishermen alike, Mahmoud is unwilling to change profession. "We have a saying 'Work hard and abandon the sea' [*Amal mnieh wa kib al-bahar*], but it's a disease. If you fish once you can't resist a fish moving its tail in water." While the maritime border between Lebanon and Israel is now actively surveilled by Lebanese and Israeli coastguards and made visible by luminous buoys, it retains the promise of permeability. The body of water that connects Tyre and Zib is not simply a barrier, but also a bridge. "We have passed," his mother told me, "but God Willing, our grandchildren will one day return to Zib by boat."

Bread and salt

The string of lights illuminating Tyre's coastline hang like beads, or a constellation in the darkness. When I point this out, Abu Hani redirects my attention to the north star above us, and with characteristic economy describes how before the advent of GPS fishermen navigated with stars. "We used stars to know north and where we were because we could see nothing but water." At that point there were few lights on the coast; they would leave before noon, drop their nets, and wait until the sun had risen before returning. A fisherman is considered skilled and expert (a "*rayes al-bahar*") once he has mastered these techniques of practical navigation (*alam al-bar*, "the knowledge of the coast"). This involves a combination of position fixing using "sights," celestial navigation, and a primitive form of dead reckoning to determine location and chart a course. Although Abu Hani equipped his boat with a GPS and sonar technologies two years ago, he continues to use familiar coastal landmarks and a weighted rope to navigate and determine sea depth. Since he started fishing in 1955 at the age of 10, he instinctively memorizes trees, electrical pylons, and buildings visible at sea, aligning points along the coast to determine his position. "This is the tree ... there is the hill ... we are between."

If living by and from the sea continues to be the fate of the poor, seventy years on it has produced richly involved, often paradoxical maritime histories in informal refugee gatherings like Jal el-Bahar. Unlike the Zebawis, fishing for Abu Hani, Hasan, and the Ibrahim family is a profession learned in exile and is the product of place. This unofficial bedouin beach camp on the outskirts of Tyre was founded in 1948 by families from the tribes of Arab al-Suweilat and Arab al-Suweitat, largely to accommodate the sheep, camels, and cows they had brought with them. In 1948, families built shacks on the shore; at the time, beachfronts were undesirable, poorly serviced and thus uninhabited. As families grew and space and resources diminished, animals were sold off and residents began to turn to the sea for sustenance. When the Ibrahim family chronicled the family's history in Jal el-Bahar, they did so through the reordering of life brought about by the advancing sea. Personal biography and historical events appeared secondary to the building of Tyre's corniche, which narrowed the beach by over a 100 meters – washing away walls, grazing pasture, and gardens – or the theft of beach sand during the Lebanese Civil War (1975–90), which necessitated the building of rudimentary sea walls out of rubble. Today, touristic development represents the most pressing threat facing the community, as the gradual privatization of beachfronts presages their eviction.

As in the Palestinian coastal camps of Rashidiyye and Naher el-Bared, fishing has become a primary – if largely illicit – source of income for refugees in Jal el-Bahar. Many residents fish illegally from the shore without permits, using small boats or car tires from which nets are suspended. Only twelve fishermen in Jal el Bahar have official permits, issued before the 1989 Ta'if Accords, when discriminatory labor restrictions were imposed on Palestinians. All Abu Hani's six sons are fishermen, and one daughter is married to a fisherman-turned-net-maker. When I first met the Ibrahim family in 2008, Hasan explained he had foregone more stable work that might have enabled him to marry so that his father could continue to go to sea. "I want him to be happy ... The sea brings problems, but if put your feet in salt water you can't leave it" (*Iza das bil mai el-malha ma'sh rah yitrikha*), he told me, as if asserting an incontrovertible truth. Now, ten years later, his father is unable to fish due to poor health and Hasan fishes alone. When I ask why, he continues: despite the collapse of the fishing industry he says hope compels him – "*Khalas*, bedouin have become seamen." In the living room, a studio photograph depicting Ibrahim, Hasan's younger brother, rising out of the sea in a white suit, eyes upon the horizon, seems emblematic of the socio-economic transformation of this community, as a culture of wealth in animals is superseded by one imagined to be at sea, or across it.

When the family gathers, conversation turns, ineluctably, to fishing. It is a mobile metaphor that animates and connects disparate elements of life – the day's catch, the thrill of the chase, changes in credit terms of a particular fishmonger and a newly discovered fishing ground form the currents that carry conversation. For both men and women, the esthetic pleasure of listening to a story of a fish artfully caught (the lines left to run loose and whipped tight, where elasticity and drag are used to tire the fish), or an unexpected haul caught just moments before returning to port, becomes a measure of social harmony and beauty. A family lexicon of phrases and anecdotes constitute intimacy and companionship and affirm community. In conversation, fishing and fish often serve as signifiers for masculine prowess, economic savvy, erotic pursuit (fish are gendered female), a divine blessing, even politics. During a recent visit to Jal el Bahar, the arrival of the "Nasrallah fish" (so-named by Israeli fishermen for its lethal sting) dominated conversation, and seemed vectored to a broader discussion of Hezbollah's power in the south, just as the inexplicable plague of "*nuffagha*" (a poisonous puffer fish) several years earlier was rumored to be the work of Israeli coast guards infiltrating Lebanese waters.

While the physical separation of Palestinian fishing families living in beach gatherings and ports makes it harder for them to access UNRWA services and heightens their marginalization, it has also afforded limited possibilities for social and economic assimilation. Abu Hani often describes his relations with Lebanese fishermen as fraught and conflictual, but also as undergirded by shared interests, notably, a commitment to resisting the encroachment of police surveillance. He is now the only Palestinian refugee with a boat registered in Tyre's port. He was able to navigate changes in the law after Ta'if by registering his boat under a Lebanese name in exchange for a yearly fee. When, in 2010, the port authority refused to renew his sea permit (*hawiyyet al-bahar*) unless he agreed to inform on fishermen using dynamite, he petitioned Tyre's fishing syndicate, dominated by Amal (the Shiite party that attacked Palestinians during the "War of the Camps" in the 1980s). As a Palestinian, Abu Hani cannot be a member of the syndicate, but years of honest, hard work have afforded him an honorary status of sorts and his predicament elicited sympathy. His refusal to spy, in spite of his vulnerable position, compelled syndicate members to intervene and his permit was ultimately renewed (Allan, 2018b).

The experience of the Ibrahim family and other Palestinian fishermen I've interviewed in Lebanon suggests that the sea is a space of solidarity and comradery, enshrined in the proverbial seaman's code of bread and salt ("*hobz wa maleh*"). Lodging a complaint in an Amal-led fishing syndicate (of which he is not a member) reflects Abu Hani's temperamental optimism, but it's also representative of certain robust, if informal, forms of recognition and reciprocity that working relations have spawned. A sporadic economy of favors prevails among fishermen, as different skills – net making, boat building, hook baiting, engine fixing, and so on – are tapped and exchanged. Historically, forms of fishing that demand large numbers of hands – such as "*jaroofi*" (now illegal, carried out with large nets from the shore, requiring at least ten men), or other forms of purse-seining in deeper waters (where boats work together to encircle schools of fish) – have forged connective webs, tying generations of Palestinian and Lebanese fishermen together.[7] Abu Hani learned to fish at the age of 10 "running after *jaroofi* fishermen on the beach" and working on Palestinian and Lebanese boats – skills he has passed on to his children and grandchildren. Solidarities forged through work, however, are also threaded through with hatred, discrimination, and bitter memories of sectarian violence. In January 2018, Abu Hani's mooring of fifteen years – a prized spot – was given to a Lebanese fisherman. When he asked for an explanation and challenged his unjust treatment, he was told the decision was final. "They took my spot because I am the only Palestinian in the port. They kick the person who is weakest."

In January 2016, Gazan fisherman Muhammad El-Sissi was killed when a storm blew his boat close to (but well within) the designated 6-mile nautical limit. The Israeli Navy responded by ramming his boat, which according to eyewitnesses, broke "like a stone dropped on an egg" (Gadzo, 2017). While Israeli officials claimed it was an accident, Muhammad's cousin, Nihad El-Sissi, argued it was intentional. "How can these mistakes happen when they have the best technological capabilities in the world?" There are now literally hundreds of documented attacks on Palestinian fishermen by the Egyptian and Israeli navies, with each side disputing the others' conceptualization of maritime space. The experiences of the El-Sissi family are prefigured in Mahmoud Zebawi's account of his father's incarceration in Atlit. With the implementation of restrictive maritime borders, the Israeli state has sought to destroy Gaza's fishing industry. Motivated in no small measure by the presence of large gas reserves and marine resources off the coast, Israel is attempting to impose and consolidate a legalistic spatial imaginary on the sea – one that is bounded and "territorialized" – turning maritime fluidity into a fixed object of cartographic, sovereign control. The familiar forms of Israeli settler colonial occupation are extended into the sea. Gaza's fisherman, who daily contest these maritime encroachments, are engaged in tenacious forms of counter-mapping that highlight the gap separating how state bodies conceptualize and control the sea – through technology and law – and how fishermen understand their work and attachments to particular waters, where movement and access is guided by custom and local knowledge.

While the fate of Gaza's fishermen is not the focus of this chapter, their experiences form part of a continuum with the histories of Palestinian fishermen displaced to Lebanon in 1948, and make vivid the stakes for those working at sea today – not only in Lebanon and Gaza, but also in Israel, where they are subject to colonial subjugation (Ben Yehoyada, 2013). The histories of Palestinian fishermen living along Lebanon's coast remind us that the sea has forged its own, distinct histories of displacement, refuge, and relation with host communities. How refugee fishermen articulate relation to place, or insist upon their right to fish in particular waters (even when this takes them across maritime borders) suggests ties to place and forms of claims-making not captured by territorial, statist logics, or rights discourse, which privileges the political over the economic. It also points to an inherent ambiguity and permeability in the way maritime borders are imagined. The social and economic ties that connected ports across Greater Syria still resonate in the histories and practices of Palestinian fishermen in Lebanon. Both in Palestine and in exile, they have constituted themselves as bearers of rights rooted in genealogies of labor at sea – in Hasan's words, the attachments that come from knowing the sea from above and below. The perception of the sea as a shared, level playing field is also reflected in the paramount role "chance" is understood to play.[8] One never knows when a sudden storm will blow one out to sea, or what one will catch, leaving open the possibility that fortunes may be turned around (in spite of one's refugee status).

Commenting on longitudinal research conducted with Palestinian refugees, Ilana Feldman exhorts researchers working in conditions of protracted displace-ment to distinguish between a "politics of living" and a "politics of life"

(Feldman, 2018). While a "politics of life" evokes the regulatory power of relief providers and governments to make distinctions between people, and determine "the sort of life people may or may not live" (Fassin, 2009), a "politics of living" allows researchers to account for the complex ways refugee recipients contest humanitarian values, state policies, and "coercive arguments[s] about how persons, communities, and claims should be enacted."[9] Like the Zebawis' returns to Zib, refugees crossing the Mediterranean today are similarly asserting the right to move in search of life and livelihood through a "politics of living" and dying.[10] Dispossessed and immiserated by decades of imperial subjugation and colonial exploitation, their crossings challenge the exclusionary politics of asylum that has sought to deny the past, and artificial boundaries separating economic from the political, migrant from the refugee, by lending historical consciousness to the "crisis of migration." Just as Mahmoud's father critiqued the validity of Israel's newly imposed maritime borders, refugees making the perilous journey from Libya to Europe contest the dehumanizing forms of statecraft through which the Global North has sought to keep them out and absolve itself from all responsibility for their fate (Tazzioli, 2014). As Smythe argues, through their actions refugees are implicitly calling for another politics, "one that does not look to state recognition and the calculated valuation of human life, but rather is generative of a new coalitional practice that can be conceived via the Mediterranean's shores rather than national borders" (Smythe, 2018 :7).

Littoral life, historically constructed as marginal to Palestinian nationalism, offers novel perspectives through which to critique landlocked imaginaries. Histories of displacement, colonial governance at sea, fishing, and socio-economic entanglements in exile unsettle the statist *idées fixes* of Palestinian experience. The lives of Palestinian fishermen – past and present, autochthonous and exilic – have been forged by occupations not only political and territorial, but also temporal and existential. Understanding them means posing new questions about the relationship of identity to place and the importance of mobility and skill to each. While statelessness, disenfranchisement, and exclusion have played a determining role in the lives of Palestinian refugees who work as fishermen in Lebanon, their experiences are also bound up with the sea, with the shifting contours of coasts and touristic development, even with weather and tides, as they wait for the wind to change, or for a new fishing season to begin. Indeed, "waiting" is as much a vocational imperative as a political one. In these moments they occupy a particular "time-space" – *zam-kanyiah* (Wick, 2016: 25) – which reflects not only patterns of work and attention, but also subjectivity.

The sea has not only played a determining role in the lived experience of displacement and refuge among coastal dwellers, but also in how return to Palestine is imagined. Mahmoud's experience of fishing with his father informs his own ties to Zib, in periplum, as it were, aboard a boat. Accounts of fishing off the coast of Zib, Acre, or Tantoura, as late as the 1970s, are examples of surreptitious returns, where refugee rights are enacted, rather than demanded and awaited.[11] These narratives also articulate patterns of attachment, belonging, and claim-making that are not rooted first and foremost in land ownership, or an imagined collective, but in patterns of mobile labor that are intrinsically fluid and often solitary. The particularities of place and embodied practice situate these accounts at an oblique angle to nationalist and statist imaginaries. Histories of maritime displacement and exile have not been invoked to challenge Zionist narratives in the way *fellaheen* culture has. But attachments to particular waters, and to lives lived by and through them, are charged in their own way with the cumulative force of experience, the political and ethnographic implications of which have yet to be traced.

Notes

1 This marginal framing of the maritime registers in the way people refer to it as marking the perimeter. The common activist chant, "From the river to the sea, Palestine will be free," is one example.

2 In speaking of coastal life, I draw a distinction between a prevailing culture of the sea, and the cosmopolitan coastal cities of Jaffa, Haifa, Acre, and Gaza.

3 The Nakba Archive is an oral history archive I co-created with Mahmoud Zeidan in 2002. Since its inception we have recorded around 475 interviews with first-generation refugees in Lebanon about their experiences. www.nakba-archive.org.

4 The quoted lines are from Canto 59, published in 1940. In *The ABC of Reading* (1934), he attributed the idea to an unnamed writer on Homer. "Another French scholar has more or less shown that the geography of the Odyssey is correct geography; not as you would find it if you had a geography book and a map, but as it would be in a 'periplum', that is, as a coasting sailor would find it" (Pound, 1934: 43–44).

5 The extraordinary photograph taken in Jaffa by Nakashion of a portly, Palestinian man being carried to boat on the shoulders of a stevedore.

6 Available at http://www.un.org/Depts/los/LEGISLATIONANDTREATIES/PDF-FILES_1983_Decree.pdf.

7 As Hasty and Peters argue ships – or boats – at sea create novel affects, geographies, and relationalities that are not apparent on land: "Whereas humans can actively shape earthly nature ... they can do so less at sea, and as such worlds on ships raise new relational geometries" (Hasty and Peters, 2012: 670).

8 "Unlike other natural resource economies ... marine fishing precludes private ownership of the raw materials of production," observes Subramanian. "To the extent that there is private ownership, it is in the technological means of production" (Subramanian, 2009: 8).

9 Cited in an interview with Elizabeth DeLuca (2017). https://culanth.org/fieldsights/1124-dilemmas-of-the-long-term-an-interview-with-ilana-feldman.

10 Tens of thousands of refugees have died trying to cross from the coast of North Africa to Europe making the Mediterranean one of the deadliest seascapes in

the contemporary world. The current practice of enumerating the deaths of refugees at sea, without being accountable for them, represents what Katherine McKittrick calls a "mathematics of unliving" (cited in Smythe, 2018: 5).

11 This enacted form of refugee activism can also be seen in the recent Palestinian border protests that began with the 2011 March of Return, where refugees have attempted to exercise their right of return (Allan, 2016).

References

Allan, D. (2018a), What bodies remember: sensory experience as historical counterpoint in the Nakba Archive. In Abdo, N. and N. Masalha (eds) *An Oral History of the Palestinian Nakba* (London: Zed Books).

Allan, D. (2018b), This is not a politics: solidarity and subterfuge in a Palestinian camp in Lebanon. *South Atlantic Quarterly* 117(1): 91–110.

Allan, D. (2016), Watching photos in Shatila: visualizing politics in the 2011 March of Return. *Visual Anthropology* 29: 296–314.

Allan, D. (2007), The politics of witness: remembering and forgetting 1948 in Shatila Camp. In Lughod, L.A. and A. Sa'adi (eds) *Nakba: Palestine, 1948, and the Claims of Memory* (New York: Columbia University Press), pp. 253–284.

Bassi, E. (2016), *An Aqueous Territory: Sailor Geographies and New Granada's Transimperial Greater Caribbean* (Durham, NC: Duke University Press).

Ben-Yehoyada, N. (2013), The men who knew too much: Sardines, skill and the labor process in Jaffa, Israel 1948–1979. *Focaal — Journal of Global and Historical Anthropology* 67: 91–106.

Dictaphone Group (2017), Camp Pause: Stories from Rashidiyyeh Camp and the Sea. Published by Jadaliyya, January 26 [online] http://www.jadaliyya.com/ Details/33964/Camp-Pause-Stories-from-Rashidieh-Camp-and-the-Sea [accessed February 4, 2017].

Fassin, D. (2009), Another politics of life is possible. *Theory, Culture and Society* 26(5): 44–60.

Feldman, I. (2012), The humanitarian condition: Palestinian refugees and the politics of living. *Humanity* 3(2): 155–172.

Feldman, I. (2018), *Life Lived in Relief: Humanitarian Predicaments and Palestinian Refugee Politics* (Berkeley: University of California Press).

Gadzo, M. (2017), Who killed Gaza's fisherman Muhammad al-Hissi? Published by Al-Jazeera, (May 7, 2017) [online] https://www.aljazeera.com/ indepth/features/2017/04/killed-gaza-fisherman-muhammad-al-hissi-170413123311286.html [accessed May 10, 2017].

Hasty, W. and K. Peters (2012), The ship in geography and the geographies of ships. *Geography Compass* 6(11): 660–676.

Malkki, L. (1992), National geographic: the rooting of peoples and the territorialization of national identity among scholars and refugees. *Cultural Anthropology* 7(1): 24–44.

Nazzal, N. (1978), *The Palestinian Exodus from Galilee, 1948* (Beirut: Institute for Palestine Studies).

Peteet, J. (1995), Transforming trust: dispossession and empowerment among Palestinian refugees. In Daniel, E.V. and J.C. Knudsen (eds) *Mistrusting Refugees* (Berkeley: University of California Press), pp. 168–186.

Pound, E. (1934), *ABC of Reading* (New York: New Directions).

Said, E. (1999), *After the Last Sky: Palestinian Lives* (New York: Columbia University Press).

Sayigh, R. (1979), *The Palestinians: From Peasants to Revolutionaries* (London: Zed Books).

Smythe, S.A. (2018), The black Mediterranean and the politics of imagination. *Middle East Report* 286(Spring): 3–9.

Stierl, M. (2017), A fleet of Mediterranean border humanitarians. *Antipode* 50(3): 1–21.

Subramanian, A. (2009), *Shorelines: Space and Rights in South India* (Stanford: Stanford University Press).

Tamari, S. (2009), *Mountain against the Sea: Essays on Palestinian Society and Culture* (Berkeley: University of California Press).

Tazzioli, M. (2014), *Spaces of Governmentality: Autonomous Migration and the Arab Spring* (Rowman & Littlefield International).

Wick, A. (2016), *The Red Sea: In Search of Lost Space* (Berkeley: University of California Press).

Wigen, K. (2007), Introduction. In Bentley, J., R. Widenthal and K. Wigen (eds) *Seascapes: Maritime Histories, Littoral Cultures, and Transoceanic Exchanges* (Honolulu: University of Hawai'i Press).

6

Privatized housing and never-ending displacement: the temporality of dwelling for displaced Georgians

Cathrine Brun* and Ragne Øwre Thorshaug**[1]

We[2] are on our way to a former student hostel at the outskirts of Tbilisi, Georgia.

We are not quite sure where our bus-stop is.

The hostel-turned-collective center is an institutional space for hosting internally displaced people (IDPs) who came from Abkhazia to Tbilisi in the 1990s. The building houses IDPs and non-IDP families. Technically the building is no longer a collective center because most residential units were privatized in 2009. When we ask the bus driver where to stop, it is, however, the description of the "IDP house" that makes him understand where he should let us off: neighbors and Tbilisians still know it as an "IDP-building."

We approach the twin blocks, there are groups of men outside, buses, *machutkas* (shared taxis), and a taxi are waiting for passengers. It is a cold December day, but the men are still outside because there is no gathering space for them indoors. We enter the building, with its open ground floor and find a coin-operated lift. But can the lift be trusted? The stairs are dark, uneven and sometimes not secured with railings, so the lift becomes the preferred option. We come out of the lift on the ninth floor to an equally dark corridor. All the wooden floors that were once there are long gone: most likely used as firewood. A window with its glass missing makes it breezy. A kind resident provides us with some light and we can identify the door we are looking for.

Salome[3] opens and her daughter – a young woman in her 20s – is also there. We enter the light, well maintained and warm room which is now the two women's home. They have fitted the room with new windows and renovated the bathroom. Across the corridor, they have built a kitchen in a box-room without windows. Their plan is to develop another room in the collective center for the daughter to occupy. A space in the corridor appropriated some time back has been sealed off and, one day, they will complete an outer wall, install windows and make it part of their home. They do not long for a return to Abkhazia; their lives are here.

Residents are gradually modifying the building, transforming rooms not meant for permanent living, constructing spaces that did not exist, building kitchens, and renovating bathrooms. There is gradual transformation of the one-time student dorm from the Soviet era, then a collective center for internally displaced persons, and now a residential building on par with any other residential building in the city. However, there is a limit to how much people can change this residence with its small living spaces, run down corridors, and crumbling structure. The building's afterlife as a Soviet era student dorm and then as a collective center continues to affect everyday lives.

Understanding protracted displacement through the dwelling

More and more refugees and internally displaced persons (IDPs) live outside the traditional humanitarian spaces of the camp and predominantly in urban areas. Accompanying this trend is a policy shift away from focusing on camps to increased emphasis on assisting people living in urban areas. In this context, there is a need to better understand the nature of current dwelling spaces for forced migrants, be it rented residences, shelters, or collective centers, such as Salome's described above. Salome represents a significant proportion of forced migrants[4] who may – with or without assistance and government or owner consent – occupy available buildings that were often not intended for permanent living. These shelters may be abandoned or unfinished buildings, buildings that were generally built with a different intention than permanent residency, such as hotels, student and workers' dormitories, kindergartens, schools, sanatoria, hospitals, factories, or storage spaces. In protracted displacement, the residents of these shelters and collective centers gradually appropriate the buildings into becoming long-term residences because there is no available solution in sight. The buildings may not be considered home at the outset, but the gradual appropriation of buildings such as Salome's represents homemaking practices that do not necessarily lead to a solution and an end to displacement (Brun, 2012).

In the current discourse around forced migration in the Middle East and Europe, there has been much emphasis on these types of temporary spaces for refugees, such as the more well-known hotel City Plaza in Athens (Kop-tyaeva, 2017). This category of living space for forced migrants is not new and has been a common practice on the Balkans (Council of Europe, 2011) and in other more urban displacement crises such as those that emerged with the dissolution of the Soviet Union. The case of internal displacement in Georgia and the privatization processes that have taken place in that context may be helpful for understanding some of the dynamics between temporality, materiality, and displacement status in this particular type of dwelling for forced migrants. In this chapter we thus explore and analyze the experience of what happens when the status of the material shelter that forced migrants occupy changes from a temporary to a permanent living space through privatization, but people's displacement status does not change accordingly.

The material for this chapter was collected between 2003 and 2015 at various times by the two authors[5] (see Brun, 2015a,b, 2016, 2017; Brun et al., 2017; Thorshaug, 2011). A central focus of our research has been on the homemaking that takes place in the temporary dwellings that people from Abkhazia have occupied since their displacement in the 1990s. In this context, people have become tied to and interact with the material dwellings in particular ways. This material dimension of social life has gained prominence in social science research (Coward, 2009; Schatzki, 2010), but has not represented a significant body of research in forced migration (Dudley, 2011). Unpacking the role of materiality in co-constituting social life provides insights into what buildings can do and the impact of the material on people's experience of displacement (Gieryn, 2002). In this chapter, we position our work in relation to the body of work described as a geography of architecture that seeks to understand the thrown-togetherness of the *material infrastructures, institutional arrangements*, and *everyday practices* that come together through dwelling in particular buildings (see Kraftl and Adey, 2008; Lees and Baxter, 2011; Thorshaug, 2018). Conceptually, our contribution is to add *temporality* to the literature on geographies of architecture. We find that understanding the interaction between the IDP status (the institutional dimension) and the building (material infrastructure) must be seen in the context of the particular experience and governance of temporalities – past, future, and everyday – that we identify in protracted displacement. Our lens is to create an understanding of how the institutional arrangements, the material infrastructure, and the temporalities come together in the process of inhabiting the building through homemaking practices that bind material and imaginative geographies together (Blunt and Dowling, 2006; Jacobs and Merriman, 2011; Kraftl, 2010). We understand homemaking as the process of "endowing things with living meaning, arranging them in space, in order to facilitate the life activities of those whom they belong, and preserving them, along with their meaning" (Young, 2005: 140–141).

In this chapter, we then take the material buildings – the collective centers for displaced people and the privatization process of those buildings – as the starting point for everyday life and homemaking. We consider the buildings as the point from which people find their bearings (Ahmed, 2006, 2010). The dwellings not only become the background to people's lives, but also represent an element of what people draw together (Jacobs and Merriman, 2011) through an everyday skillful engagement with their environment (Simonsen, 2007). This intimate co-dwelling of bodies and buildings help to shape people's horizons, their desires and ambitions (Ahmed, 2006). The building with its particular social status thus becomes a directive for the status and social position of those who dwell within it. By emphasizing the role of the building and shelter in long-term urban displacement, we are able to unpack a central dimension of forced migration and understand the policies of displacement: the interaction of forced migration status and shelter.

In the next section we describe the displacement situation for the Georgian internally displaced from Abkhazia and the institutional infrastructure around their displacement. We then introduce the collective centers and the process of transferring ownership of the dwelling spaces, referred to as a privatization process, before analyzing how people relate to the material buildings during and after the privatization process by focusing on temporal registers, material dimensions, and displacement status and how these dimensions interact through homemaking practices. We conclude by reflecting on the role of the IDP status and the privatized buildings in order to understand better the interaction of the material building with the process of unending displacement.

War and displacement: the Georgian IDPs from Abkhazia

Abkhazia and Georgia were both annexed into the Russian Empire in the nineteenth century and treated as separate republics. However, in 1931, Abkhazia was included in the Georgian Soviet Republic and lost some of its autonomy. With the dissolution of the Soviet Union in 1991, Georgia was declared an independent nation-state and Abkhazia one of its regions. Abkhaz authorities presented secession claims from Georgia in 1992. The Georgian authorities refused to let go of the Black Sea region and Georgian forces entered Abkhazia to regain the disputed territory but were defeated. In the conflict that followed, about 250,000 ethnic Georgians, approximately 46 percent of the population in Abkhazia at the time, fled their homes and were granted the status of internally displaced persons when they settled in the Georgian controlled territories of the country (Kolossov and O'Loughlin, 2011). Many IDPs settled in Western Georgia, close to Abkhazia, in and around the cities of Zugdidi and Kutaisi, but a large proportion found their way to Tbilisi where they had relatives and where there was better access to employment. Interviews for this chapter were conducted in the two cities of Kutaisi and Tbilisi.

The conflict between Abkhazia and Georgia is often described as a frozen conflict with periodic outbursts of war, such as that between Russia and Georgia in August 2008. Many scholars now believe that Georgia has lost de facto control over Abkhazia (Kabachnik, 2012) whose independence is recognized by a handful of states, including Russia. For security reasons, it has been almost impossible for ethnic Georgians to return to Abkhazia since their displacement. With the unresolved conflict, people have remained within their IDP status. It is believed that if the government of Georgia officially recognizes that the IDPs can stay rather than return, they admit that they have given up on the Abkhaz territories. Consequently, the nationalist discourse of a unified Georgia that includes the territories of Abkhazia is still strong and its IDPs play an important role in keeping Georgia's hope of regaining control over Abkhazia alive. There is a shared belief among the government, the internally displaced, and the general Georgian public that Abkhazia must stay part of Georgia and that the return of the displaced represents the only valid solution to displacement. As a consequence, the ethnic Georgians displaced from Abkhazia in the 1990s remain in the status of IDPs in Georgia.

During the more than 20 years of displacement, there have been waves of international attention and support for the IDPs. In the 1990s, international NGOs and UN organizations, such as the UNHCR, were actively present and assisted the IDPs with basic needs. However, due to the strong emphasis on return, greater long-term assistance with the possibility of integration of the IDPs into their existing living environments was not politically acceptable. In the early 2000s, after about ten years of displacement, international organizations were talking about 'temporary integration' to shed light on the problematic and temporary situation of the internally displaced and to convince the government that a more long-term strategy to assist the IDPs was necessary (Brun, 2015b, 2016). However, as we show below, it would take another decade before a more long-term strategy could be implemented.

Nearly half the Georgians who came from Abkhazia settled in collective centers, others were renting or staying with family or friends.[6] Until 2009, the collective centers were institutionalized spaces where services such as electricity and water were provided by the state. Humanitarian organizations assisted the internally displaced to make minor improvements, such as repairing communal sanitary facilities, leaking roofs, and sometimes changing windows. The collective centers presented crowded, substandard, and unhealthy living conditions, but nevertheless were spaces where people lived together. Residents had also, when they were able to, improved their living spaces themselves as much as they could. However, since their arrival in the 1990s and until 2009, no substantial changes were made to improve the substandard conditions in the collective centers.

The permanent impermanence became more and more unbearable and the government's willingness to accept longer-term strategies increased gradually. This willingness resulted in a new state strategy for IDPs launched in 2007. Here, the notion of 'durable housing solutions' became a means to provide, at least partly, a durable solution.[7] A durable housing solution, the government emphasized, was not a full local integration process, but for the displaced in the collective centers, it meant the possibility of privatizing their living spaces.

Privatization: durable housing solutions and the transfer of ownership in collective centers

With the privatization program, IDPs could buy their living spaces in the collective centers for a symbolic 1 Georgian Lari.[8] Simultaneously, buildings of commercial value, occupied by the internally displaced, could be taken over by businesses and the IDPs in those buildings were given compensation (Brun, 2016; Thorshaug, 2011).

A Working Group on Privatization[9] with members from the humanitarian community and civil society established minimum standards and legal guidelines for the spaces that could be privatized. The minimum standards were recognized by the Georgian authorities but were not systematically applied on the ground and particularly not in Tbilisi. In Tbilisi, the argument was that people were being transferred property in prime locations that would increase in value. Consequently, the government was not willing to improve conditions or attempt to fulfill minimum standards and many of the buildings that were privatized were left in a poor state.[10] Privatization was based on the number of family members that left Abkhazia. After 17 years of living in the same space, many families had increased in number, but could not access larger spaces.

Formally, people had difficulties obtaining deeds for their newly owned spaces. The authorities kept the original contract, whereas the IDPs retained an owner certificate – which is not valid as a deed (Thorshaug, 2011). Additionally, the contract only allowed one signatory on behalf of the household. However, everyone that was registered as a resident in the apartment was also included in the paperwork with a clause stating that the signatories renounced the right to make any further claims on the government concerning housing assistance. In effect, the second and third generation IDPs unintentionally gave up their rights to further assistance. Generally, information concerning legal rights became a key issue addressed by national civil society organizations (Georgian Young Lawyers Association, 2014).

Despite their concerns, most people who were offered privatization accepted. Afraid of losing the opportunity of a more permanent living space, they did not dare decline and, in the beginning, the privatization process was rapid. Some, however, were careful and reluctant: if they privatized, would they lose the right to assistance upon return and the right to compensation for their lost houses in Abkhazia? What would happen with their monthly IDP benefits? The spaces in the collective centers were small and substandard. Would this mean an end to any possibility of improving living conditions? In many ways, privatization was a mixed experience. Living in a general condition of poverty and uncertainty, privatization came with responsibilities that were difficult to fulfill, such as paying for electricity and organizing and paying for maintenance.

The idea of transfer of ownership may be understood as a very convenient way for the government to handle the IDP problem. With privatization, the government made substantial efforts to provide durable solutions for IDPs. However, privatization was also understood as a first attempt to cut off assistance and see the IDPs as economically self-reliant and less dependent on government assistance (Manning, 2009).

The privatization process took place on the basis of a particular moment in time. No needs assessment or assessment of the quality of the dwelling was undertaken before privatization papers were signed. As mentioned above, the process was rapid and many households were uncertain about what they had signed up to. Privatization was random, based on what living spaces people had access to at the time. In some ways, the transformation of the collective centers into condominiums provided a potential for the residents to integrate into the wider society. With transfer of ownership, the building is no longer an institution, but formally a residential building on par with other buildings. Residents can now apply for grants from local authorities to upgrade the building, whereas before, the internally displaced would turn to humanitarian organizations or the ministry responsible for the internally displaced. With privatization, IDP status became irrelevant vis á vis the material building. Additionally, ownership leads to control, security of tenure, and the possibility of investing in and modifying the dwelling within the limits that the material structure imposed on people. In the remainder of the chapter, we will discuss how people experienced the privatization process and what difference it may have made to the displacement experience.

Clash of temporalities, norms, and the material buildings

For the Georgians who fled Abkhazia in the 1990s, displacement represents an unending state of being where different temporalities of the past, present, and future come together but also often clash. Moreover, the buildings under consideration also represent a particular meeting point of temporalities, with their own histories and futures which tie in with the temporalities of displacement. In the context of Georgia and other post-socialist states, it has become common to consider ways in which the residue of socialism and Soviet life continue to play a role in contemporary societies (Frederiksen, 2013; Škribić Alempijević and Potkonjak, 2016; see also Benjamin, 1923/97). The afterlife of Soviet era buildings turned collective centers imprints experiences and everyday life in displaced people's privatized dwellings. With clashing temporalities in the building, people experienced a sense of exclusion and marginalization that represented a particular expression of power and status (Frederiksen, 2013; Sharma, 2014). We will describe three dimensions of clashing temporalities here: first, the histories of buildings built with a very different intention than permanent dwelling; second, clashing temporal registers in everyday life; and, third, the understanding of an ideal home that lies in the past and which is understood to be unreachable in the future.

The experience of dwelling is affected by the history and the current standards of the material building and this represents our first identification of clashing temporalities in the dwelling. Collective centers may be understood as "unhomely" (Blunt and Dowling, 2006) because they were not originally meant for family life and the living spaces have histories that are present in how people relate to them. Julia used to live in an old hospital building in Kutaisi that was a collective center until the privatization process began in 2009. She talked about how she always felt that the illnesses of patients were still sitting in the walls. While living there, she constantly worried that her children would fall ill because of this afterlife of the hospital turned collective center. She felt that she was unable to escape that history. Inevitably, the prolonged nature of displacement and later privatization meant a clash of temporalities in the building between its intention, its history, and everyday times for its current inhabitants.

With privatization, and even though people now owned the living space and controlled that space, people strove to create a home and lead a decent everyday life within the bounds of the building. Rita lived in a privatized space in a former student dorm and later collective center. She invited us in for coffee and said she would have liked to be more hospitable, but she did not have more to be hospitable with. She made an excuse for not receiving us in a 'proper way'. Her wish was to have another room for receiving guests, instead of having to receive us in her combined bedroom/dining room/living room.

> All families should have separate living rooms and bedroom. It is not normal to eat, sleep and watch TV, all in one room. If I have guests I would like to have a separate room where I could welcome them. (Interview July 2010)

The small crowded spaces represent a second clash of temporalities; the clash of everyday times, the particular and different temporal registers that are played out every day: the sleeping, eating, and hosting – the shifting of temporal registers that needs to take place in one small room is laborious, it is challenging to keep it tidy, maintain privacy and dignity, and it challenges the norms of dwelling and everyday requirements.

Making a home is about creating both pasts and futures through inhabiting the grounds of the present (Ahmed, 1999). Strategic actions are developed to fulfill normative understandings of the ideals of home, ideals developed over a life course and which shape the orientation of people in time and space. However, there are constraints on homemaking imposed by the physical structures of collective centers and thereby restricting the prospects of achieving these norms. The restrictions on homemaking in the temporary dwelling are closely connected with the experience of losing a home, wherein lies the third clash of temporalities in these privatized dwellings. To lose a dwelling that is defined as home is to lose something meaningful that extends beyond the material domain. The experience of loss is emphasized when interviewees speak of their former dwelling spaces. Dedika pointed out that even though they did not own their former house, they had enough of everything and they were content. Everything was theirs, they were in control, they had everything they needed to make home:

> It is not just about the apartment we had there, but all the things we owned, the linen, the dishes, all the things. (Interview (Dedika), July 2010)

Homes are created in the tension between the real and the ideal (Mallet, 2004). The rather idealist notions of past home that displacement may cause shape the expressions and imaginaries that people create in the dwellings of the homes they desire. The norms of the home are influenced by that past experience of home where socialist housing was not about ownership, but about the security, things, and practices that came together in a functional way in the dwelling. Consequently, drawing on past experiences of home is central to how the internally displaced are currently imagining and making home in their dwelling spaces. The experience of loss does not only involve the material property they have left behind but also the wider social context of the community and the social relations that constituted it. With the privatization process, it was the unhomely spaces in the collective centers that were supposed to become permanent homes, and in the next section we turn to understanding how the privatization process influenced homemaking practices in more material ways.

Materiality and institutional manifestations

The co-constitution of everyday life and the material occurs through making the living spaces in collective centers inhabitable and more home-like spaces (Brun, 2012). This process of inhabitation (Krafll and Adey, 2008; Simonsen, 2012), that reached a new stage with privatization, contributed to a re-orientation in time and space. The dwelling became a more permanent residence with an outlook of staying put rather than returning. Ownership represented the possibility of investing in the dwelling. With help from remittances, Salome, from the beginning of the chapter, replaced her windows, renovated the bathroom, and appropriated space across the corridor to build a kitchen. However, some of her neighbors who had also privatized their spaces had no economic opportunity to make improvements and had a very different perspective on living with this particular material environment. For them, the bad air quality that came from the air ducts was unhealthy due to mildew and other pollutants after years of use. The residents had health problems because of the building and would "suffocate to its history," a neighbor of Salome said. He continued: "we are stuck here, we cannot return to our homes, we cannot afford to move to a better place."

Most people we interviewed had made the most of the limited space in the collective centers, despite the limitations for improvements. Many are confined to very few square meters, often only one room where all the activities of family life are performed as described above. Partitioning of a room is a common practice. Curtains are used to divide a space, walls are lined with different wallpaper to separate the bed area from the kitchen table, for example. Beds are made into sofas during the day. Through a laborious process, separate spaces are clearly demarcated for different everyday activities to help cope with the clashing temporalities.[11]

From the time the internally displaced first occupied the collective centers, and long before privatization, people made considerable efforts to personalize the space as much as possible and to organize it in ways that supported everyday routines and habits. Here, the role of particular objects from the past and the present came together, such as the few photographs the family had managed to bring or get through friends after displacement, a cup from their wedding presents brought with them when they fled. Preservation, modification, and appropriation of a dwelling are important for the emotions with which people invest their living spaces. "It is mine because I worked on it" was a common statement in interviews conducted both before and after transfer of ownership. Modification led to identification with the living space. Through homemaking, the dwelling spaces served as a material anchor for a sense of agency.

Despite ownership, however, the building continues to act as a marker of identity and a particular social status. The afterlife of previous uses and statuses associated with the building, its reputation, in addition to the size, style, and location of the building continue to determine an inhabitant's position in the social hierarchy. As alluded to at the start, everyone knows which are the IDP houses. Interviewees frequently express that they feel the negative social stigma of living in a collective center, even though it is technically not a collective center anymore. The collective center was an exceptional structure in Tbilisi. It represented a kind of "villagization" (Manning, 2009) of the city, an erosion of the Tbilisian urban culture together with the conflict arriving at the city with the internally displaced. The privatized spaces in the former collective centers are not easily freed from this exceptional status, but are coded by the wider population as houses for those who have fled:

> I don't feel like IDP in any other sense than living here. It is this apartment that makes me IDP. (Mariana, interview July 2010)

Tamar had a similar experience, and this was transferred to the next generation, such as her son who does not feel like an IDP outside the house:

> When he (her son) is out he forgets that he is an IDP. Once he comes back and sees this building, he becomes an IDP again. The house makes you IDP, it is humiliating. Once there was a delegation from the Christian Democrats who visited the building. One of them is a friend of our son. When she met him here, she was very surprised and started to cry: "I never thought you were IDP," she said. (Interview August 2010)

Collective centers are considered a material manifestation of a particular sense of loss and deprivation and the privatization process did not necessarily change this experience. In the former collective centers, the displacement experience is a continuous presence in people's everyday lives through the marginal and substandard living spaces. Perhaps with time, the stigma attached to the former collective centers will change. Inhabiting the privatized living spaces in the former collective centers has created new possibilities for homemaking and people may feel at home there, but from the interviews with Mariana and Tamar in 2010 to the encounter with the bus driver on the way to visit Salome, the former collective centers are still associated with displacement.

Conclusions: temporalities of protracted displacement

We should not take for granted that if people stay long enough in one place, they will get used to the space and be happy there. Daily activities and interactions that happen in and around people's dwellings contribute to people's sense of belonging, but more than twenty years after their displacement, the majority of the internally displaced in Georgia continue to express the hope of returning (UNHCR, 2015). However, as we have shown elsewhere, many do not think this return will happen in their lifetime (Brun, 2015b; Thorshaug, 2011). Living with a dominant discourse of return challenges the possibility of creating a sense of belonging. Being an IDP in Georgia has been associated with long-term dependency on aid in the context of a public discourse that overlooks IDPs' complex and translocal attachment to place. Displaced people, despite being citizens, feel out of place because they are associated with the place they have been displaced from rather than where they currently live (Brun et al., 2017). After many years of displacement, there are few benefits left in the IDP category; most humanitarian organizations have moved on to other displacement situations, but the category lives on (Brun et al., 2017).[12] The temporary living spaces in collective centers were closely associated with institutional arrangements around the temporary status of "internally displaced persons." The question is: to what extent did the privatization process contribute to changing this status?

The material dwellings for displaced people represent politically significant spaces that help to make sense of the history, sociality, and status of internal displacement. Dwelling as a political issue has been particularly significant in the Georgian government's response to and settlement of IDPs in temporary dwellings that have remained temporary in tandem with their IDP status. Starting from geographies of architecture that focus on the interaction between the material infrastructure, institutional arrangements, and everyday practices, we have shown that privatization did to some extent enable people to develop their lives based in the material building. Salome felt at home in the former collective center on the outskirts of Tbilisi, her closest friends were her neighbors, her daughter had a job nearby, and her son and husband were buried in the neighborhood. She had found her bearings, the privatized room was the center of her homemaking, and her plans for the future were to stay there.

However, the unchanging nature of the buildings, where old statuses cling to buildings that were built and inhabited with a different temporal orientation than permanency, contribute to a continued clash of temporalities in and after the privatization process. People become stuck in a material structure that they cannot escape, where everyday times clash in these small, substandard spaces. What we have thus shown in this chapter is the power of particular temporalities produced in the interaction between homemaking and the material buildings during protracted displacement.

The nature of the dwelling spaces occupied by displaced persons becomes central to the displacement experience; we can understand social life and practices through the material building. The case we have presented has a resemblance to other urban displacement settings. Often, in situations of displacement, buildings not intended for permanent dwelling are occupied as residences. People make uninhabitable spaces habitable through occupation. However, many of these dwelling spaces remain marginal spaces, always attached to a particular form of temporality: an impermanence that clings to the building even though displacement seems never-ending. The politicized nature of forced migration and the unwillingness of nation-states to resolve situations of protracted displacement become manifest in the conditions of these material buildings. Privatizing substandard dwellings that continue to represent marginalized lives cannot alone solve and end displacement.

Notes

1 Equal authorship.
2 Brun and research assistant.
3 All names used are pseudonyms.
4 We have been unable to identify exact numbers of how many forced migrants occupy such dwellings.
5 We did not conduct fieldwork together, but the different periods of fieldwork built on each other's insights and we spent time in the same buildings and worked at times with the same interpreter. Throughout all our research we had greater opportunities for interviewing women than men. Women were more often at home in their dwelling and were often more willing to share their experiences with us. The material thus reflects a particular gendered perspective where women and homemaking in the dwelling spaces that they occupy become the focus of regard.
6 For more on internally displaced Georgians in rented accommodation, see Brun 2016.
7 A durable solution here refers to the accepted term "durable solutions to internal displacement," an analogy to the better known durable solutions for refugees (return, local integration, and resettlement). The government of Georgia used the term "durable housing solution," although they did not fulfill the accepted criteria for a durable solution as an end to displacement. For a relevant critique of durable solutions, see Brun and Fábos (2017).
8 1 Georgian Lari is 0.38 USD (oanda.com 28 October, 2017).

9 The UNHCR led a group that established minimum standards for space, quality, and facilities. The information regarding this process is based on interviews with stakeholders such as government officials, international humanitarian organizations, and national civil society organizations.

10 The rehabilitation of collective centers took place before or during privatization in the western regions of Georgia. The concentration of money and effort toward the western regions of Georgia must also be understood to be because the politics of settlement of IDPs is geared towards the western regions – which are closer to Abkhazia – but also because this avoids further urbanization in Tbilisi.

11 Some families managed to appropriate more rooms in the collective center. There was some buying and selling of rooms before privatization which paid off in the sense that families were generally able to privatize whatever space they controlled at the time of transfer of ownership. In these cases, separation of activities was easier and privatization gave a better position; those with enough space did get a good deal, although for the majority this was not the case.

12 We have defined these processes of exclusion as "abjection" – forms of state control and boundary making that exclude members from the very things that require their inclusion and lead to a type of ambiguous citizenship that emerges from protracted situations of displacement. For more on this discussion, see Brun et al. (2017).

References

Ahmed, S. (2010), Orientations matter. In Bennett, J., P. Cheah, M.A. Orlie, and E. Grosz (eds) *New Materialisms: Ontology, Agency, and Politics* (Durham, NC: Duke University Press.)

Ahmed, S. (2006), Orientations. Towards a queer phenomenology. *GLQ: A Journal of Lesbian and Gay Studies* 12(4): 543–574.

Ahmed, S. (1999), Home and away. Narratives of home and estrangement. *International Journal of Cultural Studies* 2(3): 330–331.

Benjamin, W. (1923/1997), The task of the translator. *TR: traduction, terminologie, redaction* 10(2): 151–165. (Translated by Steven Rendall.)

Blunt, A. and R. Dowling. (2006), *Home.* (London: Routledge).

Brun, C. (2016), Dwelling in the temporary: the involuntary mobility of displaced Georgians in rented accommodation. *Cultural Studies* 30(3): 421–440. Special issue on (Im)mobilities of Dwelling, edited by Meier, L. and S. Frank.

Brun, C. (2015a), Home as a critical value: From shelter to home in Georgia. *Refuge* 31(1): 43–54.

Brun, C. (2015b), Active waiting and changing hopes. Toward a time perspective on protracted displacement. *Social Analysis* 59(1): 19–37. Special issue on Conflict, mobility and uncertainty edited by Horst, C. and K. Grabska.

Brun, C. (2012), Home in temporary dwellings. In Smith, S.J., M. Elsinga, L. Fox O'Mahony, O. S. Eng, S. Wachter, and R. Dowling (eds) *International Encyclopedia of Housing and Home* (Oxford: Elsevier), pp. 424–433.

Brun, C. and A.H. Fàbos. (2017), 'Mobilising home for long term displacement: a reflection on the durable solutions.' *Journal of Human Rights Practice* 9(2): 177–183.

Brun, C., A.H. Fàbos, and O. El Abed. (2017), Abject citizenship: when categories of displacement collide with categories of citizenship. *Norwegian Journal of Geography* 17(4): 220–232.

Council of Europe. (2011), Alternatives to Europe's sub-standard IDP and refugee collective centres. Council of Europe, Parliamentary Assembly, Committee on Migration, Refugees and Displaced Persons. Provisional version [online] http://website-pace.net/documents/19863/168397/20140313-RefugeeIDP-EN.pdf/a64c8a95-bbd9–49ba-89e6-c8b2364486db [accessed 7, January 2018].

Coward, M. (2009), *Urbicide. The Politics of Urban Destruction* (Abingdon: Routledge).

Dudley, S. (2011), Feeling at home: producing and consuming things in Karenna refugee camps on the Thai-Burma border. *Population, Space and Place* 17: 742–755.

Frederiksen, M.D. (2013), *Young Men, Time and Boredom in the Republic of Georgia* (Philadelphia: Temple University Press).

Georgian Young Lawyer's Association (2014), *State Policy on Providing Housing for the IDPs.* (Tbilisi: GYLA).

Gieryn, T.F. (2002), What buildings do. *Theory and Society* 31(1): 35–74.

Jacobs, J. and P. Merriman. (2011), Editorial. Practicing architectures. *Social & Cultural Geographies* 12(3): 211–222.

Kabachnik, P. (2012), Wounds that won't heal: Cartographic anxieties and the quest for territorial integrity in Georgia. *Central Asian Survey* 31(1): 45–60.

Kolossov, V. and J. O'Loughlin. (2011), After the wars in the south Caucasus state of Georgia: economic insecurities and migration in the 'de facto' states of Abkhazia and South Ossetia. *Eurasian Geography and Economics* 52(5): 631–654.

Koptyaeva, A. (2017), Collective homemaking in transit. *Forced Migration Review* 55: 37–38

Kraftl, P. and P. Adey. (2008), Architecture/affect/inhabitation: geographies of being-in buildings. *Annals of the Association of American Geographers* 98(1): 213–231.

Kraftl, P. (2010), Geographies of architecture: the multiple lives of buildings. *Geography Compass* 4(5): 402–415.

Lees, L. and R. Baxter. (2011), A 'building event' of fear: thinking through the geography of architecture. *Social & Cultural Geography* 12(2): 107–122.

Manning, P. (2009), The hotel/refugee camp Iveria: symptom, monster, fetish, home. In Van Assche, K., J. Salukvadze, and N. Shavishvili (eds) *City Culture and City Planning in Tbilisi: Where Europe and Asia Meet* (Lewistone: Mellen Press).

Schatzki, T. (2010), Materiality and social life. *Nature and Culture* 5(2): 123–149.

Sharma, S. (2014), *In the Meantime. Temporality and Cultural Politics* (Durham, NC: Duke University Press).

Simonsen, K. (2012), In quest of a new humanism: Embodiment, experience and phenomenology as critical geography. *Progress in Human Geography* 37(1): 10–26.

Simonsen, K. (2007), Practice, spatiality and embodied emotions: an outline of a geography of practice. *Human Affairs* 17: 168–181.

Škribić A.N. and S. Potkonjak (2016), The Titoaffect. Tracing objects and memories of socialism in postsocialist Croatia. In Frykman, J. and M.P. Frykman (eds) *Sensitive Objects. Affect and Material Objects* (Lund: Nordic Academic Press), pp. 107–123.

Thorshaug, R.Ø. (2018), Arrival in-between: analyzing the lived experiences of different forms of accommodation for asylum seekers in Norway. In: Meeus, B., B. van Heur, and K. Arnaut (eds) *Arrival Infrastructures* (Cham: Palgrave Macmillan).

Thorshaug, R.Ø. (2011), Interminably Displaced? Home-making Practices among Georgian IDPs in Collective Centres in the Context of Privatization. M. Phil thesis, Department of Geography, Norwegian University of Science and Technology, Trondheim.

UNHCR (2015), After 23 years, still hoping for a better future. UNHCR, http://www.unhcr.org/uk/news/latest/2015/6/559166596/23-years-still-hoping-better-future.html, [accessed September 25, 2017].

Young, I.M. (2005), *On Female Body Experience: Throwing like a Girl and Other Essays* (New York: Oxford University Press).

7

Voice through exit: Syrian refugees at the borders of Europe and the struggle to choose where to live

Chiara Denaro

In the seven years since the Syrian revolution began, more than 400,000 people have lost their lives and the number of internally displaced persons (IDP) has surpassed 7 million (IDMC, 2017). In addition, according to data provided by the UNHCR (2018a), more than 5.4 million Syrian citizens have crossed the border into neighbouring countries[1] and are registered as refugees in the Middle East and North Africa (MENA) region.[2] While most neighbouring countries were still reachable without a visa before 2013, by the beginning of 2016 there was no legal way out of Syria (Vio, 2016), and although significant transformations occurred in the region, Syrian refugees continued to move in search of safe countries.

As demonstrated by the available data, reaching Europe was even more difficult[3] and the vast majority arrived through irregular migration routes, mainly articulated around three corridors (eastern, central and western Mediterranean), with Greece, Italy and Spain being the main access points into Europe. In spite of the presence of legal barriers imposed by the Schengen Border Code and Dublin III Regulation, once the refugees reached the southern European countries, most of them attempted and managed to continue their journeys through so-called internal secondary movements with the aim of reaching central and northern EU countries and being able to choose their final destinations (Denaro, 2016a, 2016d, 2016e).[4]

Drawing on Hirschman's famous paradigm of 'Exit, Voice and Loyalty' in dialogue with the autonomy of migration theory, subaltern studies and critical citizenship studies, this chapter examines how Syrian refugee voices emerged as they left their homeland and carved out de facto escape routes towards northern Europe. In particular, their active engagement with a legal framework perceived as oppressive – with respect to their demands for freedom of movement – is conceptualised as a 'voice through exit' in an attempt to give an account of the agentive processes, struggles and claims that emerged during migration. Working with empirical references from a three-year multi-sited ethnography with Syrian refugees in the southern European border zones (Italy, Spain and Greece), with an extended look at transit countries (Turkey, Egypt and Morocco), this chapter analyses the mechanisms, events, tools and processes through which refugee voices emerged during their migrations.

The multi-sited ethnography was part of my PhD research, entitled 'Limits and borders of the right to asylum in the Mediterranean space. Ethnography of some escape routes from Syria', which analysed – in parallel with the mechanisms through which refugees' agency has developed – the content of the right to asylum in three border zones of southern Europe (Lesbos, Sicily and Melilla) in order to shed light on its variable contours.[5]

Research fieldwork utilised semi-participant observation activities – which included volunteering within different projects – and the realisation of 60 in-depth interviews with refugees and 30 with different relevant stakeholders. During these activities, I had the opportunity to collect more than 300 units of audio-visual material – mainly pictures and video – and to discuss their content with refugees.[6]

Understanding refugees' experience of voice through exit requires supplementing Hirschman with more recent theorisation about the concepts of voice and escape. Voice here is intended to be a fundamental component of human agency resulting from the interactive processes between speakers and listeners (Couldry, 2009), while escape – a core concept in theories on the autonomy of migration – indicates the ability of migrants to autonomously choose their mobility trajectories by challenging the present configuration of control (Mezzadra, 2006; Papadopoulos et al., 2008). While several authors have already addressed the agency of refugees living in camps, the voices of refugees on the move, as well as the experiential dimension, have been less explored.

How have the voices of refugees materialised? How did they engage with a legal framework perceived as oppressive? And how did they manage to affect certain social structures by carving out different escape routes? I refer in particular to the functioning of EU internal borders, as well as to the more general configuration of the spaces that refugees crossed during their transit in terms of relationships with traditional and non-traditional actors. Moreover, what were the main communication tools? And what were the mechanisms and interactions through which they took shape? And finally, who were the actors listening to these voices?

The transformation that took place in Syrian information during the revolution and war (Cottle, 2011; De Angelis, 2011) is part of my analytical background. In particular, I hypothesise that phenomena such as citizens improvising as reporters, photographing and filming the escalation of violence on their smartphones to bypass the limits imposed on the flow of information by Syria's progressive inaccessibility to foreign journalists (Ruiz de Elvira Carrascal, 2014; Yassin-Kassab and Al Shami, 2016) could have had an influence on the ways in which refugee voices emerged in terms of language and communication tools, but also with regard to the principle values and concepts at the core of their demands.

After explaining the theoretical framework in which the analysis takes place – namely the politics of voice in refugee studies – and providing an overview of Syrian mobility from the MENA region to Europe, as well as the migration routes as contexts of refugee agency, the chapter proceeds with an analysis of certain significant events and practices through which refugees expressed their voices; acts of peaceful resistance, public demonstrations and hunger strikes could all be found on the migration corridors to Europe, and the protests were swiftly reported on social media. Words, pictures and audio-visual messages materialised in several kinds of interactions: with me as researcher and observer and with activists, volunteers and other institutional and non-institutional actors involved in refugee reception and migration flow management.

A broader look at the contemporary migration studies debate suggests that the issue of refugee voice is quite crucial, especially in the context of what Mezzadra (2015: 2) defined as an 'epistemic crisis', namely 'the growing instability of many categories and epistemic partitions' such as certain dualistic oppositions – 'forced vs. voluntary migration' and 'regular vs. irregular migration' – which no longer seem to be an adequate account of what is a complex reality. The analysis of refugee voices sheds particular light on the structural overlapping between the forced and voluntary components in each migration (and life) path, and contributes to the recognition of agency and political subjectivity in forced migrants, too often represented as speechless emissaries (Malkki, 1996) and agency-less individuals (Sigona, 2014).

The politics of voice in refugee studies

Drawing on Hirschman's conceptualisation of voice as an alternative to exit and its re-elaborations in the field of migration studies, this section addresses some key components of the debate on the politics of voice in refugee studies, bringing them into dialogue with the literature on the autonomy of migration – in particular with the concept of escape – and with critical studies on agency.

Voice is at the heart of several academic works, including Albert Hirschman's essays (1970, 1978), in which the author gives an account of the consumer's possible reaction to unfavourable market conditions: exit, voice and loyalty. In Hirschman's original work, voice was defined as 'any attempt at all to change, rather than to escape from, an objectionable state of affairs, whether through individual or collective petition to the management directly in charge, through appeal to a higher authority with the intention of forcing a change in management or through various types of actions and protests, including those that are meant to mobilize public opinion' (1970: 30). While the author first conceptualises voice as residual and an alternative to exit (1970: 36), he later recognises the possible usefulness of an 'elusive optimal mix' between those responses, in which 'exit and voice alternate as principal actors' (1970: 120–126).

Hirschman's theory has been re-elaborated in several fields, including migration studies, through the new conceptualisation of 'voice after exit' (Fargues, 2011; Newland, 2010), but it has never been applied to refugees on the move. Similarly, most ethnographies addressing the refugee voice – or more correctly, refugee voices – focus their attention on the demands expressed by refugees living in camps (Feldman, 2008; Malkki, 1996) or in countries of resettlement (Moulin, 2012). Mechanisms of voice after exit, in particular inside diaspora communities, have been analysed by Newland (2010), who underlines their influence both in the host countries and the countries of origin (2010: 3). The idea of voice as capable of influencing processes of change in countries of origin is also present in Fargues' work, which – by focusing on the causal relationship between exit, intended as migration, and voice, as a *prise de parole* during revolutionary processes – argues that the Arab revolutions would not have been possible without the establishment of the previous exit paths of Arab youth from their patriarchal societies.[7]

The tie between migration and revolution emerges as a key issue in Van Hear's article (2015), which stresses the need to further examine the role of diaspora communities as a transnational dimension of social mobilisation in the Arab revolts, the connection between migration and political contestation and the bond between immigration and mobilisation. The close interrelation between human mobilities and mobilization is a fundamental element of autonomy in migration literatures (Mezzadra, 2006, 2015; Papadopoulos et al. 2008), which attempt to overturn the interpretative framework that presents migrants as victims with limited decision-making autonomy, and migration phenomena as the primary outcomes of the interaction between push and pull factors.

One core concept in the autonomy of migration is that of escape, which highlights the subjective dimension of migration processes in opposition to their deterministic interpretations (Mezzadra, 2006: 18), and represents 'a mode of social change that is simultaneously elusive and forceful enough to challenge the present configuration of control' (Papadopoulos et al., 2008: xiv, 52). From Edward Said, who denounced the denial of the 'permission to narrate' to Palestinian refugees (1984), to Chakravorty Spivak who, in her essay 'Can the subaltern speak?', uses the concept of epistemic violence to give an account of the processes through which 'men and women among the illiterate peasantry, the tribals, the lowest strata of the urban subproletariat' are systematically silenced (Spivak, 1988: 33), the mechanisms for allocating narrative power have been identified as very pervasive control devices that are able to marginalise subaltern experiences and deprive them of political subjectivity.

In particular, the limited access of refugees to narrative power has been at the core of several studies. Malkki (1996) explains how certain kinds of humanitarian interventions – with related dominant discourses, technical language and organisational features – may contribute to the representation of refugees as de-historicised and de-humanised, by reducing them to 'speech-less emissaries', helpless individuals in need of someone who can speak for them. It is as if their knowledge, using Foucault's word, was inadequate or insufficiently elaborated to give an account of their situation and was therefore worthy of disqualification and subjugation (Foucault 1980: 82).

On the other hand, the same humanitarian apparatus has been identified by Ilana Feldman as an opportunity and site of resistance that may, incidentally, offer refugees ordinary tools to present claims of recognition (2008). Her work pays particular attention to the mechanisms and tools used by refugees to win political attention, which she defines as 'visibility practices', an approach at the core of this chapter.

Finally, in this analysis of the strategies used by refugees to make their voices heard along their migration paths, Couldry's engagement in 're-thinking the politics of voice' (2009) has been a fundamental inspiration. More than a mere 'irreducible part of human agency' (2009: 580), according to the author, voice is the result of an interactive process, where speakers and listeners are equally important in bringing the message to light, through processes of co-production. In Couldry's view, Chakravorty Spivak's famous question about whether the subaltern can speak – or, in more general terms, 'who will speak?' – is less crucial than 'who will listen?', since only through the presence of listeners can the voices of the people be registered (Couldry, 2009).

In the case of the Syrian refugees, I will argue in the following paragraphs that the main sites of expression for their voices, through interaction and dialogue with both new and old listeners, were the border zones and migration routes from the MENA region to Europe. During 2013 and 2014, these routes became spaces of agency and political subjectivity, where refugees performed different escape attempts aimed at eluding a number of dominant social, economic, political and legal structures, from the violent, authoritarian Syrian regime, to the oppressive, discriminatory socio-economic policies enacted by the Egyptian government (Denaro, 2016c); from the obstacles preventing access to safe countries legally put in place by the current border regimes, to the restrictions imposed by the Dublin Regulation. At the core of their claims, which they attempted to present using multiple tools and strategies aimed at making their voices heard, were human rights. Freedom of movement was perceived as an essential prerequisite to enjoy the true right to asylum, which would only materialise in the countries that they imagined were sufficiently safe to restart their lives.

Syrian refugees and escape routes: from the MENA region to Europe

The millions of Syrians who have been rendered refugees have been faced with a rigid legal framework, limiting their mobility both to and around

Europe. Beginning in 2011, Syrians started to flee to Lebanon, Turkey, Jordan, Iraq, Egypt and the North African countries. Reception conditions in the MENA region were heterogeneous. People were accommodated in official camps (Turkey, Jordan, Iraq), non-official camps (Lebanon) and abandoned and rented houses (all the MENA countries). Even the legal status of the refugees shifted constantly, determining differing access to health services, social aid, work and education (Un Ponte Per, 2015). As the refugee population increased, each host country began placing restrictions on legal permanence and implementing discriminatory policies and practices. At the same time, it was becoming more and more difficult to envision an end to the war, and the idea of returning home became increasingly less realistic every day.

Syrian refugees started arriving in Europe from the very beginning of the revolution, but their presence along the central Mediterranean corridor became more visible and significant in the summer of 2013 and this continued to be the route most travelled by Syrians throughout 2014 (Amnesty 2014a; IOM, 2014). The start of 2015 signalled the re-opening of the Turkish seaborne routes to Greece, which had been almost completely closed since 2006 because of the strong presence of the border and coast guard agency, Frontex, promoting daily pushbacks at sea, while the border between Turkey and Greece became more permeable than ever (Amnesty, 2014b; Goodwin Gill, 2011; Pro Asyl, 2013). The western Mediterranean corridor was also affected by the movement of Syrian refugees from Morocco to Spain via the enclaves of Ceuta and Melilla, which totalled around 11,000 people between 2013 and 2016. Except for the first phase of Syrian refugee arrivals via the land borders between Morocco and Spain (2013), the possibility of leaving the enclaves was subject to the presentation of an asylum claim, which was processed in a short space of time and usually with positive results. Nevertheless, most Syrian refugees decided to continue onwards to northern Europe, although detailed official data on this movement are not available.

Between 2013 and 2016, Italy, Greece and Spain served as the main access points to Europe and transit countries for refugees. The limitations to refugee mobility imposed by the Dublin Regulation were not a sufficient deterrent factor to keep Syrians from continuing on to northern Europe. As confirmed by comparative data about the number of seaborne arrivals and the number of asylum claims presented by Syrian refugees, most continued their journeys to the central and northern EU countries.[8] They did this by escaping identification, refusing to provide fingerprints, declining to claim asylum in the first country reached, organising hunger strikes and demonstrations and by interacting with new and old actors who were involved in the management of incoming migration flows.

The beginning of 2016 was marked by new policies and practices aimed at interrupting the eastern Mediterranean migration corridor and the so-called Balkan route, in the context of the domino-like closure of internal European borders and the EU–Turkey agreements. These restrictive measures were implemented after the refugees had strongly challenged the Dublin Regulation by leaving first arrival countries and going to Germany and other countries in the north. Their movements created a crisis for both the Schengen system and the EU's principle of solidarity (Crawley, 2016), and refugee voices finally began to emerge through a multiplicity of mechanisms, tools and interactions.

Refugee voices through exit: four case studies

The communication practices of Syrian refugees often mixed different goals, from requests for help in cases of human rights violations, such as rescue at sea, to more politicised expressions of grievances through demonstrations and hunger strikes, to opposition to a legal framework they perceived as oppressive – represented by the Dublin Regulation. Their claims took shape through the use of different communication tools, including digital technologies, and through different kinds of interaction with relevant stakeholders in the management of migration flows, as well as civil society actors encountered at different stages along their journeys.

This section uses empirical evidence from four case studies to highlight some of the mechanisms and interactions through which Syrian refugee voices emerged as they made their way to northern Europe. The first is a peaceful demonstration organised on board a Danish merchant vessel in Maltese waters. The second is the 'case of the missing fingerprints' in Italy, in which Syrian refugees refused to be fingerprinted so that they could claim asylum elsewhere. The third case is a sit-in and hunger strike organised in Athens's Syntagma Square by Syrian refugees who wanted to continue on to central and northern Europe. Finally, the fourth case concerns Syrian and Syrian-Palestinian refugees detained in Karmooz, a police station near Alexandria, who organised demonstrations and disseminated them on social networks as part of their efforts to be released.

The selection of the four case studies has been led by three main criteria: (i) the cooperation amongst refugees and activists; (ii) the wide use of audio-visual material by refugees, as a fundamental tool for the expression of voice; and (iii) the relevance of the selected cases in exemplifying the capability of refugee voice to positively challenge oppressive dominant structures.

Refugees on a Danish merchant vessel: Maltese waters

On 25 October 2014, during a shift with Watch the Med Alarm Phone, I followed the case of a Danish merchant vessel, the Eleonora Maersk, which rescued a ship in distress with hundreds of Syrian refugees on board. The ship had left Egypt several days before and at the point of rescue was in Maltese waters. When the refugees heard that they were going to disembark in Malta, they organised a demonstration, creating banners and posters with available materials, on which they wrote explicit demands and requests for help: 'We have the right to choose where to live' and 'We want international protection from Denmark' (Figure 7.1, 7.2). One man attempted suicide, declaring that 'he did not sell a kidney to end his journey in Malta'.[9]

The refugees wanted to disembark in Italy, which they considered gave them the best chance to continue their journey to northern Europe. At the suggestion of a number of activists and thanks to the captain, who allowed them to make calls using the ship's satellite phone, some of them tried to demand international protection from Denmark from on board the vessel. During the protest, the refugees took many pictures, which they sent to activists who had received their SOS and who were following the case (N.S. and Watch the Med Alarm Phone). The activists forwarded the photos to the local and international media in an attempt to mobilise political opinion. In the end, the Syrian refugees were allowed to disembark in Italy (Denaro, 2016b).[10]

According to what emerged from the in-depth interviews conducted at border zones, the right to choose the country in which one lives was in part rooted in the concept of 'survivor', which was used by many refugees as a self-definition. People who had survived the war, the dangerous land border crossings and, finally, the lethal sea crossings were inclined to reach for what they deemed 'the best option', in order to justify such a risk to their lives.

> We are survivors. Do you understand what I mean? We are survivors. Firstly we survived our army's shooting during demonstrations, then Assad's bombs on our houses, then again the violence at the border crossing with Turkey, and finally the lethal sea crossing to Greece. And now, we are determined to go right to the end. We lost everything and now we want to choose where to re-start. We do not have anything to lose anymore. (Interview with A.A. 32, Syrian refugee woman, Idomeni, 2 September 2015)

The question of fingerprints: Sicily

Protests against the Dublin Regulation, led by refugees who wished to continue their journeys northwards, started in Italy in the summer of 2013, and a fundamental point of tension with the authorities was the question of fingerprints. The first attempts to challenge the Dublin Regulation, by not providing fingerprints, date back to June 2013, when a small group of Syrians took part in the demonstrations organised by refugees from the Horn of Africa (Brigida, 2013). A second, more widely documented case of refusal occurred at the former Andrea Doria School in Catania, where refugees had been accommodated after the shipwreck on La Playa beach on 10 August 2014, in which six people lost their lives. This event was followed by others: the case of Palacannizzaro, a sports arena in Catania, where 100 detained refugees organised a demonstration and hunger strike between 7 and 17 October 2013 (Carnemolla, 2013); the case of the first aid and reception centre (CSPA) in Pozzallo (Tomassini, 2013); and the case of the Centre

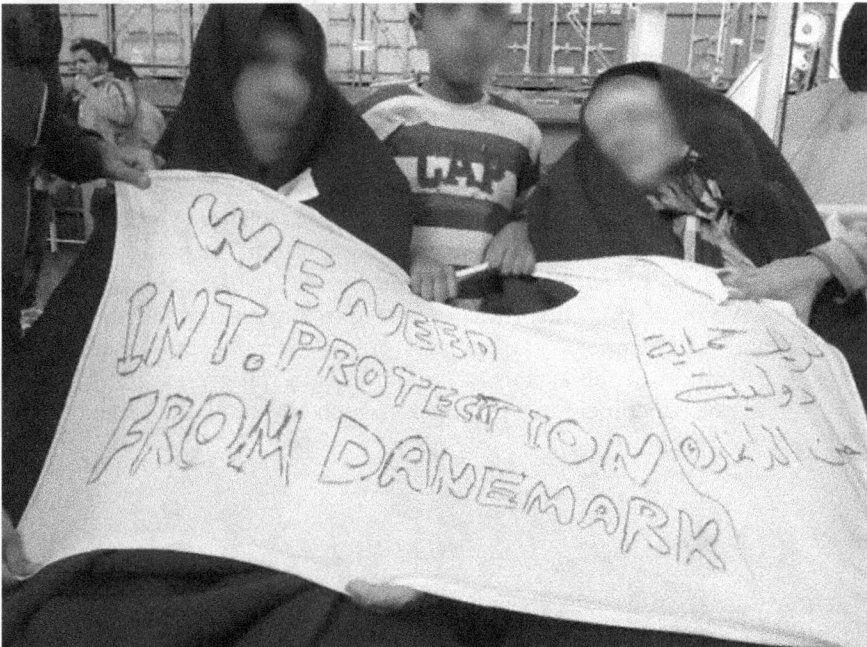

7.1 and 7.2 Danish merchant vessel 'Eleonora Maersk', 25 October 2014.

for Asylum Seekers and Refugees (CARA) in Crotone. According to the eyewitness accounts collected by associations, individual activists, journalists and lawyers, the Italian police had tried to collect the refugees' fingerprints through use of force. Several injuries were reported, especially after audio-visual material documenting the violence became public (Denaro, 2016d).

Beginning in late 2013, the Italian authorities started to 'let Syrian refugees go', by ceasing systematic fingerprint collection upon disembarkation. The Catania train station became a space of transit where activists offered various kinds of support to refugees to help them reach the North (Denaro, 2016d). Their tasks included purchasing food, water, phone cards and train or bus tickets to Milan to help ensure that the refugees did not fall into the hands of land smugglers.

Protests in Syntagma Square: Athens

Another case of demanding the right to continue to travel to central and northern Europe was seen in the demonstrations in Syntagma Square in Athens, which were organised by Syrian refugees in November 2014. The protests lasted for more than one month and took the form of a permanent sit-in and hunger strikes (Figures 7.3, 7.4).

Greece's inadequacy as an asylum country was one of the fundamental causes of the protests, while the core demands included allowing the refugees to reach the North legally. Greece, which had been sanctioned with two sentences by the European Court of Human Rights (ECtHR) for violating the prohibition of inhumane and degrading treatment and the collective expulsions of asylum seekers, still suffered from systemic deficiencies in providing access to asylum procedure and reception facilities (Denaro, 2016a). Due to the almost complete lack of a reception system, the living conditions for refugees unquestionably failed to meet the standards established by EU directives (AIDA, 2016). The primary results of the Syntagma Square protests included the establishment of a fast track procedure to quickly examine and positively respond to the asylum claims of Syrian refugees, enabling them to obtain a travel document in a few weeks, which in turn allowed free circulation around Europe.

Karmooz refugees

The fourth case study concerns the Syrian and Syrian-Palestinian refugees detained in Karmooz police station (Alexandria, Egypt), who – through the production of audio-visual material and its dissemination via social media – managed to create a network of solidarity and be resettled in Germany. In 2014, after the democratically elected president Mohammed Morsi was overthrown by a coup, the detention of refugees, which was an old practice

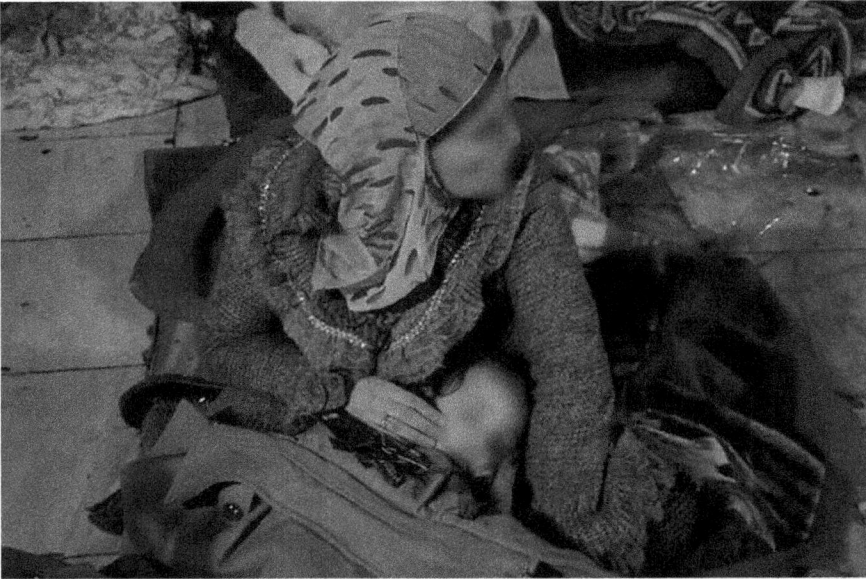

7.3 and 7.4   Refugees in Syntagma Square.

used for people from Sudan and the Horn of Africa, was extended to Syrians. Many of them were arrested during attempted departures by sea, whether real or presumed, and brought to local police stations (Denaro, 2016c, 2016d).

In November 2014, due to an argument between Egyptian and Turkish smugglers on the Turkish route from Mersin to Italy, at least 300 people were forcibly disembarked in Egypt and immediately arrested. During their detention in the Karmooz police station, which lasted more than seven months, they organised several protests and documented them on social media. Syrian refugees who had a passport had been deported to Lebanon and Turkey; those who did not have a passport or were Syrian-Palestinians remained in Egypt. The latter group created a Facebook page during their detention and started to spread their story through the use of pictures and videos, in order to acquire international solidarity and, indeed, many foreign newspapers told their story.

> The police are using methods of psychological pressure to make us accept the deportation. For example, they transferred 23 people to the prison of Al Qanater to convince them to be repatriated to Syria [...] In this police station they put us in three rooms, one for women, one for children and one for all the men. They did not let us see the sun. Only a half an hour for one day a month, when they took us to the top of the station and then brought us back down. (Interview with M.D. Syrian-Palestinian refugee, detained in Karmooz, 23 May 2015)

In the case of the Karmooz refugees, the protests and hunger strikes were documented on the Facebook page 'Karmooz Refugees', which was constantly updated with very well edited pictures (Figure 7.5, 7.6). This effort was aimed at building relationships with the outside world, especially with NGO members and journalists.[11] In the end, they reached their goal; the protest organisers managed to build significant relationships with international NGOs and journalists and to maintain high levels of attention regarding their case. At the end of May 2015, they were finally freed and transferred to Germany.

The idea of the Facebook page was discussed during an interview with its creator. Its existence confirmed the ever-growing direct involvement of refugees in advocacy actions, a phenomenon noted concerning the reception of SOS calls from sea and other forms of activism in countries of destination (Newland, 2010).

> I hope that this Facebook page could be a starting point, an inspiration, an idea, for refugees and detainees. I have seen too much injustice against them. When they moved me to the prison at Al Qanater, I met other people in even worse situations than me. Refugees who had been jailed for more than a year, simply because there was no country willing to accept them. Egypt proposed only repatriation or jail. There are people who are unfairly detained, without having committed any crime. I would like to try to help them to bring their voice outside, Insh'Allah, when I have my freedom. (Interview with M.D., a Syrian-Palestinian refugee, detained in Karmooz, 23 May 2015)

7.5 Hunger strike in Karmooz police station.

The emergence of refugee voices: communication tools, interactions and strategies

Drawing on evidence from the four case studies presented above, this section analyses how refugee voices emerged, focusing on three fundamental issues: the most used communication tools – such as new technologies and social media – interactions between refugees and other relevant actors and the main strategies put in place.

The most essential tools of communication between the refugees and their listeners were pictures and videos, namely the same privileged language used during the Arab revolts (Denaro, 2016b). Looking at the pictures taken by the refugees and published on social media, it is clear how their content openly contrasted the narratives being relayed in the dominant political discourses and by the mainstream mass media. On the Eleonora Maersk, at Catania station and in Syntagma Square, Syrian refugees contradicted their representation as desperate boatpeople by presenting themselves as agents, true protagonists in their migration and ready to negotiate and resist a legal framework perceived as unjust. Other images accurately 'photographed reality', keeping memory safe, spreading awareness about a specific situation and seeking solidarity, aid and support.

7.6   Karmooz police station, 11 November 2014.

In-depth interviews with experts on the Syrian context have highlighted the continuity between the documentation work done during mobilisation and the work carried out during the refugees' journeys to Europe (Denaro, 2016b).

Why have refugees being washed with a pump in Lampedusa been filmed by a Syrian man? Perhaps other people would not have thought to do that

… Syrians have been organizing demonstrations for four years, and they film during the demonstrations and they try to use those recordings to denounce to the world what is happening in Syria […] they have got into the habit of documenting the reality, and the production of audiovisual material is, precisely, part of that kind of mobilization […] They usually use these kinds of tools to document, sometimes to request help, sometimes to make allegations and also to preserve memory and understand where they have gone wrong. However, I think that the work of documenting mobilizations is reflected in the subsequent phase of the journey. (Interview with F.R., Syrian journalist, 20 May 2015, Rome)

Indeed, some of the interviewees defined the practice of self-documentation in terms of 'personal inclinations', or acquired habits, which while closely connected to their original context, was also interpretable in light of the widespread habit among young people of recording and sharing their everyday life through digital technologies and social networks.

Moreover, this practice should be framed as part of the age of new technologies and the Internet. Young Europeans record and share when they go out at night, or they have a coffee with friends and, of course, when they travel. This is their everyday life. For Syrians it is the same. But for many of them, their everyday life is made up of borders, camps, lethal journeys and reception centres. (Interview with F.R., Syrian journalist, 20 May 2015, Rome)

Mechanisms of production and the dissemination of images varied in space and time, depending on the socio-geographical contexts where they were produced and in relation to the interlocutors who were imagined to be listeners.

The kinds of relationships that existed between refugees and other actors, such as activists, journalists, volunteers, lawyers and average citizens, played an important role in the content of the images. The systematic interaction of Syrian refugees with a wide array of listeners was one of the most novel aspects of the socio-political environment in which the refugees' voices emerged. These listeners were institutional and non-governmental, individual and collective, old and new actors in the migration field, politicised or apolitical.

More than the protests themselves, which I analysed in the four case studies, Nick Couldry's understanding of voices as interactive processes between speakers and listeners was fully confirmed by some of the refugee listeners who were interviewed.

It is always a co-production. It is something that we do together. Some people are very aware of their rights and not without reason. If they are Afghan, many of them had already been in the UK and had a clearer idea of their rights in the EU, or if they are Syrian, and maybe from a higher social class. People who arrive directly from Pakistan have no idea of their capacity to speak or to act. They even have to ask for your advice about that [...] They want to say something, but they have to find out what their rights are. (Interview with Y.A., Italian teacher, activist for the LasciateCIEntrare campaign, 15 May 2015)

From a methodological perspective and starting with the assumption of voice as an interactive process, I will briefly consider three kinds of dialogue or interaction between refugees and various listeners with different roles and missions who partially contributed to determining the content and messages: (i) me as a researcher; (ii) volunteers–activists; and (iii) institutional actors.

The first kind of interaction was with me, as a researcher and activist, and took place during in-depth interviews and the collection of life stories. The first question I generally posed was, 'When did you leave Syria?' This was a starting point from where people could recount their entire journey, feeling free to share (or not share) feelings, reflections and considerations concerning their condition as refugees, their expectations, their plans and their dreams for the future. The richness and detail of the personal accounts that they shared with me was impressive and cut across a wide range of issues: exiting Syria, living conditions in neighbouring countries, migration routes through the Mediterranean, reception conditions in southern EU border zones. Their narratives were often supported by pictures and videos, which they had taken during their journeys in order to remember particularly significant steps in their lives or to document violations, difficult living conditions or situations perceived as inhumane.

The second kind of dialogue took shape within the interactions with volunteers and activists involved in various roles in the reception of the refugees. Audio-visual material in this case was aimed at supporting complaints and claims for help and at documenting human rights violations and desperate living conditions. Nawal Soufi, Mussie Zerai and Watch the Med Alarm Phone are some examples of the individuals and associations involved in a quite new form of activism, which I have termed 'critical sea watching'.[12] They received SOS signals from out at sea, called the coastguards, provided interpretation (between themselves and the people on the boats), monitored the rescues and reported cases of pushbacks or missing refugees. These volunteers and activists engaged with new, quite novel forms of solidarity when compared to the past.

The common array of tasks generally carried out by volunteers and activists, such as the provision of first aid, health assistance, food and clothes, was progressively extended through different and innovative ways of supporting people on the move. The main components were the provision of information concerning migration routes to facilitate transit to the North, the involvement of civil society in search and rescue operations, transnational advocacy and taking (socio-legal) charge of particular cases of human rights violations or illegitimate detentions.

At the same time, the tasks of the listeners, who heard the demands for help and support, multiplied. On the one hand, so-called old actors became involved in new tasks, such as the No Borders activists and volunteers who had traditionally supported migrants; on the other hand, completely new actors, such as independent activists who received no organisational support and improvising volunteers with no previous experience in refugee reception, appeared on the scene.

The internet, social media and digital technologies were basic infrastructures in the communication between refugees, volunteers, activists and other professional figures, such as journalists and lawyers. Pictures were shared not only on Facebook and Twitter, but also through WhatsApp and Viber. The audio-visual material disseminated on social media channels was based on collective narration, requests for help and complaints. Exemplary cases include the Karmooz Refugees,[13] Syrian and Palestinian refugees in Libya ('boycott the boats of death – refugees from one death to another')[14] and Syrian refugees in Melilla.[15]

A very different kind of interaction was the third type, in which the voices of the refugees mixed with those of institutional actors, such as local authorities and national police forces. Acts of passive resistance (e.g., resisting fingerprinting), demonstrations, sit-ins and hunger strikes were all spaces of negotiation and conflict where refugees demanded what they considered their rights. The cases of the peaceful demonstrations organised on the Danish merchant vessel and in Syntagma Square are both examples of open negotiation with the authorities, where the Syrian refugees were able to partially obtain their goals. A similar process occurred in the mass refusal to give fingerprints to the Italian authorities, culminating in the cessation of this step in the refugee process for Syrians and the prospect that they could continue their journeys. It is possible to read these events in terms of a transformation of dominant social structures, in which Syrian refugee agency and voices were able to partially modify the consolidated praxis and modus operandi.

The involvement of the listeners was aligned with the goals and circumstances underlying each expression of voice, delineating agentive strategies. In many cases, refugee voices were aimed at requesting help and/or rescue and denouncing human rights violations, as well as the inhumane situations experienced during their migration. Cases of illegitimate detention, beatings, forced identifications, pushbacks at sea, sea crossings, shipwrecks and shameful reception conditions were generally documented with pictures and videos, and then shared through digital technologies (WhatsApp, Viber) and on social media (Facebook, Twitter). Their content was, in part, a result of the interaction between refugees and their listeners (activists, volunteers, lawyers).

In other instances, refugee voices emerged through acts with more explicit political content; demonstrations, hunger strikes and sit-ins were organised by refugees along their migration routes, and they were essentially aimed at demanding that they be allowed to continue their journeys to the countries they had imagined to be their final destinations. Refugee requests to choose the country where they wanted to live clashed with the prescriptions imposed by the Dublin Regulation and emerged within the framework of interactions with other stakeholders involved in managing incoming migration flows.

In most cases it was not possible to draw a clear line between the goals and circumstances of the voices, but it was interesting to identify the mechanisms overlapping between them: reports, requests for help and rescue, claims for rights and freedoms, expressions of will and identity. Voices and agency emerged through individual or collective acts, with different levels of politicisation, but certain goals and demands were transversal to the different migration contexts and exit routes in which they took shape. In many cases, refugee voices and agency materialised in acts of resistance against a legal framework perceived as oppressive and unjust. The main demands made by the refugees included the possibility of overcoming the limitations imposed on their mobility and the exercise of their right to choose their destination countries.

Concluding remarks

This chapter examined the emergence of the voices of Syrian refugees along their multiple exit routes from Syria to and throughout Europe. The voices are seen as expressions of agency that took shape in various contexts, the result of interactions with several listeners, and emerged as acts of resistance to a legal framework perceived as unjust. The main innovative development was the widespread use of audio-visual material, an essential component of what Feldman defined as 'visibility practices' and passed along through social media and new technologies. More than being the only means to document uncomfortable living conditions and often fatal journeys, the photos taken and shared by refugees contained new meanings of what a refugee is – namely an agent, a speaking subject, the protagonist of one's own life – and new attributes with respect to the past: courage, resilience, determination.

This subjectivity took shape through a kaleidoscope of complex interactions, among refugees – as the main speakers – and a multiplicity of stakeholders, new and old listeners, activists and volunteers and institutional and non-governmental counterparts, by generating voices as a result of dialogues where messages were essentially co-defined.

In particular, a key implication of these emerging voices was their ability to challenge and, in certain cases, affect how various dominant structures functioned, as regulated by the law. This was made possible through alliances with solidarity activists, lawyers and new listeners, as well as through processes of negotiation with some authorities or peaceful resistance and conflict with others. These voices seemed to fully contain the subversive potential inherent in the concept of escape routes and attributed to all human mobilities by the autonomy of migration theorists. Still more significant, perhaps, is the ability of refugee voices to challenge the dualistic opposition between forced and voluntary migration by revealing the continuous overlap between these two components in each migration as a reflection of the deeply entwined aspects of human lives.

Notes

1 The inter-agency information-sharing portal Syrian Refugee Regional Response contains disaggregated data concerning the primary hosting countries, namely Turkey, Lebanon, Jordan, Iraq, Egypt and the North African countries (UNHCR, 2018a, 2018b).
2 The total number of Syrian refugees is about six and a half million people (UNHCR, 2018a, 2018b).
3 Between April 2011 and January 2018, the number of asylum claims presented by Syrian citizens was less than 1 million across the entire continent (UNHCR, 2018a, 2018b).
4 The most sought-after countries were Sweden, Germany, Norway, the Netherlands and Denmark.
5 To this purpose, I put the question of *access* at the core: access to the territory of a supposedly safe country, access to the asylum procedure and access to first reception.
6 Audio-visual material was collected through three different channels: (i) during in-depth interviews with refugees, who decided to share it with me as visual support of their narratives; (ii) during volunteering with different networks of activists; and (iii) through social networks (i.e., Facebook pages managed by refugees).
7 Newland examines the advocacy processes undertaken by these communities, the causes they promoted, the communication tools and financial means that they used. Fargues interprets the emigration of young people as a causal factor in the outbreak of the Arab revolutions; they were rupture points in terms of loyalty, something promoted and strengthened in patriarchal societies.
8 See Frontex (2015) for data on sea arrivals disaggregated by nationality, and EUROSTAT (2016) for data on asylum claims presented, by year and nationality.
9 The case was referred to as 'Watch the Med Alarm Phone' by the activist N.S. who was in direct contact with the refugees on board and who received the pictures and voice messages via WhatsApp.
10 See also: http://www.strettoweb.com/2014/10/incredibile-malta-immigrati-si-rifiutano-sbarcare-vogliamo-litalia-arrivano-catania/204368/.
11 The Facebook page 'Karmooz Refugees' is still active today and documents other cases of refugee detention in Egypt and abroad. See https://www.facebook.com/karmooz48/?fref=ts.

12 See also the official page of the Alarm Phone project: http://alarmphone.org/
    en/.
13 See also: https://www.facebook.com/karmooz48/.
14 See also: https://www.facebook.com/damlage2/.
15 See also: https://www.facebook.com/ملیلیه-فی-السوریین-اوضاع-Refugiados-Sirio
    s-en- Melilla-427999480637961/?fref=ts.

References

Amnesty International (2014a), *The Human Cost of Fortress Europe* (London: Amnesty) [online] http://www.amnesty.eu/content/assets/Reports/EUR_050012014__Fortress_Europe_complete_web_EN.pdf [accessed 25 November 2014].

Amnesty International (2014b), *Greece: Frontier of Hope and Fear. Migrants and Refugees Pushed Back at Europe's Border* (London: Amnesty International, 2014b) [online] http://www.sos-europe-amnesty.eu/content/assets/docs/Greece_Frontier_of_Hope_and_Fear_Avril_2 014.pdf [accessed 1 June 2014].

Asylum Information Database – AIDA (2016), 'Mapping asylum procedures, reception conditions and detention in Europe' [online] http://www.asylumineurope.org [accessed 28 August 2015].

Brigida, V. (2013), Lampedusa, vincono gli eritrei. No alle impronte digitali. *La Repubblica* (21 Luglio 2013) [online] http://www .repubblica.it/cronaca/2013/07/21/news/lampedusa_vincono_gli_eritrei_no_alle_impronte_digitali-63432090/ [accessed 23 November 2014].

Carnemolla, D. (2013), Sicilia – Diritti sempre più violati: da Catania testimonianze di migranti ed attivisti e a Siracusa violenti pestaggi della polizia e reclusione forzata. *Melting Pot Europa* (14 August 2013), [online] http://www.meltingpot.org/Sicilia-Diritti-sempre-piu-violati-da-Catania-testimonianze.html#.VDpmF0u6zK9 [accessed 15 November 2016].

Cottle, S. (2011), Media and Arab uprisings of 2011: research notes. *Journalism* 12: 247–259.

Couldry, N. (2009), Rethinking the politics of voice: commentary. *Continuum: Journal of Media & Cultural Studies* 23(4): 579–582.

Crawley, H. (2016), Managing the unmanageable? Understanding Europe's response to the migration crisis. *Human Geography* 9(2): 13–23.

De Angelis, E. (2011), The state of disarray of a networked revolution. The Syrian uprising's information environment. *Sociologica* 3: 1–24.

Denaro, C. (2016a), I rifugiati siriani sulle rotte via mare verso la Grecia. Riflessioni sul transito e sullo svuotamento del diritto d'asilo. *Mondi migranti* 1(1): 97–117.

Denaro, C. (2016b), We have the right to choose where to live. Agency e produzione di material audiovisuale nei percorsi di fuga dalla Siria. *Mondi migranti* 2(1): 123–145.

Denaro, C. (2016c), The reconfiguration of Mediterranean migration routes after the war in Syria: narratives on the Egyptian route to Italy and beyond. In Ribas-Mateos, N. (ed.) *Spaces of Refugee Flight: Migration and Mobilities after the Arab Spring in the Eastern Mediterranean* (Cheltenham: Edward Elgar Publishing).

Denaro, C. (2016d), Agency, resistance and (forced) mobilities. The case of Syrian refugees in transit through Italy. *REMHU, Revista Interdisciplinar de Mobilidade Humana* 24(47): 77–79.

Denaro, C. (2016e), Syrian refugees' reception in Southern Europe; the shifting content of the right to asylum in Lesvos, Sicily and Melilla. *Refugee Watch Special Issue on Syrian refugee crisis.*

EUROSTAT (2016), Asylum and first time asylum applicants by citizenship, age and sex. Annual aggregated data (2008–2015) [online] http://ec.europa.eu/eurostat/web/asylum-and-managed-migration/data/database [accessed 7 August 2016].

Fargues, P. (2011), Voice after exit: revolution and migration in the Arab world. Migration Information Sources (Fiesole: Migration Policy Institute) [online] http://www.migrationinformation.org/Feature/print.cfm?ID=839 [accessed 13 May 2015].

Feldman, I. (2008), Refusing invisibility: documentation and memorialization in Palestinian refugee claims. *Journal of Refugee Studies* 21(4): 498–516.

Foucault, M. (1980), *Power/Knowledge. Selected Interviews and Other Writings 1972-1977* (New York: Pantheon Books).

Frontex (2015), Annual Risk Analysis 2015 [online] http://frontex.europa.eu/assets/Publications/Risk_Analysis/Annual_Risk_Analysis_2015.pdf [accessed 6 July 2015].

Goodwin-Gill, G.S. (2011), The right to seek asylum: Interception at sea and the principle of non-refoulement. *International Journal of Refugee Law* 23(3): 443–457.

Hirschman, A.O. (1970), *Exit, Voice, and Loyalty: Responses to Decline in Firms* (Cambridge, MA: Harvard University Press).

Hirschman, A.O. (1978), Exit, voice, and the state. *World Politics* 31(1): 90–107.

Malkki, L.H. (1996), Speechless emissaries: Refugees, humanitarianism, and dehistoricization. *Cultural Anthropology* 11(3): 377–404.

Mezzadra, S. (2015), The proliferation of borders and the right to escape. In Jansen, Y., R. Celikates and J. de Bloois (eds) *The Irregularization of Migration in Contemporary Europe. Detention, Deportation, Drowning* (London–New York: Rowman & Littlefield), pp. 121–135.

Mezzadra, S. (2006), *Diritto di fuga: Migrazioni, cittadinanza, globalizzazione* (Verona: Ombre corte).

Moulin, C. (2012), Ungrateful subjects? Refugee protests and the logic of gratitude. In Nyers, P. and K. Rygiel (eds) *Citizenship, Migrant Activism and the Politics of Movement* (Abingdon: Routledge), pp. 66–84.

Newland, P. (2010), *Voice after Exit: Diaspora Advocacy* (Washington, DC: Migration Policy Institute).

IOM (2014), *Fatal Journeys. Tracking Lives Lost during Migration* (Geneva: IOM) [online] http://publications.iom.int/bookstore/free/FatalJourneys_CountingtheUncounted.pdf [accessed 25 November 2014].

Papadopoulos, D., N. Stephenson and V. Tsianos (2008), *Escape Routes: Control and Subversion in the Twenty-first Century* (London: Pluto Press).

Pro Asyl (2013), Pushed back [online] http://www.proasyl.de/en/press/press/news/pro_asyl_releases_new_report_pushed_back/ [accessed 20 June 2015].

Ruiz De Elvira Carrascal, L. (2014), Retour sur la révolte syrienne: conditions de départ et prémières mobilisations. *Annuaire Français des Relations Internationales* 15: 673–689.

Said, E.W. (1984), Permission to narrate. *Journal of Palestine Studies* 13(3): 27–48.

Sigona, N. (2014), The politics of refugee voices: representations. In Fiddiah Qasmiyeh, E., G. Loescher, K. Long and N. Sigona (eds) *The Oxford Handbook of Refugee and Forced Migration Studies* (Oxford: Oxford University Press), pp. 369–382.

Spivak, G.C. (1988), Can the subaltern speak? In Nelson, C. and L. Grossberg (eds), *Marxism and the Interpretation of Culture* (Urbana: University of Illinois Press), pp. 21–78.

Tomassini, V. (2013), I siriani e il campo pestaggi. *Il Fatto Quotidiano* (17 October 2013): 14.

UNHCR (2018a), Syria Regional Response. Inter Agency information sharing [online] http://data.unhcr.org/syrianrefugees/regional.php [accessed 2 January 2018].

UNHCR (2018b), Refugees/Migrants Emergency Response: Mediterranean [online] http://data.unhcr.org/mediterranean/regional.php [accessed 2 January 2018].

Un Ponte Per (2015), Out of the Borders. Rifugiati siriani in Medio Oriente e Nord Africa [online] http://docplayer.it/12659884-Out-of-the-borders-rifugiati-siriani-in-medio-oriente-e-nord-africa.html [accessed 1 September 2016].

Van Hear, N. (2015), Dépasser la defection et la prise de parole dans la region euro- méditerranéenne. In Schmoll, C., H. Thiollet and C. Wihtol de Wenden (eds) *Migrations en Méditerranée* (Paris: CNRS), pp. 371–379.

Vio, E. (2016), No way out: How Syrians are struggling to find an exit. *IRIN* (10 March 2016) [online] https://www.irinnews.org/special-report/2016/03/10/no-way-out-how-syrians-are-struggling-find-exit [accessed 1 September 2016].

Yassin-Kassab, R. and L. Al Shami (2016), *Burning Country. Syrians in Revolution and War* (London: Pluto Press).

8

The global refugee camp: coinciding locales of refuge among Sahrawi refugees in North Africa

Konstantina Isidoros

Research and scholarly debates focus on refugees as the Other, always kept at arm's length, at a distant site somewhere in a Global South, usually trying to get into the Global North. They are perceived as people fleeing from a supra-local site of crisis, either as internally displaced people (IDPs) within their local nation, or on to an external host and then further onwards into the global arena – moving from dystopic local to utopian global in a unilineal motion, between local to national via transnational spaces. Somewhere in between, they usually end up in refugee camps in a distant local (if not as asylum seekers in hosted suspension), to be 'managed as undesirables' (Agier, 2011) with their stop-motions discursively isolated as dis(placements). Yet, wherever they are situated, refugee camps are still treated as local places of 'bare life' in a parochial 'state of exception' (Agamben, 1998), even though refugees have been recognised with agency 'negotiating' (Pasquetti, 2015) and circumventing external impositions of control (Kibreab, 1993).

Meanwhile, as the local seems to be perpetually captured in looking out and moving to the global, the lenses of analysts and humanitarians are perpetually refracted from global sight to local site. What is in this different movement of site and sight: where the humanitarian world moves in the opposite direction, from the global into the local? What brings these two worlds to 'collide' in a camp intended for refuge, where one body (usually conducting the work of humanitarian aid, infrastructure building and research) moves out of choice towards refugees who had moved without choice? What happens at this 'conjuncture of stars' within the refugee camps, when the global humanitarian experts come face to face with the local? And is the provision of refuge really unilineal and one-sided? Mauss (1967) showed how gifts are never 'free'. As this chapter will show, neither is receiving humanitarian assistance free. Given the intensive humanitarian–developmentalist flurry of activity and infrastructure building in refugee camps, which is part of a monolithic, global Northern politico-economic regime (Idris, 2016), who are the 'real' occupants of a refugee camp; who is really dependent on whom? In the 1990s, sociologists Robertson (1997) and Wellman and Hampton (1999) first cemented glocalisation as meaning 'the simultaneity – the co-presence – of both universalising and particularising tendencies', commenting that 'the particular is what makes the universal work'. Meanwhile anthropology, expanding this with its hallmark ethnographic particularism, expressed scepticism with the idea of 'absolute' globalisation and found rich sources of ethnographic evidence of glocalising encounters.

This chapter homes in on one group of Sahrawi refugee camps in North Africa where large agglomerations of both refugees and humanitarian 'aid' workers/volunteers come face to face. On the Algerian desert border, following a frozen Spanish de-colonisation due to the Moroccan invasion of two-thirds of the 'Spanish Sahara' territory (now called the Western Sahara) between the 1960s and 1970s, the Sahrawi have been employing international law and human rights alongside their traditional desert nomadic encampments to construct their nascent nation-state. Due to Morocco's breach of international law in its military occupation of the Western Sahara, the Sahrawi are classified under international law as refugees. Their traditional way of life as nomadic tent dwellers has changed to becoming refugees dwelling in UNHCR canvas tents in what have come to be called 'refugee' camps. This is where a year-round diaspora of international humanitarians arrives to provide food aid and other developmental assistance projects. I explore an interplay of global social relations – at once reciprocal and at cross-purposes – between the Saharawi as refugees and self-made citizens of their nation-state 'in waiting', and their external visitors, who together make these camps a pivotal point of 'glocal' engagement. Theoretical debates about heterotopia (Foucault), friction (Tsing) and cool grounds (Allen) help to discern the conceptual importance of observing an intriguing globality being reproduced in these refugee camps. This interplay makes the camps a simultaneous site of different 'refuges'. At ground level, while these refugees are technically the primary benefactors of refuge, in actuality they are the chief providers of it, having to manage, mediate and safeguard the visiting humanitarian body. The 'local' keeps the vulnerable 'global' safe and fed where it is out of depth in this politically and ecologically harsh environment of the Sahara Desert.

The food aid that has travelled so far suddenly transforms into what feeds and nurtures the visitors themselves – the humanitarians only have the refugees' food aid supplies for consumption in a desert ecology far from conventional urban spatialities. Tsing's (2005) thesis on 'friction' and 'zones of awkward engagement' serves as a useful metaphor to catch sight of the diverse encounters and contradictory social interactions between humanitarian apparatus and refugee camp infrastructure, specifically the 'grey area' *between* the humanitarians and the refugees themselves. At this conjuncture, it is the local that is feeding the global. I highlight food here as an easily visualised example, where it conventionally arrives into the hands of the refugees through numerous pathways, moving from the global givers through their international distribution routes, towards the local receivers. The encounter involves far more than food as these international bodies move towards the refugees – the refugees receive these humanitarians in the act of local 'traditional' hospitality in many other ways too, helping these visitors to circulate through the geopolitics, regional culture and harsh Saharan desert ecology. They also help the visitors live and survive in the desert and its camps by the very fact that for at least three millennia, the Sahrawi have been first and foremost highly experienced desert tent-dwellers and nomadic circumnavigators of the Sahara Desert, North Africa and far beyond (i.e., long before they 'became refugees' in 'refugee tents').

Foucault (1971, 2004, 2009) also circulated around philosophies of utopia/dystopia/heterotopia which intriguingly map onto theoretical debates about the glocal and Tsing's 'awkward zones'. Drawing from his deliberations on the 'order of things', four aspects stand out as relevant to this discussion about refugees and humanitarians in camps as their *mutual refuges*. Foucault proposed that heterotopias: (i) mutate at different historical junctures; (ii) juxtapose incompatibilities in a single space; (iii) relate to other spaces in terms of illusion or compensation; and (iv) presuppose a system of entry, exit, distance and penetration. This makes utopias illusory and heterotopias 'localisable'. Another way that Foucault explained heterotopias was as spaces of otherness possessing some essence of *irrelevance*. Mead (1995: 13) further expanded this to: 'Utopia is a place where everything is good; dystopia is a place where everything is bad; heterotopia is where things are different – that is, a collection whose members have few or no intelligible connections with one another.'

My argument, drawing on eleven years of research among the Sahrawi in North Africa, finds instead that their dystopian camps can be observed as having become a globalised humanitarian utopia. On the one hand, a year-round visiting 'humanitarian body' moves from their own diverse international locales, flying into and converging on the camps as one global entity with powerful biopolitical ideas about developing the Sahrawi as dystopic refugees. They need to remain dystopic to continue to fulfil the humanitarians' goals. The refugees, however, do not find living in tents in the Sahara anything unusual – what is dystopic is the technical failure of international law and geopolitical breach of sovereign territorial law. These refugees have their own utopian ambitions to build their nascent nation-state from their desert camps, which serve as their biopolitical and legal 'GPS point' on the global geopolitical map, as a mutually and positively reinforcing entity as refugee-*citizens*. I use this dual term to denote an intertwining over the last forty years of their self-made project of nation-statehood, its resulting reconfiguration of themselves as citizens of the Sahrawi Arab Democratic Republic (SADR/RASD) and their considerable diplomatic efforts to have this identity achieve international legal–political recognition. While they are still not recognised as a formal nation and state by the United Nations, they have created their own 'passports' in the form of Sahrawi identity cards (which are also recognised as viable identity documents by Algeria, Spain and Mauritania). The camps, therefore, represent two oppositional goals between two different human groups 'occupy-ing' them. In the eyes of the arriving humanitarians, the Sahrawi are only – can only ever be – refugees. To the Sahrawi, they are citizens of their nation-state-in-waiting receiving the humanitarians as *visitors*. Meanwhile, the Sahrawi as refugee-citizens happen to be agile nomadic 'movers' and skilled tent- and camp-dwellers, living in their own idiosyncratic world as millennia-old 'global nomads'. They are in fact, in the true sense of their own world view, emerging as nomad-citizens at this juncture along their historical continuum; 'refugee' is simply an add-on necessitated by an external outcome of global politics and international human rights jargon at this contemporary point of their continuum. Although the Sahrawi refugee camps are places in which the Sahrawi 'as refugees' and the humanitarian visitors do make con-nections, where the camps are the local point of meeting face-to-face, the camps are actually a fully-fledged nation-state, albeit awaiting full international legal recognition. It seems an unintelligible othering where the vision and goals of each are irrelevant and at cross-purpose to each other. This may explain why we have not yet noticed how camps are, or have been becoming, new global refuges for more than 'just refugees', and more specifically as 'glocalising' places of heterotopia.

I make one contradistinction to other sites where, for example, more individual encounters occur as asylum seekers already in the Global North are moving through local–national legal processes. The implication of this distinction is to analytically move further beyond the view of refugee camps as simply local places of bare life, where scholarship has become influenced by Foucauldian biopolitics and biopower and progressed into arguments such as those around 'humanitarian governmentality' (Butler and Athanasiou, 2013),[1] which propounds top-down ideas of camp inhabitants being rooted in an inexorable localism and managed by global apparatuses of control. The humanitarian encounter in the Sahrawi camps never recognises that the Sahrawi are in far more 'control'. The humanitarian entity needs to feel needed, thus the interplay between who is 'refuge-ing' who can be analogously visualised as my earlier question – who is really feeding who? At a very base level of 'bare life', humanitarian visitors could not biologically survive in this Sahara Desert without the millennia-old desert experience and survival skills of the Sahrawi. It is the Sahrawi's self-project of 'state-building' that builds basic accommodation, toilets, cooks food and provides the safety needed by these visitors.

Global refugees and localising humanitarians

Having occupied the western territories of the Sahara Desert for at least three millennia, the Sahrawi are arguably 'global nomads', actors in and agents of human globalisation along the historical continuum; linked into

ancient networks of trade and seafaring routes and situated between the rise
and fall of pre-colonial North African and Sub-Saharan monarchies and
emirates (As-sa'd, 1990; Lydon, 2009). Locally, as skilled nomadic pastoralists
and warrior cameleers, their command of long-distance trading across the
trans-Saharan economy developed powerful political links across North Africa.
Part of their territory, the Spanish Sahara, was colonised by the Spanish; and
during Spain's failed de-colonisation process in the late 1960s and early
1970s, Morocco invaded – creating a long war from 1975 to a United Nations-
led ceasefire in 1991 (see Zunes and Mundy, 2010). Those Sahrawi within
the Spanish Sahara and many in southern Moroccan regions fled to safety;
some of whom made their way towards Tindouf, a strategic military town
inside the Algerian desert border. These early encampments grew into more
formalised refugee camps, first assisted primarily by the ('local') Algerian
Red Crescent (ARC).

One of the first foreign visitors to fly in was Dr Barbara Harrell-Bond
(1981) to report to Oxfam on camp conditions. Harrell-Bond opens her
report by framing it very much as her visit *to* the Sahrawi. After contextualising
her arrival, first encounters, food, lodgings and transportations – as the
provisions of Sahrawi hospitality to *her* – she focuses the rest of the report
on the Sahrawi themselves, their culture, war story and early administrative
system and educational and health programmes in the camps. In closing, she
notes a moment visiting Moroccan prisoners being held in a Sahrawi prison:
'Several journalists took down names and addresses. One visitor asked them
about the food they were given in prison. One replied: "We are all Muslim
and it is not polite for a guest to talk about the hospitality of his host"'
(Harrell-Bond, 1981: 12). Next, she records one prisoner saying they have
eaten better in the prison than back in Morocco. This captures an early reference
to the analytical complexity of deciding what one is terminologically focusing
on: who is host to whom, whose refuge it is, and how we untangle the
simultaneity of refuges.

These early refuges have since grown into six large refugee camps. One
is Rabuni, variously described as the 'government', 'administrative' or 'politico-
administrative' centre, which is not really seen as 'residential' because it presides
over the formal and symbolic structures of a nascent nation-state – the parliament, presidential office and other governmental buildings, warehouses for
international aid provisions, the radio, television and press services, the National
Archive, central hospital and several human rights associations. As San-Martin
perceptively states in his ethnographic monograph, 'Rabuni is not a camp,
but essentially the *capital city* of the Saharawi Republic' (2010: 154–155,
original emphases). Rabuni also serves as the original and still preferred
logistical arrival point of foreign visitors, with a large Protocol Centre from
which foreign groups and project teams are first organised and assigned
various Sahrawi guides, translators, drivers and so forth. The other camps
are perceived by the external gaze as more familiarly like residential camps,
filled with the woman–child complex that easily depicts 'family'. However,

Rabuni possesses its own idiosyncratic residential cycle, shaped by Sahrawi workers who come into the camps to work within this nascent state infrastructure. These mostly male workers (as conventional breadwinners) stay for weeks or months before returning to see their families in the neighbouring residential camps. Rabuni is briefly intersected by momentary cycles of arriving visitors who are temporarily lodged in the transitory Protocol Centre (i.e., a Sahrawi provision to enable a human being to make a 'home for a day') before being transferred to other camps, or for a few foreign aid workers who are based there at a live-in office for more than a few weeks.

In debates about what makes a refugee camp, there has been a disciplinary shift in terminology. When Harrell-Bond first founded the Refugee Studies Centre at Oxford, the key word 'refuge' was used in the study of humanitarian policy and practice to focus solely on refugees inside such refuges. In *The Birth of a 'Discipline': From Refugee to Forced Migration Studies* (2009), Chimni chronicles an important change from refuge to movement-as-migration, underscoring the puzzling and illogical paradoxes today: we now recognise the analytical intricacies of protracted refugeehood as equalling permanent impermanence and permanent temporariness (see also Picker and Pasquetti 2015 on durability). But the recent European refugee crisis signals a shift from concern of the distant Other safely 'warehoused over there' (Smith, 2004) to the Other suddenly on the move; a shift in Other Words of migrants from Other Worlds who do not want to be the sitting-waiting refugee anymore, but strike further out from incorporeal (dystopian) refugee camps to reach the world beyond that holds the promise of a full-bodied (utopian) life. Discussion of refuge in its old sense seems redundant to me because at the very least we might want to start thinking instead about refugees on the move. In which case, the Sahrawi are experts as nomadic 'movers' *and* as hosts.

Global disorder and local order

Over the past sixty years, both humanitarian and development policies and practices have received critical scholarly scrutiny ranging from romanticised ideals of imagined futures to demonised criticism of destructive myths in what is seen as a failed chapter in the history of Western modernisation and its ideology (Escobar, 1995). No longer moored to colonial science, but having become anchored in rising postcolonial human displacement, development agencies have been seen to revise and reframe their neocolonial policies and procedures to legitimate their own political and moral positions (Mosse, 1996). Post-development theory critically conceptualises development as a regime imposed on Third World peoples through the North's intervention in the South (Rahnema and Bawtree, 1997). Development models unleash the social re-engineering of undeveloped by developer, producing hierarchies in which scientific knowledge trumps indigenous knowledge (Escobar, 1995; Ferguson, 1990), while the language of 'participatory' or 'bottom-up' principles sustains development hegemony 'behind the beguiling rhetoric of "people's control"' (Ferguson, 1990; Mosse, 2004: 643). In line with Foucault's notion of fields of knowledge that are constructed as politically neutral (1971; cf. Escobar, 1995), development discourse has become heavily critiqued for creating powerless and dependent subjects through the intervention of global players establishing governmental and administrative control over refugee camps and the inhabitants within.

A new body of critical literature emerged to track the emergence of humanitarianism, equally criticised as the new neocolonial project of the ailing postcolonial development mission. Increasing refugee numbers since the Cold War have contributed to the continued survival and political interests of what has now grown into a Western 'refugee regime' (Harrell-Bond and Mahmud, 1996). From this conscious policy shift by Western governments and their international agencies has emerged the newly termed 'third sector', private professional development organisations and the voluntary sector, regarded as a viable humanitarian alternative to the disparaged industry of development (Goonatilake, 2006). Scholarly attention has shifted to questioning the role and political economy of these new foreign and privately funded NGOs by drawing attention to the prevalence of NGO myths as preserving 'the previous era of developmental orthodoxy' (Gardner and Lewis, 1996: 108–109). Western countries have turned to closing their borders and using the refugee regime to *contain* refugees within developing countries (as Smith's 2004 'refugee warehousing' and Kibreab's 1993 'dependency syndrome').

The 'old' *raison d'être* of refugee camps may have been to provide external assistance and protection, but it was always criticised as a global order needing a local disorder to scaffold the humanitarian existence. This centres on Western humanitarian [il]logic, such as the UN and UNHCR tied to donor states who serve as powerful Security Council members, to whose higher geopolitical script refugees remain inextricably linked (Loescher, 1993: 138). Critical refugee studies scholars had already long questioned whether refugee camps provide security or sustain dependence at all, determining that confined and artificial camps not only thwart refugees' abilities to make indigenous decisions for dealing with insecurity, but also force a greater dependence on refugees that increases global insecurity (Horst, 2006: 77).

The Sahrawi did not wait for the global order to arrive, they set their first camps up almost twenty years before Dr Barbara Harrell-Bond made an official aid agency visit (and this is what impressed her). The main reason this happened, which is little credited in studies of the Sahrawi case, is that they were already experienced nomadic movers and camp-dwellers. This is quite different to, say, working- and middle-class Syrians in flight, used to very different 'comforts' of a modern, urban infrastructure that is (variously) plumbed into a pre-existing state structure. The Sahrawi case also serves to demonstrate an ironic fallacy in Western promises and statements about developmental goals, humanitarian 'resilience' and 'global security' (the latter being the old security paradigm of 'you stay far away from us and we'll come to you to deliver the aid'). Development by the Global North and its international agencies is impossible without security and peace. Humanitarian action and military intervention are no longer neutral – nor separate (Castles, 2003). Despite making every effort to build a nation-state and self-initiate the transformation from refugees to citizens, the Sahrawi remain 'trapped' as refugees by that same original humanitarian illogic. If the humanitarian–development nexus truly wanted to 'assist' the Sahrawi, it would logically be encouraging them to succeed in establishing a stable nation-state. In many ways, by taking action themselves, the Sahrawi are trying to reverse a global disorder that imposes upon them not to establish a local order. Instead, a symbiotic glocal order emerges in their humanitarian encounter to reposition themselves as a new locale on the world stage. One of the ways they do this is by taking control of the failed humanitarian thesis by applying its geopolitical vocabulary and logistics 'onto' themselves. Yet, on the ground, this has the very ordinary and subtle effect of hospitably encouraging visitors to the camps, taking control of their logistical movement in a dangerous, not so easily accessible political geography, and presenting and performing the structures of modern political nation-state architecture. There is no such thing as a free gift – receivers can be just as adept at managing a gift to wrest control out of the givers. At the same time, they have to use the humanitarian gift to feed, house and keep safe the humanitarians as additional recipients.

Refuge among refugees

Protocol Centres in the Sahrawi refugee camps are single-storey compounds made of desert sand bricks and mud rendered with large, locked metal entrance gates primarily for the safe housing and feeding of visiting foreigners. Sometimes, I chose to allocate specific time-frames to live in a few out of curiosity about these spaces containing international foreigners who come to the camps mostly for aid work – as disparate and numerous NGOs, but also as informal humanitarian-interest groups of students, musicians and artists, as well as political representatives and journalists, film-makers, photographers and occasional academic Masters and PhD students from around the world. Other times I ended up moving through different Protocol Centres when I joined Sahrawi interlocutors as they worked for these visitors as drivers, guides and translators during the annual cultural and music festivals and political anniversary commemorations. These centres are where thousands of visitors arrive, make a temporary home and leave from, year in and year out. They seemed to me to be rather like global bubbles sitting in a unique locale. They are in every respect refuges run by refugees; global nomads providing temporary refuges for localising humanitarians.

In one particular visit back to a longstanding host family in 2013, after a few days a daughter of my host family asked me if I needed to do anything in particular (i.e., for research). We had been gradually catching up on mutual family news and I had settled back into the womenfolk's daily routines, social visits and visitors. A few days later, she asked me again if there was anything I needed to do; again, I said no, that it was just good to be back. After another few days, her father asked me 'The women say you haven't gone out, isn't there anything you want to do or see?' Again, I said no, that it was good to just relax with everyone. 'But don't you want to go outside?' I answered that I had, that we had been very busy: to visit family friends, to the shops … I appealed to his wife to confirm we had been very busy. He seemed unconvinced and took a fatherly tone: 'I will ask the girls to take you for a walk at sunset.' Yet again, I insisted he did not need to arrange this, I was just happy to 'stay at home'. I assured him this was in fact a very busy activity and I joked that I could do with a little more idleness, which triggered his rumble of laughter. He looked across to me and held my gaze to pinpoint a profound thought: 'Ah … you seek refuge among refugees.'[2]

I have often reflected back on his poetic and pointed play of words between refuge and refugee. Visitors form a year-round flow; their 'movement' into these camps comes from the outside in, from one type of global into a perceived local. As *refugees* without internationally legal identities (i.e., passports), the Sahrawi do not have that kind of freedom of movement. Neither do they as refugees travel to examine, interview and survey their visitors. However, they do possess a different global which the visitors cannot move freely through (without danger). The Sahrawi as refugees are entirely responsible for the logistical movement, housing, feeding and safety of visitors. They also have to work for (or with, in 'bottom-up' humanitarianism) visitors, who cannot complete their projects without Sahrawi physical, logistical and oral assistance. Not only do they need the Sahrawi to be *there*, they need them to *be* refugees (see again Horst, 2006 and Harrell-Bond, 2002). In another aspect, every year and particularly during the Christian Easter vacation, Spanish families travel to the camps to visit their 'Sahrawi family'. This is a product of up to 10,000 Sahrawi children since 1988 having been hosted by the longstanding, humanitarian Spanish *Vacaciones en Paz* programme.[3] In the reverse Easter journey, the Sahrawi become hosts, friends and 'family' to these humanitarian actors. The camps yet again serve as a refuge in a hostile ecology, but in reverse – as a humanitarian apparatus to welcome the humanitarians – which illuminates intriguing paradoxes of who is a host, who is really in control, and the circular use of the humanitarian 'gift'.

Worldwide careers, livelihoods, small businesses, global finance and philanthropic sentiments screen millions of people moving up and down long chains of the global humanitarian–developmental industry (Carbonnier, 2015; Els and Carstensen, 2015; Verdirame et al., 2005). Each actor needs to make a 'profit' – whether a salary or a business revenue yield or a good feeling – out of individual sentiments of compassion, kindness, concern, morality, benevolence. But humanitarianism is not free – there is no such thing as a free gift (Mauss, 1967 [1923]). Humaneness (Harrell-Bond, 2002) requires viability and a profit and loss accounting system whether financial or sentimental. If Sahrawi refugeehood disappeared overnight, so too would the visitors; so who is really 'feeding' who? There is simply no other reason to visit the geographical location of the camps in its arid desert ecology. Humanitarian tourism occurs while the site is 'live', but this geographical location is not a tourist site in and of its self. In the very local of the global, a miniscule form of humanitarian economy plays out in little payments to individual Sahrawi drivers, guides, translators, hosts and shop keepers. Or, to easily switch this around: of Sahrawi agency tapping into these global scraps.

Cool grounds, global refuge

The word refugee implies and has come to define and label those seeking/needing refuge, but refract the analytical lens and it is not hard to see refugees equally as providers and benefactors of refuge. Refugee camps can be conveyed as a rich research 'enclave' belonging to and inhabited as much by the omnipresent humanitarian external body envisioning its abstracted refugee. The Sahrawi in their wider geopolitical context experience a complex stress to manage the technical politico-legal mirage of the humanitarian entity in their midst. Even in their most basic category as refugees (to use the external body's binary classification), they are having to manage, mediate and control that humanitarian body.

In his 1996 study of the Mursi's self-representation of their 1979 migration from their Ethiopian homeland in response to severe droughts, Allen first proposed the idea of the Mursi as a people 'in search of cool ground'. This is achieved through networks of social relations, where safety can be sought among those trusted networks. The renewal of war-fractured survival strategies and the cultural fabric of life will require these same networks. At the onset of the 1975 Moroccan invasion, the early sites of the Sahrawi refugees' 'cool grounds' were in initial encampments scattered throughout the conflict zone, such as at Um Dreiga. Those at Um Dreiga fled again when Morocco dropped phosphorous bombs, and shortly afterwards the Algerians offered Polisario the Tindouf location. In Allen's sense, cool grounds are stop-motion sites of temporary refuge for those in flight. But like all refugee settlements in their early stages, when the Sahrawi first began setting up the camps at Tindouf, just inside the Algerian desert border, they were crowded into improvised lines of makeshift tents with only one doctor and little food (San Martín, 2010: 567). Mercer (1979: 19) reported that initially there were twenty-two scattered camps made up of informally positioned tent clusters and by 1979 the camps had begun to be more formally regrouped – that is, the Sahrawi began to reorganise *themselves* – into the first three main settlements named after those in the homeland, Layoune, Dakhla and Smara. That was in the 1970s when the aid regime was in its nascent form and a lot slower to arrive; today, it has virtually anticipated your arrival.

Camps are never marked on conventional maps; they are always an invisible cartography known only to those who live there or those who have a reason to travel there. Cartographically, separate maps are created to denote these exceptional places to the humanitarian world. The entirely-out-of-the-way camp does not need to be identified to the rest of the world, and is only exceptionally delineated for those who need it. This 'comfort map' becomes delineated as a cool ground exclusively for the use of the travellers (or specialised commentators from afar). The exceptional local only appears selectively in the global which relies upon the concrete existence of that local for its own existence and success. The exceptionalism of the local becomes persistently demoted as camp, not city (Baker et al., 2012; UNHCR 2014).

Allen did not intend a 'cool ground' to mean a formal, highly infrastructured refugee camp, but wanted to capture the stopping places along the unseen movement of people, at the times and along the routes of danger and difficulty that few journalists and photographers would risk. Expanding Allen's insight to reverse the picture somewhat, refugeehood and camps are lives and places that few from the Global North would want to experience. Most visitors to refugee camps will be related to the humanitarian–developmental regime. My argument here is that once a formal camp has been determined, we should then be able to observe another cycle of stop-motion arrivals of the humanitarian–development nexus. The Tindouf refugee camps and the journey to get there also become a series of cool grounds for visitors, to whom the Sahrawi are the main providers of food and safety. The infrastructural development of refugee camps must also incorporate the needs of visitors' own expectations of life(style). The Sahrawi Protocol Centres are just this – somewhere bearing some cultural familiarities for visitors' own infrastructural expectations. Here, the local safeguards and feeds the global; the global is vulnerable and out of depth in this political and ecological environment, for only the Sahrawi have the millennia-old skills to know how to live, navigate and survive such environments.

Glocal encounters across refugee thresholds

So, who really inhabits these camps? As Sahrawi refugees engage with this Global Coming into the camps, they engage as active agents with the distant global world. But the above also illuminates the Sahrawi refugee camps not just as local points of refuge for 'the locals' but also simultaneously as global spaces into which arrive a year-round international diaspora – a global space of international actors meeting, working and living with each other, made and unmade in their cyclical transits in and out of the camps as *their* (temporary) locales. This is where different international visitors encounter each other, collaborate on projects and artistic events, socialise in Protocol Centres and produce a continual stream of discourse, humanitarian reports, films and photographs about the Sahrawi.

In 2007, I had been travelling through the desert towards Tindouf. The timing was propitious as it fell on an annual political–cultural festival, and I was invited to join foreign delegates for a meal in a large cultural tent with Sahrawi political representatives present as the hosts. I had occasionally heard over that year that there was another anthropologist from the University of Cambridge doing research in the camps. I sat on one of the deep cushions laid out in rows for us visitors with large platters of food and soft drinks positioned along these several rows of cushions, and each group of people leaned towards the nearest platters to eat. Sometime later my gaze kept glancing across to the back of a female, dressed in Sahrawi female clothing. I could not see her face but something distinct, which I cannot put my finger on, drew my attention to her. A while later I made my way towards her to sit on the cushion between her and other attendees. 'Alice Wilson, I presume?' I joked and was delighted when she turned and said yes. The significance of this is how the global animatedly meets itself in this distant local. Visitors from thousands of local sites amalgamate in the camps as the central global location, like little sub-worlds linking Foucault's heterotopia to his [dis]order of things (1971) and Malkki's (1995) 'national [dis]order' of things. They would never have met elsewhere. Yet in many ways, one does not have to be physically there for locals to create the camp population as a discursive global. The range of glocal actors in the Sahrawi case is colossal, from institutions such as the International Court of Justice (ICJ) meeting in 1974 to determine the Sahrawi right to self-determination, to international lawyers and jurists (Botha et al., 2010), UN and UNHCR to international aid agencies, and NGOs to small disparate humanitarian groups and occasional academic researchers. While both (foreigner and refugee) encounter each other in mutual need, and those needs can be extraordinarily different, the camps can transform into a paradoxical global locale.

Yet in the Sahrawi story, visitors engage in little politicised action for *resolving* 'the other matter': self-determination is left in the hands of the United Nations, whose Security Council members are precisely involved in maintaining irresolution (Zunes and Mundy, 2010; see also Hyndman, 2000). The Sahrawi *as* citizens of a nascent nation-state are actively engaged in 'receiving' the coming visitors as part of a much higher goal of realising self-determination and territorial sovereignty – gifts are never free. I have no intention to reduce the Sahrawi predicament as refugees, but the Sahrawi are engaged in a higher level, intellectual and strategic goal that supersedes – supplants, surpasses, displaces – refugeehood. Refugeehood is en*trap*ment, nation-state becomes en*camp*ment, where structurally *refugee* camps are 'dependency traps', but those within it exercise political agency to experientially move beyond such entrapment. When visitors come towards the Sahrawi, they approach them as refugees, but the Sahrawi receive them as much, much more. A sensitive visit by UN Secretary General Ban Ki-moon on 5 March 2016, just before his retirement, was captured in a particular photo-graphic image taken by Farouk Batiche for Agence France-Presse (AFP).[4]

The UN Secretary General approaches Ahmed Boukhari, United Nations Representative for the Frente Polisario,[5] two global actors, engaged in and encountering each other regularly on the geopolitical world stage and in its international legal corridors in places like New York, Washington and the EU. Yet here Boukhari emerges in a traditional male gown billowing in the desert breeze from a traditional nomadic camel- and goat-hair tent, walking with hand outstretched to welcome Ki-moon. This meeting was about much more than just simply 'being refugees'; the camps are also actually, technically, a 'floating' nation-state headquartered physically and symbolically in the camps. While formally, technically not acknowledged as a legitimate, legal structure in the world order (and no element of humanitarian aid assists the Sahrawi to construct their nation and state while in exile), it is quietly admired and recognised behind the 'global' scenes – thus the significance that Ki-moon chose to visit the Sahrawi nation-state. Likewise, less distinguished visitors are not just living in 'camps', they are in a real and live nascent (local) nation-state where the battle is to position it onto the global, geopolitical world stage. In this context, the Sahrawi Arab Democratic Republic is actively involved with the global political platform, with its governmental ministers and political representatives regularly positioned overseas and navigating international corridors such as the UN, the European Union and the African Union.

A highly comparative study is McConnell's research on the exiled Tibetan government practising statecraft while excluded from formal Indian state politics, legally unrecognised and lacking territorial jurisdiction, and deploying practices of peace, diplomacy and mediation while in a geopolitical margin (McConnell, 2016). While very comparative to the Sahrawi case, the Sahrawi have full territorial jurisdiction of one third of their original, Spanish-decolonising territory, and are only in an international legal 'technical margin'. This is because the other two thirds of territory were illegally invaded by Morocco which stopped the de-colonisation process from being completed. The difference in these two cases is that while the Sahrawi 'State' cannot be formally recognised by the UN until Morocco's breach of international law on territorial occupation is resolved, both the Sahrawi nation and state are pretty much accepted by all (but Morocco) as legally valid and as the rightful heirs to the 'Spanish Sahara' (Western Sahara, today). In relation to this chapter, this is another aspect that is 'suspended' in how the humanitarians fly to, circulate through and engage with the Sahrawi, as *refugees*. While the Sahrawi are refugees in one obvious sense, they are technically not refugees – but citizens in waiting, in tented nomadic encampments.

But when can one be classified as global or local? Another interplay here, but at the lowest ground-level in comparison to the above ethnographic picture, is between global actors connecting with each other in a very local camp of mutual refuges – or, thousands of visitors interacting between their simultaneous locals to create the desert camp as the global point refuges. While the camps can be too primitively collapsed as the 'ultimate' local (so far removed from the Global North's 'smart' agglomerations of population), and as simply about low-level economic provision of humanitarian aid, instead there is a wide-scale circumnavigation between global visitors meeting each other at the same airport terminals, flights, Protocol Centres, 4x4 jeeps and tents. These Sahrawi camps and the transit points as refuges for the stop-motion movement of foreign visitors heading towards them are simultaneous – or oscillate between – 'non-places' (Augé, 1995) with the Sahrawi adjusting domestically as 'refugees for the humanitarians' while organising internationally as citizens of their nation-state for themselves. The globality of the camps has expanded Agamben's original proposition ('state of exception', 1998), to be a *'nation-state'* of exception, as (refugee)-citizens, where visitors are ironically 'meeting the Sahrawi State' but rarely, truly, recognising it or the Sahrawi as citizens of that state.

This illuminates the various apparatuses and directions of control that are encountered by and imposed over Sahrawi refugees. Foreigners arriving in the midst of the Sahrawi are Foucault's (1988) 'political technology', part of a humanitarian regime whose structural policies are used as instruments of power to shape individuals. Post-conflict reconstruction rarely leads to the restoration of the pre-conflict situation, but rather to new and often problematic social relationships. While refugee 'containment' and 'warehousing' (Krever, 2011: 589; Smith, 2004) expands across humanitarian aid, peace-keeping missions and military intervention, camps are Tsing's awkward zones of friction in global social relations. Counterpoising traditional social theory about global flows and networks in the action of refugees in flight 'coming into' the camps (Castells, 1996), humanitarians also 'fly into' camps, bringing their myriad locals to amalgamate into a dynamic international setting. The early Chicago School's and Park's 1928 'catastrophe theory' of swarming border-crossing migrants and Refugee Studies' theories – such as Smith's 2004 'refugee warehousing' and Kibreab's 1993 'dependency syndrome' – apply as much to the year-round humanitarians teeming towards refugee camps. These camps are as much refuges for them as they for the refugees. The Sahrawi camps contain different geographies of refuge that are simultaneously transnational as they involve diaspora populations of foreign volunteers and international intervention forces 'in transit' through the camps. In this way, camps become 'transit points' of refuge to these arriving global actors.

Conclusion

Scholarship on refugees has naturally tended to focus the analytical lens on refugees on-the-move or as static inhabitants of camps. But what of those others who move through the camps, which here I have referred to as visitors and foreigners? Analytical distinctions of the global and the local help to open up new ways of seeing the various actors on the ground. The Sahrawi camps offer an intriguing empirical sight of a site in which there exists a global circulation of humanitarian people visiting them as 'refugees', yet these refugees are engaged in nation-state forming and see themselves as citizens actively managing this foreign circulation as it enters their camps. Moreover, the Sahrawi are far from 'fixed' refugees – they are experienced nomadic movers and camp-dwellers. Geographically located in a desert, it is perhaps the humanitarian visitors who are the real refugees, the camps serving them as much as they intended the camps to serve 'the refugee'. In this ecologically harsh Sahara setting, the arriving humanitarians are very much the 'needy' population, heavily reliant on the Sahrawi for food, shelter and safety.

In the perplexity of the experience and circumstances that refugees find themselves, and as researchers visiting, observing and studying them, seeking refuge among them and receiving (dependent upon) their hospitality, it is to academic grandfathers like Agamben and Foucault that we naturally seek intellectual refuge from in trying to make sense of the despair of it all. Although Foucault spoke around a wide range of spaces, such as religious colonies, ships and asylums, he also made references to cemeteries, gardens, Muslim ablutions and baths (*ghusl* and *hammam*), prisons, museums and festivals – all of which can be found in the Sahrawi camps. And these are places that those visiting the Sahrawi also seek out, or invariably come across/enter/examine, in the huge variety of humanitarian–development projects that are started in the camps. However, the relationship between development and humanitarianism seems to continue to grow and become one, rather than remain (morally?) apart. Now, as Sezgin and Dijkzeul (2016) demonstrate, a new humanitarianism is developing with considerable variation, such as faith-based, armed, *for*-profit as well as the (problematic) idea for *humanitarian* development. Problematic because, in the Sahrawi instance, any development projects have nothing to do with the 'real' development the Sahrawi want, which is to build their nation-state.

These anomalies signal a 'new' reason(s) for the global order to need local disorder more than ever: to revise the script of the humanitarian gift into a *new* form of development. The frisson between displacement and development is that the latter now needs to perpetuate the former (cf. Otto and Weingärtner 2013; Streets 2011; and the 'relief-development continuum' in Haider 2014). One subtle way this has been demonstrated recently has been in the argument about the 'European crisis' – are they migrants or refugees?[6] This heated linguistic anomaly signifies a subtle policy and practice shift but far more serious international legal consequences. The growing application of the UN's sustainable development goals (SDGs) to migrants becomes complexly extended in its application to refugees when no one can seem to agree whether a human being is a refugee or a migrant. This can be seen in the 'grey literature' of organisations that are beginning to develop indistinguishable development–humanitarian 'goals' (see, for example, UNDP, 2015) when '[…] the displaced require development interventions' (Christensen and Harild, 2009: 11).[7] This has serious implications because, until now, refugees had distinct classifications from which to draw on (or be applied to) recognisable international legal protection; 'migrants' have never had them. Particularisms are becoming muddied, but what appears to be the new phenomenon in the development–humanitarian nexus is of humans *resolutely* on the move, clearly wetting the developmental appetite where developing the Other can now be usefully obscured behind indistinctions of 'movement'. The 'old' *raison d'etre* worked well when they stayed still and waited for the global humanitarian regime to arrive to rapidly construct the local refuge.

This new world dis-order of humans-on-the-move can instead be seen as millions of local movements towards and seeking entry into global refuges, wherein the refugees themselves may bear considerable responsibilities and authorities to 'govern' in 'other' ways. In anthropological terms, the Sahrawi camps are places that embody many glocal refuges for both local (i.e., regional) populations seeking new locales, as well as distant-locals arriving into the camps as the global meeting point. The problem with analytical sight:site has been to see lots of disordered locals moving towards a presumed global order. But the latter is made up of its own locals with their own local disorders. Nevertheless, at the macro-level, the old terminologies seem to have as powerful a significance as before – the undeveloped moving towards the developed, the Global South turning its gaze more determinedly towards the Global North. With populations now on the move, perhaps ideas of refuges can be revised as equally capable of being on the move. Much like the Sahrawi nomads, who have long been 'connecting up the dots' of their traditional tented camps as mobile refuges that together create global flows, interconnections and their own worldly encounter.

If we were to stop seeing camps as 'local' but instead as part of a new global, we might be able to refract our analytical lenses to re-envision how the glocal was at play all along and how it will be in future intriguing ways. Certainly, the Sahrawi refugees have long been skillfully 'managing the humanitarians' and feeding them with their own aid provisions since around the 1980s. The local–global 'flows' of relations, are ironically transposed when one realises just who really is dependent upon whom. For the humanitarians could never have survived in these desert camps without the refugees' assistance in the first place.

Notes

1 The field known as anthropology of development (note: *not* 'development anthropology') and subsequent 'critical' refugees studies scholars such as Horst (2006) provide the founding literature to my point here.
2 The data in this study uses the local Berber–Arabic dialect of Hassaniya, English, French and Spanish. The Sahrawi are fairly multilingual due to their ancient long-distance trading and colonial encounters. It helps as a researcher in this fieldsite to be adept in these three European languages and learn Hassaniya locally. In this conversation, the father and daughter liked to speak

English with me and fluently engaged in perceptive word-play ('refuge among refugees').

3 See the Spanish arm of the UNHCR (ANCUR) https://eacnur.org/blog/refugiados-saharauis-40-anos-de-vida-en-los-campos/ (accessed December 2017).

4 Farouk Batiche/AFP/Getty Images, editorial number of photo: 513897884. www.gettyimages.co.uk/license/513897884 (accessed May 2016).

5 Boukhari is one of the most senior members of the Polisario, his title signifies the political leadership of the government of the Saharawi Arab Democratic Republic (SADR).

6 See Alexander Betts' discussion in the *Washington Post*: 'Is it time to ditch the word "migrant"?' (24 August 2015) (accessed 12 July 2017).

7 For another example, see the charity UNA-UK's piece 'Displacement and development. The fate of displaced people and the achievement of the SDGs are closely intertwined' 1 March 2016, www.sustainablegoals.org.uk/displacement-and-development/ (accessed 12 July 2017).

References

Agamben, G. (1998), *Homo Sacer: Sovereign Power and Bare Life*. Translated by D. Heller-Roazen (Stanford: Stanford University Press).

Agier, M. (2011), *Managing the Undesirables: Refugee Camps and Humanitarian Government* (Cambridge: Polity Press).

Allen, T. (1996) (ed.), *In Search of Cool Ground: War, Flight and Homecoming in Northeast Africa* (London: James Curry).

As-sa'd, Muhammed Al Muhtar W. (1990), Émirats et espace émiral maure: le cas du Trârza aux XVIIIe-XIXe siècles. *Mauritanie, entre arabité et africanité, Revue des mondes musulmans et de la Méditerranée* 54: 53–82.

Augé, M. (1995), *Non-places: Introduction to an Anthropology of Supermodernity* (London: Verso).

Baker, I., N. Card and N.A. Raymond (eds) (2012), *Satellite Imagery Interpretation Guide: Displaced Population Camps* (Cambridge, MA: Harvard Humanitarian Initiative).

Botha, N., M. Olivier and D. van Tonder (eds) (2010), *Multilateralism and International Law with Western Sahara as a Case Study* (Pretoria: Unisa, University of South Africa).

Butler, J. and A. Athanasiou (2013), *Dispossession: The Performative in the Political* (Cambridge: Polity Press).

Carbonnier, G. (2015), *Humanitarian Economics: War, Disaster and the Global Aid Market* (London: Hurst & Company).

Castles, S. (2003), Towards a sociology of forced migration and social transformation. *Sociology* 37: 13–34.

Castells, M. (1996), *The Rise of the Network Society: The Information Age: Economy, Society, and Culture, Volume I* (Oxford: Blackwell Publishers).

Chimni, B.S. (2009), The birth of a "discipline": from refugee to forced migration studies. *Journal of Refugee Studies* 22(1): 11–29.

Christensen, A. and N. Harild (2009), Forced displacement: the development challenge. Conflict, Crime and Violence Issue Note, Social Development Department, The World Bank Group.

Els, C. and N. Carstensen (2015), The humanitarian economy [online] https://www.local2global.info/research/the-humanitarian-economy/the-humanitarian-economy-2 [accessed 19 December 2019].

Escobar, A. (1995), *Encountering Development: The Making and Unmaking of the Third World* (Princeton: Princeton University Press).

Ferguson, J. (1990), *The Anti-Politics Machine: 'Development', Depoliticization, and Bureaucratic Power in Lesotho* (Cambridge: Cambridge University Press).

Foucault, M. (2009) [1966], *Le corps utopique – Les hétérotopies* (Clamecy: Éditions Lignes).

Foucault, M. (2004) [1966], Utopies et heterotopias (CD: INA, Mémoire Vive).

Foucault, M. (1988), The political technology of individuals. In Foucault, M., L.H. Martin, H. Gutman and P.H. Hutton (eds) *Technologies of the Self: A Seminar with Michel Foucault* (Amherst: University of Massachusetts Press).

Foucault, M. (1971), *The Order of Things* (New York: Vintage Books).

Gardner, K. and Lewis, D. (1996), *Anthropology, Development, and the Post-modern Challenge* (London: Pluto Press).

Goonatilake, S. (2006), *Recolonisation: Foreign Funded NGOs in Sri Lanka* (New Delhi, London: Sage Publications).

Haider, H. (2014), *Conflict: Topic Guide*. Revised edition with Rohwerder, B. (Birmingham: GSDRC, University of Birmingham).

Harrell-Bond, B.E. (2002), Can humanitarian work with refugees be humane? *Human Rights Quarterly* 24(1): 51–85.

Harrell-Bond, B.E. (1981), The struggle for the Western Sahara, Part III: the Sahrawi people. *Africa* 39: 1–13.

Harrell-Bond, B. and Mahmud, N. (1996), Refugees and Other Forcibly Displaced People in Africa: A Background Paper for the IFRC's Pan-African Conference (Oxford: Refugee Studies Centre).

Horst, C. (2006), *Transnational Nomads: How Somalis cope with Refugee Life in the Dadaab Camps of Kenya* (Oxford: Berghahn).

Hyndman, J. (2000), *Managing Displacement: Refugees and the Politics of Humanitarianism* (Minneapolis: University of Minnesota Press).

Idris, I. (2016), Economic Impacts of Humanitarian Aid. GSDRC Helpdesk Research Report 1327 (Birmingham, UK: GSDRC, University of Birmingham).

Kibreab, G. (1993), The myth of dependency among camp refugees in Somalia. *Journal of Refugee Studies* 6(4): 321–349.

Krever, T. (2011), "Mopping-up": UNHCR, neutrality and non-refoulement since the Cold War. *Chinese Journal of International Law* 10(3): 587–608.

Loescher, G. (1993), Protection and humanitarian action in the post-Cold War Era. In Zolberg, A.R. and P.M. Benda (eds) *Global Migrants, Global Refugees: Problems and Solutions* (New York, Oxford: Berghahn).

Lydon, G. (2009), *On Trans-Saharan Trails: Islamic Law, Trade Networks, and Cross-Cultural Exchange in Nineteenth-Century Western Africa* (Cambridge: Cambridge University Press).

Malkki, L.H. (1995), Refugees and exile: From "Refugee Studies" to the national order of things. *Annual Review of Anthropology* 24: 495–523.

Mauss, M. (1967) [1923], *The Gift: Forms and Functions of Exchange in Archaic Societies* (Norton Library: New York).

McConnell, F. (2016), *Rehearsing the State: The Political Practices of the Tibetan Government-in-Exile* (West Sussex: Wiley Blackwell).

Mead, W.R. (1995), Trains, planes, and automobiles: the end of the postmodern moment. *World Policy Journal* 12(4): 13–31.

Mercer, J. (1979), *The Sahrawis of Western Sahara* (London: Minority Rights Group).

Mosse, D. (2004), Is good policy unimplementable? Reflections on the ethnography of aid, policy and practice. *Development and Change* 35(4): 639–671.

Mosse, D. (1996), The social construction of people's knowledge in participatory rural development. In Bastian, S. and N. Bastian (eds) *Assessing Participation: A Debate from South Asia* (New Delhi: Konark).

Otto, R. and L. Weingärtner (2013), Linking relief and development: more than old solutions for old problems? Policy and Operations Evaluation Department (IOB) Study, Netherlands Ministry of Foreign Affairs.

Pasquetti, S. (2015), Negotiating control. *City* 19(5): 702–713.

Picker, G. and S. Pasquetti (2015), Durable camps: the state, the urban, the everyday. *City* 19 (5): 681–688.

Rahnema, M. and V. Bawtree (1997), *The Post-Development Reader* (London: Zed).

Robertson. R. (1997), Comments on the global triad and glocalization. Paper presented at the Globalization and Indigenous Culture Conference, Institute for Japanese Culture and Classics, Kokugakuin University, Tokyo.

San Martín, P. (2010), *Western Sahara: The Refugee Nation* (Cardiff: University of Wales Press).

Sezgin, Z. and D. Dijkzeul (2016), *The New Humanitarians in International Practice: Emerging Actors and Contested Principles* (London; New York: Routledge).

Smith, M. (2004), Warehousing refugees: a denial of rights, a waste of humanity. World Refugee Survey (Washington: US Committee for Refugees), pp. 38–39.

Streets, J. (2011), *Donor Strategies for Addressing the Transition Gap and Linking Humanitarian and Development Assistance: A Contribution to the International Debate* (Berlin: Global Public Policy Institute).

Tsing, A.L. (2005), *Friction: An Ethnography of Global Connection* (Princeton: Princeton University Press).

United Nations Development Programme (UNDP) (2015), *Guidance Note: A Development Approach to Migration and Displacement* (Washington: UNHCR).

United Nations High Commissioner for Refugees (UNHCR) (2014), *UNHCR Policy on Alternatives to Camps* (Washington: UNHCR/HCP).

Verdirame, G., B.E. Harrell-Bond, Z. Lomo, H. Garry and A. Sachs (2005), *Rights in Exile: Janus-faced Humanitarianism* (Oxford: Berghahn Books).

Wellman, B. and K. Hampton (1999), Living networked on and offline. *Contemporary Sociology* 28(6): 648–654.

Zunes, S. and J. Mundy (2010), *Western Sahara: War, Nationalism and Conflict Irresolution* (New York: Syracuse University Press).

Part III

Scales of intervention

9

Out-sourcing refuge: distance, deferral, and immunity in the urban governance of refugees

Jonathan Darling

For the large majority of the British population, asylum seekers are abstract figures. For many people it is incredibly rare to knowingly come into contact with an asylum seeker. As such, an awareness of forced migration comes almost exclusively through media coverage and political rhetoric. At the same time, much discussion of asylum seekers reduces them to an economic language of costs, efficiencies, flows and 'burdens', such that managing forced migration becomes a 'numbers game' played by the state on behalf of its citizens (Darling, 2014a). This process of abstraction is not new, as Malkki (1995) and Bauman (2016) remind us, yet in recent years it has grown in spatial and political significance as measures to interdict asylum seekers have become more prominent. From the growth of border walls (Jones, 2012), to the emergence of technological measures for sorting and classifying migration (Salter, 2004), the reassertion of border control as a matter of securitisation has had profound effects on the possibilities of seeking, and finding, refuge (Jones and Johnson, 2016). In this chapter, I argue that one of these effects has been to distance, both physically and discursively, asylum seekers from the countries they seek refuge in, and from the citizens they seek refuge among.

In exploring this landscape, I focus on the accommodation of asylum seekers in the UK, to argue that we witness the internalisation of attempts to keep asylum seekers at a contained distance, physically, morally and politically. In doing so, this chapter offers a critical consideration of how logics of bordering, which maintain such distance 'outside' the traditional boundaries of the territorial state (Bialasiewicz, 2012; Collyer and King, 2015), are reflected in forms of distancing '*within*' the nation-state. The chapter foregrounds two key contributions to understanding the politics of refuge. First, the account of distance central to this chapter draws on the biopolitical thought of Roberto Esposito (2008) and his examination of immunology as a desire for security. Yet unlike previous analyses of immunisation (Vaughan-Williams, 2015), I turn this lens inwards to explore Esposito's (2011) account of immunity as a specific *relation to* difference, exemplified through the UK's asylum seeker dispersal system. Second, the chapter makes a case for the urban application of immunisation. This is not to limit the reach of this frame of thought, but is rather to respond to two significant trends. On the one hand, the enforced mobility of asylum seekers to some UK cities as a means to conditionally fulfil international obligations. And on the other, the privatisation of housing and support for asylum seekers. Together, I argue that these trends represent attempts to immunise society against the relation to difference that a *common* obligation might imply. It is this common obligation to others – a responsibility to recognise and negotiate alterity rather than to avoid or displace it – which has been argued to characterise the politics of the city and its demands of proximate diversity (Amin, 2012; Wilson and Darling, 2016). On this basis, the chapter argues that the biopolitics of immunisation 'within' the nation-state has significant implications for how we understand urban democracy. In doing so, I foreground the risks that a concern with immunity at all costs may pose for democracy (Derrida, 2005), and argue that such risks are borne most painfully by those at the margins of the nation-state.

In making this argument, the chapter develops as follows. I begin with the biopolitical thought of Esposito to argue that an interplay between community and immunity is central to understanding borders, identity and difference. I then advance this understanding through arguing that in the off-shoring of asylum, we witness the development of an immunising distance between the nation-state and asylum seekers. With this in mind, I turn to asylum seeker support and accommodation in the UK. Here, distance and deferral are produced as a means of neutralising a perceived threat. The significance of this argument is that in maintaining distance, and seeking to selectively incorporate a perceived threat in a regulated manner, the dispersal of asylum seekers holds an immunitary function that runs counter to claims about the democratic nature of urban life (Magnusson, 2011). Building on these insights, I conclude by arguing that Esposito's attempts to articulate an affirmative biopolitics may offer politically salient openings to consider how identifying the limits of immunity can expose opportunities for different responses to refuge.

Immunological borders and the rejection of community

In exploring the role of distance in shaping the politics of refuge, I draw on Esposito's affirmative biopolitics that is situated between the vitalist and thanatopolitical positions that, following Foucault, have often been argued to have shaped work on the biopolitical (see Agamben, 1998; Foucault, 1997). Esposito has thus been argued to be a '(post)biopolitical' thinker, whose work unpacks how 'the negation and affirmation of life – are not separate from each other, but part of the same biopolitical logic' (Vaughan-Williams, 2015:

9). Esposito's work thus explores how attempts to protect and preserve life may, in their extreme, come to produce its negation. He argues that this negation is not a perversion of biopolitics as a way to secure life, but rather forms a fundamental part of how the preservation of life operates, always at a risk of undoing that which it seeks to preserve (Esposito, 2011). To develop these debates in the context of asylum, it is necessary to first consider some of the key contours of Esposito's work, most notably the constitutive tension between community and immunity.

Esposito's biopolitical work is centred around three linked texts, *Communitas* (2010), *Immunitas* (2011) and *Bios* (2008), which together explore how an immunitary logic may be argued to operate throughout modern biopolitics. In making this case, Esposito's analysis begins by returning to the concept of community and recasting this as a shared experience of the improper and of obligation. Drawing on Nancy (1991), Esposito rejects an understanding of community as a shared identity or group to which one adds oneself:

> Against every temptation to conceive of community in terms of the 'authentic' or the 'proper', as the self-appropriation of one's own essence conducted by man, or by entire peoples, community always has to do with an inauthentic or improper modality. What is the 'common' if not the improper, that which does not belong to anyone but instead is general, anonymous, indeterminate. (Esposito, 2013: 45–46)

Esposito argues that the basis of community is not a combined identity or set of shared attributes. Rather, members of a community are tied together by a common *munus* – a task, duty, or gift that 'is to be given rather than received' (Esposito, 2013: 14). Tracing the root of community to *communitas*, and *communitas* to *munus*, Esposito argues that the *munus* represents a common 'reciprocity or "mutuality"' of giving that assigns the one to the other in an obligation' (Esposito, 2010: 5). As such, '*communitas* is the totality of persons united not by a "property" but precisely by an obligation or a debt; not by an "addition" but by a "subtraction"' (Esposito, 2010: 6). In this way, *communitas* represents a decentring of the subject at the expense of a mutual obligation to the collective. For Esposito (2013: 14) we 'need community because it is the very locus or, better, the transcendental conditions of our existence, given that we have always existed in common'. Community is here founded on the binding of members together through an 'obligation of reciprocal donation' that necessarily 'jeopardizes individual identity' (Esposito, 2008: 50), through exposing self-identity to contact with others. The implication of this line of thought is that community is experienced as a risk to the self, an opening and obligation to otherness that connects members but that also exposes them to both the risk of unknown transformation and to a recognition of the incompleteness of self-identity (see Wilson, 2017).

It is from this account of exposure that Esposito (2011) focuses on how protective responses to community are formed. Tracing connections across both legal and biomedical accounts, Esposito argues that it is in the claim and condition of immunity that community meets its constitutive other. Thus 'if the members of a community are characterized by an obligation of gift-giving thanks to the law of the gift … immunity implies the exemption from or the derogation of such a condition of gift-giving' (Esposito, 2006: 50). Immunity in legal terms refers to an individual who is exempt from obligations towards others and, as such, immunity is always an attribute that is '"proper," in the specific sense of "belonging to someone" and therefore "un-common"' (Esposito, 2011: 6). It is this 'un-common' nature which means that immunity enables the individual to defend and retain their self-identity against the exposure of *communitas* and its binds of duty. Immunity allows for the reestablishment of those boundaries of the self that are otherwise threatened by communal bonds, and thus '*immunitas*, to the degree it protects the one who bears it from risky contact with those who lack it, restores its own borders that were jeopardized by the common' (Esposito, 2008: 50).

At the same time, Esposito (2011) relates the legal lineage of immunity to its biomedical understanding to suggest that immunity has become a central modality of biopolitics. In this context, immunity is selectively inclusive;

> the immune mechanism functions precisely through the use of what it opposes. It reproduces in a controlled form exactly what it is meant to protect us from … life combats what negates it through immunitary protection, not a strategy of frontal opposition but of outflanking and neutralizing. (Esposito, 2011: 8)

Immunity, via the production of antigens, operates through the selective and controlled inclusion of a threat so as to develop a response to it. In doing so, the threat becomes 'somehow part of the body', it is never fully removed, but has been 'shifted, diverted, deferred', such that for 'life to remain as such', it 'must incorporate a fragment of the nothingness it seeks to prevent' (Esposito, 2011: 8). Working across these two readings, Esposito (2011) argues that immunity presents a distinct relation to otherness, one that seeks to protect and retain self-identity through the selective incorporation, pre-emption and neutralisation of threats. It is this combination that Esposito (2008) argues makes immunity a fundamental logic behind biopolitical interventions in humanitarianism, the war on terror, and the politics of migration. The protection of life requires the simultaneous negation of life, or, more specifically, of certain lives over others (Butler, 2004).

The significance of this turn to the immunological is twofold. First, it is clear that the forms of pre-emptive neutralisation that immunity represents are increasingly at the heart of many political fields (Amoore, 2013; Grove, 2014; Salerno, 2017). As Esposito (2013: 60) argues; '[w]hat is important [today] is inhibiting, preventing, and fighting the spread of contagion wherever it presents itself, using whatever means necessary', and as such 'everywhere we look, new walls, new blockades, and new dividing lines are erected against something that threatens, or at least seems to, our biological, social, and environmental identity' (Esposito, 2013: 59). Second, the immunological is important as it presents a series of risks alongside its protective claims. Work on the political dangers of autoimmunity as a condition in which immunitary measures negate that which they would otherwise protect has exposed the risks of immunity in terms of democracy (Derrida, 2005), and in terms of public culture and urban life (Sloterdijk, 2014). Similarly, articulations of refugee mobility into Europe as a 'crisis' that threatens European democracy (Crawley, 2016), and that frames refugees as a potential 'disease' on Europe and its institutions, present one example of how immunitary logics can shape discussions of the 'health' of democratic life (Bauman, 2016). Immunity therefore risks not only its harmful negation in the form of autoimmune responses – a condition that Esposito argues typified the thanatopolitical logic of Nazi biopolitics (Esposito, 2008) – but also the restriction and containment of life in ever more enclosed spheres of limited exposure to difference. Contra to the risky openness of *communitas*, when expanded as a logic across social and political life, 'immunity encages life such that not only is our freedom but also the very meaning of our individual and collective existence lost' (Esposito, 2013: 61). In this way, Esposito argues that forms of communal exclusivity seek to avoid the life affirming but risky nature of 'common existence' (Esposito, 2013: 44). We might see this avoidance of 'common existence' in discussions of a growth in urban enclavism and the hardening of urban borders, such that cities have been argued to become central within a geography of aversion to difference (Graham, 2010; Shapiro, 2010).

It is perhaps unsurprising that Esposito's work has been used to explore a range of contemporary political issues. In part, this appeal comes from the contradictory tensions that Esposito exposes at the heart of attempts to immunise life, offering an account that does not dismiss the desire for protection that immunisation promises, but that foregrounds the risks that come with protection. Thus, in interpreting border controls Vaughan-Williams (2015: 13–14), argues that from an immunological perspective, 'EU border security practices are neither intrinsically "good" nor "bad", but precisely a biopolitical immune system with Janus-faced potentialities'. The critical point, Vaughan-Williams suggests, is that immunisation is a necessary process that contains within it potentialities that may both enhance and diminish life. This apparent neutrality in theory is of course problematic in practice. The 'Janus-faced potentialities' of EU border practices have all too often been actualised through deadly forms of border enforcement, racist modalities of security and surveillance, and the discursive production of migrants as a biological 'threat' to Europe. In such a context, the tensions of immunology come to the fore, with Esposito (2013: 62) arguing that; 'we need immune systems. No individual or social body could do without them, but when they grow out of proportion they end up forcing the entire social organism to explode or implode.' In the remaining parts of this chapter, I want to develop the implications of this argument for understanding how distance and deferral are employed as immunological tools in the governance of those seeking refuge.

Externalisation, off-shoring, out-sourcing

In exploring the immunitary biopolitics of contemporary refuge, we might turn first to recent work that has highlighted the use of extraterritorial spaces as tools in the interdiction of refugees (Collyer and King, 2015). From the use of island detention centres and off-shore processing zones (den Heijer, 2012; Loyd et al., 2016), to international agreements designed to redirect and contain the mobility of refugees (Dickson, 2015; Rajaram, 2003), measures to manage refugee mobility have increasingly focused on maintaining the distance between refugees and the nation-states of the Global North. In this context, as Crawley (2016) argues, Europe's response to the apparent 'refugee crisis' must be read as both a collective denial of responsibility, and a collective desire to externalise refugee processing and support.

Across this work, two core trends are evident. First, is the enrolment of often remote territories as sites of border enforcement (Bialasiewicz et al., 2009; Mountz, 2011). Examples include the use of island states such as Nauru and Manus as detention facilities by the Australian government (Rajaram, 2003), a renewed agreement between Italy and Libya to contain migrants in Libya and halt onward migration (Dearden, 2017) and, more broadly, the European Union's co-option of Southern Mediterranean and North African countries into a regional geography of securitised migration management, with EU leaders in 2017 offering support to Chad and Niger in promoting enhanced border control measures (Collyer, 2016; Samuel, 2017). Second is the simultaneous enrolment of private actors in the process of migration management and border enforcement. This includes the establishment and running of immigration detention facilities (Hiemstra and Conlon, 2017), the coordination of deportation regimes (Andersson, 2014), and the effectiveness of private security firms in influencing policy priorities (Martin, 2017; Menz, 2011).

Taken together, these trends reflect aspects of the spatial exclusivity, enclavism and border maintenance that Esposito (2008, 2013) associates with an increasing 'immunological drift' in contemporary politics. In the context of the extraterritorial management of asylum, it is the establishment of distance that serves an immunitary function, as a governance tool that mediates, filters and halts the potential circulation of perceived threats (Esposito, 2006). A turn to the extraterritorial, the off-shore and the out-sourced is thus a turn to establishing and employing distance as an immunitary device. In physical terms, this occurs through the enforced mobility of asylum seekers to marginal spatial locations and their containment and confinement, such that the visibility of asylum and refuge is diminished to those within the nation-state. Importantly, the spatial marginality of asylum this creates serves to hinder attempts to organise political campaigns or activism around the experiences of asylum seekers. While social media and digital technologies do allow the communication of testimony and the mobilisation of counter-narratives (Whitlock, 2008), the proximate relations and support that advocacy and activism are often built upon are denied in these instances (Gill, 2009). At the same time, the privatisation of migration management serves to decouple potential links between asylum seekers and the state to which they may address claims for refuge. Privatisation acts as a means to defer responsibility from the state onto a contractor acting in the name of that state. This is a distance that the state can decide to bridge at key points, through communicating decisions on cases or detaining individuals (Darling, 2014b), but this is rarely a reciprocal arrangement.

While processes of distancing illustrate aspects of an immunological border politics operating 'outside' the traditional territorial boundaries of the nation-state, there is also a need to examine the mirroring of such processes 'within' the nation-state. And, in doing so, to move beyond a focus on the continuation of detention measures within the UK as a means of containment (Gill, 2009) to consider how policies to house asylum seekers draw cities into relation with asylum as a political concern. Importantly, these are interlinked, rather than distinct, domains of immunological practice, and this is significant because Esposito's (2011) account of immunity is not simply about filtering and excluding difference, but rather it represents immunisation as a particular relation *to* difference. Immunity is intimately linked to the risks and potentialities of community. Yet focusing solely on bordering practices that establish distance extraterritorially does not enable an analysis of this relation, as the immunitary biopolitics enacted here is one that is enclosing, exclusive and averse to contact. This first set of examples must thus be supplemented with an engagement with Esposito's (2011) second reading of immunity as a biomedical condition. It is here that a more complex relation with community is established, highlighting that immunity may be a relation of closeness and distance at one and the same time, as it necessarily 'entails the presence of a negative driving force (the antigen) which it must not simply eliminate, but rather, recognize, incorporate, and, in this fashion alone, neutralize' (Esposito, 2011: 160). To explore this argument, I turn to the UK's asylum dispersal programme.

Regulating the other 'within'

Since 2000, the UK has operated a dispersal system for the accommodation of asylum seekers. This means that after an initial period in temporary reception centres, asylum seekers are relocated to towns and cities across the country to be accommodated while awaiting decisions on their asylum claims (Robinson, 2003). The location and type of accommodation provided is on a 'no choice' basis, and this lack of autonomy has been argued to mean that dispersal serves to further marginalise and socially isolate asylum seekers, as links with existing social networks are often broken through enforced mobility (Bloch and Schuster, 2005; Hynes, 2009; Hynes and Sales, 2010).

It is in the structuring of dispersal that we see the first parallel to the immunological politics of distance noted in the extraterritorial context above. While in theory dispersal was established as a policy to ease a perceived 'burden' on London and the south east of England, and promote a more equitable distribution of asylum seekers across the country, the reality has been one of significant regional and local disparities (Home Affairs Committee, 2017; Phillips, 2006). In its earliest guises this disparity came from a distribution of local authorities able to enter into agreements with the UK Home Office to accommodate asylum seekers. This required local authorities to have existing and available social housing stock that could be used at relatively short notice. The result was a landscape of dispersal focused predominantly on de-industrialised cities across the north of England, Scotland and Wales. Cities like Glasgow, Leeds, Sheffield, Cardiff, and Newcastle viewed dispersal as a way to both meet a demand from the Home Office for accommodation, and at the same time enable otherwise hard-to-let social housing to generate an income. The result was a radical shift in the geography of asylum support in the UK, as asylum seekers who had been free to seek support from any local authority under previous legislation, were now required to make centralised claims and await transport to newly established dispersal locations (Weber, 2012). Importantly, such locations were not accustomed to the support requirements of asylum seekers and were areas themselves suffering from multiple forms of vulnerability, underinvestment, territorial stigmatisation and pressure on social care and support services (Darling, 2016a, 2016b; Phillips, 2006).

Dispersal thus represents a policy that manages the mobility of asylum seekers, through fixing them to specific and known addresses, and that places asylum seekers in often physically and institutionally marginal urban locations. For these locations, dispersal was also the first point at which cities and their populations came into any sustained contact with asylum seekers in the UK, thus demanding the development of new forms of support, knowledge and often intercultural competencies. Unlike the immunological distancing evident in policies of extraterritorial processing and detention, dispersal could be argued to reflect a meeting of the nation-state's obligations to those seeking asylum, and the establishment of a proximate relationship between asylum seekers and the state. The internalisation of asylum seekers that dispersal represents – an accommodation within – might be seen as a counter to the immunitary externalisation noted so far. However, if we consider the conditions that manage such incorporation, from enforced mobility and regular reporting requirements to restrictions on the right to work and study (Darling, 2011), dispersal might be read in the biomedical sense of an immunitary function as much as in a legal sense. Considering both of these readings of immunity allows us to explore how dispersal interweaves relations of proximity and distance in ways not immediately obvious in the extraterritorial case. It also highlights how immunisation is shaped by the urban contexts through which it is operating.

In the legal sense, as a signatory of the 1951 Refugee Convention, the UK has a duty to provide accommodation and basic support to those who have sought asylum and who have not yet been given a decision by the state. Yet, at the same time, it bears no duty to make that accommodation, or that experience, a comfortable one. Indeed, it has been argued that measures such as dispersal and arbitrary detention are intended to ensure that the asylum process is an unwelcoming one so as to act as a deterrent (Bloch and Schuster, 2005). In this sense, dispersal does not effect a legal immunity, it does not evade responsibilities and obligations in the way that many extraterritorial measures may do. However, in the biomedical sense we might consider how dispersal enables elements of a perceived mobile threat to become part of the body politic, albeit on a temporary and conditional basis. This incorporation serves two purposes. First, it enables the management and regulation of mobility such that a tolerance towards the perceived threat of asylum seekers can be developed. The language of tolerance is significant here not simply because it carries with it biomedical associations, but because those associations have informed political critiques of tolerance as an assumed virtue of political liberalism. Indeed, as Brown (2006) argues, the role of tolerance in 'regulating aversion' and managing difference through practices of conditionality and containment serves to maintain hierarchies of power and position (Wilson, 2014). As a mode of 'regulating aversion', dispersal provides a means of managing an exposure to difference that is legally required. The geography of dispersal thus serves to insulate some towns and cities from ever coming into contact with asylum as a lived experience, while others become a focal point for such contact (Cheshire and Zappia, 2016). Second, dispersal offers a way to both meet an international obligation, and to avoid the risk of unwanted contact or the articulation of wider responsibilities. In this sense, dispersal illustrates many of the characteristics of the liberal governance of refuge more broadly, of an intertwined system of 'compassionate repression' (Fassin, 2005), humanitarian borders (Little and Vaughan-Williams, 2017; Williams, 2015) and the binding together of obligation *and* avoidance – a simultaneous closeness and distance that can arise only through the careful regulation of those allowed within the body of the nation-state.

Privatisation and the aversion of the common

If dispersal has served as a policy that establishes an immunological tension of inclusive exclusion, the nature of this process changed significantly in 2012. Up until this point, in the majority of cases accommodation for asylum seekers was provided either directly by local authorities or through mixed consortiums that retained local authority involvement. In 2012, the Home

Office signed a series of six centralised contracts passing accommodation and support to three private contractors: the multinational security services company G4S, the international services company Serco and the accommodation partnership Clearel. Together, these contracts were known as COMPASS (Commercial and Operating Managers Procuring Asylum Support). Announced in the context of a government-wide austerity drive, the COMPASS contracts became a key means through which the then UK Border Agency sought to make 'efficiency savings'. Here I want to focus on the effects of privatising dispersal as an expression of an immunological politics. To do so, I draw out three effects of privatisation.

First, the process of privatising dispersal has served to displace and defer responsibility for asylum seekers. Privatisation has meant that local authorities no longer have a clear role in engaging with asylum seekers dispersed to them. Together with the cuts to local authorities that austerity has affected across the UK (Hamnett, 2014; Kitson et al., 2011; Newman, 2014), this has meant that local authorities no longer have the remit, nor the capacity, to form a significant part of the dispersal process. The effects of this have been to remove the knowledge, experience and integration expertise of local authorities from the landscape of dispersal (Darling, 2016b), and to transfer responsibility for vulnerable individuals to providers who are both new to this field and who lack the contextual knowledge and expertise that is required to support asylum seekers effectively. At the same time, the three centrally contracted providers of COMPASS employ a range of subcontracting chains and networks in order to provide and procure properties to meet the needs of the Home Office. This has had the effect of both deferring responsibility between agencies and making the clear attribution of accountability opaque, and of ensuring that complaints about property standards, locations and the treatment of asylum seekers by staff are hard to maintain as complainants are passed between subcontractors, providers, and the Home Office (Darling, 2016a; Scottish Refugee Council, 2014). The first effect of privatization has thus been to displace responsibility for asylum seekers from a local authority model that, while far from perfect, was more directly, and visibly, accountable to both asylum seekers and other residents.

Second, it is important to recognise the political message that is sent by the privatisation of accommodation for asylum seekers. Privatisation not only removes the issue of asylum support from public visibility, it also transmits a message that this is an area of policy that can be, and should be, made profitable for those providers well-placed to meet the terms of a contract. In effect, the accommodation and support of vulnerable individuals becomes not a public concern or responsibility, but a site of market exchange, calculation and demands for efficiency (Darling, 2016a). This is an intervention which can itself be argued to form a minor part of a much broader biopolitical project to govern populations in the name of national economies and to assign value to life according to calculations of a potential return on any investment (Murphy, 2017; Povinelli, 2011). The importance of this shift in accommodation is both in how it illustrates the transmission of neoliberal market logics into new domains of public policy, and in how a focus on economic efficiency can serve to present those domains of policy as managerial matters of limited public concern. Privatisation therefore plays a key role in the post-democratic de-politicisation of public policy (Crouch, 2004; Darling, 2014a, 2016a), as market-orientated solutions are posed as 'common sense' responses to an increasingly wide array of issues (Brown, 2015). The post-democratic nature of dispersal as a policy arena rarely discussed beyond the narrow specifics of numbers and limits serves to further distance asylum seekers from the multiple publics that they live alongside, and from imaginaries of alternative ways of providing support (Darling, 2016a). While at the same time, dispersal and asylum policy risk becoming further elements within an argued de-politicisation of urban governance, whereby issues of social rights, services and entitlements are removed from public deliberation and positioned as primarily managerial concerns (MacLeod, 2011). In this context, the ability to politically articulate a sense of common cause across diverse interest groups, and to position the rights of asylum seekers alongside other struggles for rights to the city, is made all the more challenging.

Third, while the politics of asylum have always been shaped by categories of legal status and perceived 'worthiness' for support (Sales, 2002), the privatisation of dispersal accommodation has extended the projection and impact of such distinctions ever more starkly. In response to the humanitarian crisis in Syria, in 2015 the UK government announced plans to establish the Syrian Vulnerable Persons Resettlement Scheme (SVPRS), a refugee resettlement programme to take 20,000 Syrian refugees from the region and resettle them in the UK. The SVPRS was to run on the basis of accommodation and support provided by local authorities, in contrast to the privatised provision of the dispersal process. The effects of which has been the establishment of a two-track system of accommodating refugees and asylum seekers, despite warnings that such a system would cast those already in the asylum system as less 'deserving' of support (Home Affairs Committee, 2017). The morally normative distinctions established here, between those who 'wait' to be resettled and those who move without prior authorisation, are both problematic and longstanding within the politics of refuge (Zetter, 2007). However, the privatisation of one element of this process, and its provision by a number of companies known for their security work, serves to add suspicion and doubt to the legitimacy of entitlements to support for those in the asylum system. The removal of one side of this two-track system from public provision further questions its legitimacy as a matter of collective responsibility.

Each of these elements of privatisation has in some way contributed to the production and maintenance of distance between asylum seekers and both the state and the public in the UK. Be that through the deferral of responsibility for addressing the concerns of asylum seekers, through the roll-back and regression of public services equipped to support asylum seekers, or through the discursive framing of asylum seekers as 'burdens' to be managed by private security contractors rather than social care professionals or public servants (Darling, 2016a). In each case, the privatisation that COMPASS puts in place has not radically altered dispersal policy itself; it has instead served to further insulate that policy from both criticism and from the proposal of alternative models of accommodation and support. For if dispersal operates as a policy that attempts to manage and control a set of obligations to others, then privatisation establishes a set of barriers between those obligations and the nation-state. Privatisation operates as an immunitary device, a way to offset and defer responsibility to other actors on the one hand, and at the same time a way to present the issue of asylum as one that is precisely 'un-common', not a collective or common concern that would require forms of solidarity to emerge in response. The effect is not to fully immunise the nation-state from its obligation to asylum seekers, but rather to encase and enclose obligations in cycles of contractualism and economic efficiency, and in doing so to increasingly remove them from the realm of public consideration. Such tendencies have been argued to lie at the heart of the 'post-democratic city', wherein opportunities for articulating an urban commons of political influence that responds to the claims of citizens and non-citizens alike have been narrowed. Through dispersal and its privatisation, accountability and responsibility for the lives of asylum seekers are removed from any remaining sense of this urban commons, as asylum seekers are discursively positioned as subjects of private authority, at a remove from the cities in which they are accommodated. If responsibilities are displaced to contracted private actors, they are also expected to bear the risks of not fulfilling those responsibilities. In this way concerns over poor housing standards, abusive treatment within the asylum system, and inadequate support can all be out-sourced, without the risk that such concerns become amplified and broadened into critiques of the dispersal process itself.

Privatisation therefore helps to immunise as it enables the issue of asylum accommodation and support to be contained and enclosed – a meeting of contractual obligations that does not become a call for communal identification with others. This is the insulating loss of *communitas* that Esposito (2010) fears when a drive to immunisation takes precedence over all else, when the relation that immunity describes is experienced as only a regulatory barrier and not also as a point of contact. What is lost in this context is an exposure to others in ways not directly managed by a system of enforced mobility, or by a contractual relationship that conditions the forms contact will take. The immunitary logic that shapes dispersal as an inclusive exclusion within seeks to avoid the contingency of urban life. Immunity in this context aims to avoid the encounter as a potentially transformative site of disruption and shock (Wilson, 2017; Wilson and Darling, 2016). Encounters make a difference through exposing the self to otherness in unprepared-for ways (Wilson, 2017), and in doing so they challenge the self-identification of immunity and speak once again to the bonds of *communitas*, of mutual obligations, ties and the fundamentally *insecure* status of the self.

Conclusion

In this chapter, I have highlighted three ways in which an immunitary biopolitical logic intersects with the politics of contemporary refuge. In particular, I argued that practices of distancing, the deferral of responsibility, and the privatisation of state functions each serve to produce immunitary borders within and beyond the territorial limits of the nation-state. Yet the aversion these borders express is never complete, neither practically nor philosophically. Rather, immunity is also about a conditional and often life-affirming incorporation that may protect the body from potential threat. It is here, in the conditional incorporation of asylum seekers, that immunitary biopolitics operates 'inside' the nation-state. Distance still plays a role in this context, but it is also transformed into a displacement of responsibility and a privatisation of support, such that asylum becomes a private, rather than a public, matter. Importantly, as I have argued, through this process asylum becomes a geographically uneven urban concern. Dispersal establishes a fragmented geography of immunisation in which cities exposed to the needs of those seeking refuge enable others to ignore and evade such needs. In the UK, this fragmented geography of contact forms part of a wider landscape of urban inequality and territorial stigmatisation, which has been argued to categorise marginal populations according to normative measures of productivity and desirability (Tyler, 2013). The labelling of asylum seekers as 'burdens' for cities to bear is thus mirrored in the stigmatisation of welfare claimants, such that attempts to affect the mobility of the poor through housing policy present a similar logic of selective mobility and social cleansing (Cheshire and Zappia, 2016; Waquant, 2009). It is only in beginning to explore the connections across these different spaces and articulations of the immunological that the nature of biopolitical borders may be fully understood.

There is, of course, a need for caution here too. Not least in being cognisant of the pitfalls of using a biological language in relation to the politics of asylum. This is a tension that has surrounded many recent attempts to account for the biopolitical dimensions of contemporary bordering, from the terminology of waste and excess matter (Bauman, 2003), to the less-than-human designation of a 'zoopolitical' border (Vaughan-Williams, 2015). In cautiously taking forward an account of the immunitary politics of asylum, there is a need to address two further concerns that I have only briefly sketched. First is the need to explore more fully the implications, both conceptual and practical, of autoimmunity and its excesses of violence and destruction given the centrality of this condition to political readings of immunisation (Derrida, 2005; Deutscher, 2013; Esposito, 2008). Second is the need to detail how attempts at immunisation may be resisted, challenged or reworked through the agency of those in the asylum system. For example, we might ask whether immunisation is open to inversion, to pose the question of how asylum seekers may seek to not only be part of the common obligations of community, but may also wish to evade such obligations and find ways to immunise themselves against the violence of the state.

In concluding, however, it is important to note that Esposito's (2008) account of biopolitics is one that seeks an affirmative relation with difference. While immunity can enclose, stultify and impede life, Esposito (2011: 166) notes that immunity is also central to a 'conception of identity as a system open to the challenges of the outside world'. Returning to a biomedical account of immunity, he argues that the immune system is one that relies upon communication in order to function. It is a system of constant alteration and change, of bodily becoming and learning as new elements are taken into account and bodily responses modified in relation to them. Thus;

> The equilibrium of the immune system is not the result of defensive mobilization against something other than self, but the joining line, or the point of convergence, between two divergent series. It is not governed by the primacy of the same over the like and the like over the different, but by the continuously changing principle of their relationship. In this sense, nothing is more inherently dedicated to communication than the immune system. Its quality is not measured by its ability to provide protection from a foreign agent, but from the complexity of the response that it provokes: each differential element absorbed from the outside does nothing but expand and enrich the range of its internal potential. (Esposito, 2011: 174)

Viewing immunity as a system of communication and transformation, a system with a constitutive requirement of exposure, might propose an account of biopolitical borders that seeks not to abandon protection or evade immunisation, but rather that seeks to negotiate an exposure to difference that is recognised as common. It is precisely this complex interplay between communication, transformation, exposure and protection that is lost in the attempts to immunise the nation-state from its obligations to those seeking asylum that I have discussed throughout this chapter. In each of these cases, from the extraterritorial distancing of refugee lives, to the deferral of responsibility for asylum seekers to private interests, it is the 'equilibrium of the immune system' (Esposito, 2011: 174) that has been reworked to serve the interests of some over those of others. While is it important to explore ways to rebalance such an equilibrium, recognising the limits of immunity and the promises made on its behalf presents a critical first step in the politics of refuge.

References

Agamben, G. (1998), *Homo Sacer: Sovereign Power and Bare Life* (Stanford: Stanford University Press).

Amin, A. (2012), *Land of Strangers* (Cambridge: Polity Press).

Amoore, L. (2013), *The Politics of Possibility: Risk and Security Beyond Probability* (Durham, NC: Duke University Press).

Andersson, R. (2014), *Illegality, Inc. Clandestine Migration and the Business of Bordering Europe* (Oakland: University of California Press).

Bauman, Z. (2016), *Strangers at our Door* (Cambridge: Polity Press).

Bauman, Z. (2003), *Wasted Lives* (Cambridge: Polity Press).

Bialasiewicz, L. (2012), Off-shoring and out-sourcing the borders of Europe: Libya and EU border work in the Mediterranean. *Geopolitics* 17(4): 843–866.

Bialasiewicz, L., C. Dahlman, G.M. Apuzzo, F. Ciuta, A. Jones, C. Rumford, R. Wodak, J. Anderson and A. Ingram (2009), Interventions in the new political geographies of the European 'neighbourhood'. *Political Geography* 28(2): 79–89.

Bloch, A. and L. Schuster (2005), At the extremes of exclusion: deportation, detention and dispersal. *Ethnic and Racial Studies* 28(3): 491–512.

Brown, W. (2015), *Undoing the Demos: Neoliberalism's Stealth Revolution* (Boston: MIT Press).

Brown, W. (2006), *Regulating Aversion: Tolerance in the Age of Identity and Empire* (Princeton: Princeton University Press).

Butler, J. (2004), *Precarious Life: The Powers of Mourning and Violence* (London: Verso).

Cheshire, L. and G. Zappia (2016), Destination dumping ground: the convergence of 'unwanted' populations in disadvantaged city areas. *Urban Studies* 53(10): 2081–2091.

Collyer, M. (2016), Geopolitics as a migration governance strategy: European Union bilateral relation with Southern Mediterranean countries. *Journal of Ethnic and Migration Studies* 42(4): 606–624.

Collyer, M. and R. King (2015), Producing transnational space: International migration and the extra-territorial reach of state power. *Progress in Human Geography* 39: 185–204.

Crawley, H. (2016), Managing the unmanageable? Understanding Europe's response to the migration 'crisis'. *Human Geography* 9(2): 13–23.

Crouch, C. (2004), *Post-democracy* (Cambridge: Polity Press).

Darling, J. (2016a), Privatising asylum: neoliberalisation, depoliticisation and the governance of forced migration. *Transactions of the Institute of British Geographers* 41(3): 230–243.

Darling, J. (2016b), Asylum in austere times: instability, privatization and experimentation within the UK asylum dispersal system. *Journal of Refugee Studies* 29(4): 483–505.

Darling. J. (2014a), Asylum and the post-political: domopolitics, depoliticisation and acts of citizenship. *Antipode* 46(1): 72–91.

Darling, J. (2014b) Another letter from the Home Office: reading the material politics of asylum. *Environment and Planning D: Society and Space* 32: 484–500.

Darling, J. (2011), Domopolitics, governmentality and the regulation of asylum accommodation. *Political Geography* 30(5): 263–271.

Dearden, L. (2017), 'EU plans to keep migrants in Libya would trap thousands in 'catastrophic conditions', Germany warns.' *The Independent* (4 May 2017) [online] http://www.independent.co.uk/news/world/europe/refugee-crisis-migrants-libya-italy-europe-mediterranean-sea-eu-libya-deal-detention-camps-torture-a7718346.html [accessed 23 October 2017].

den Heijer, M. (2012), *Europe and Extraterritorial Asylum* (Oxford: Hart Publishing).

Derrida, J. (2005), *Rogues: Two Essays on Reason*. Translated by Naas, M. and P-A. Brault (Stanford: Stanford University Press).

Deutscher, P. (2013), The membrane and the diaphragm: Derrida and Esposito on immunity, community, and birth. *Angelaki* 18(3): 49–68.

Dickson, A. (2015), Distancing asylum seekers from the state: Australia's evolving political geography of immigration and border control. *Australian Geographer* 46(4): 437–454.

Esposito, R. (2013), *Terms of the Political: Community, Immunity, Biopolitics* (New York: Fordham University Press).

Esposito, R. (2011), *Immunitas: The Protection and Negation of Life* (Cambridge: Polity Press).

Esposito, R. (2010), *Communitas: The Origin and Destiny of Community* (Stanford: Stanford University Press).

Esposito, R. (2008), *Bios: Biopolitics and Philosophy* (Minneapolis: University of Minnesota Press).

Esposito, R. (2006), Interview. *Diacritics* 36(2): 49–56.

Fassin, D. (2005), Compassion and repression: the moral economy of immigration policies in France. *Cultural Anthropology* 20(3): 362–387.

Foucault, M. (1997), *The History of Sexuality Volume 1: The Will to Knowledge* (London: Penguin).

Gill, N. (2009), Governmental mobility: the power effects of the movement of detained asylum seekers around Britain's detention estate. *Political Geography* 28(3): 186–196.

Graham, S. (2010), *Cities Under Siege: The New Military Urbanism* (London: Verso).

Grove, K. (2014), Agency, affect, and the immunological politics of disaster resilience. *Environment and Planning D: Society and Space* 32(2): 240–256.

Hamnett, C. (2014), Shrinking the welfare state: the structure, geography and impact of British government benefit cuts. *Transactions of the Institute of British Geographers* 39(4): 490–503.

Hiemstra, N. and D. Conlon (2017), Beyond privatization: bureaucratization and the spatialities of immigration detention expansion. *Territory, Politics, Governance* 5(3): 252–268.

Home Affairs Committee (2017), Twelfth Report of Session 2016–17, Asylum Accommodation (London: House of Parliament).

Hynes, P. (2009), Contemporary compulsory dispersal and the absence of space for the restoration of trust. *Journal of Refugee Studies* 22: 97–121.

Hynes P. and R. Sales (2010), New communities: asylum seekers and dispersal. In Bloch, A. and J. Solomos (eds) *Race and Ethnicity in the 21ˢᵗ Century* (Basingstoke: Palgrave), pp. 39–61.

Jones, R. (2012), *Border Walls: Security and the War on Terror in the United States, India, and Israel* (London: Zed Books).

Jones, R. and C. Johnson (2016), Border militarisation and the re-articulation of sovereignty. *Transactions of the Institute of British Geographers* 41(2): 187–200.

Little, A. and N. Vaughan-Williams (2017), Stopping boats, saving lives, securing subjects: humanitarian borders in Europe and Australia. *European Journal of International Relations* 23(3): 533–556.

Loyd, J., E. Mitchell-Eaton and A. Mountz (2016), The militarization of islands and migration: tracing human mobility through US bases in the Caribbean and the Pacific. *Political Geography* 53(1): 65–75.

Kitson, M., R. Martin and P. Tyler (2011), The geographies of austerity. *Cambridge Journal of Regions, Economy and Society* 4(3): 289–302.

MacLeod, G. (2011), Urban politics reconsidered: growth machine to post-democratic city? *Urban Studies* 48(12): 2629–2660.

Magnusson, W. (2011), *Politics of Urbanism: Seeing Like a City* (London: Routledge).

Malkki, L.H. (1995), Refugees and exile: from 'refugee studies' to the national order of things. *Annual Review of Anthropology* 24: 495–523.

Martin, L. (2017), Discretion, contracting and commodification: privatisation of US immigration detention as a technology of government. In Conlon, D. and N. Hiemstra (eds) *Intimate Economies of Immigration Detention: Critical Perspectives* (London: Routledge), pp. 32–50.

Menz, G. (2011), Neo-liberalism, privatization and the outsourcing of migration management: a five-country comparison. *Competition & Change* 15(2): 116–135.

Mountz, A. (2011), The enforcement archipelago: detention, haunting, and asylum on islands. *Political Geography* 30: 118–128.

Murphy, M. (2017), *The Economization of Life* (Durham, NC: Duke University Press).

Nancy, J-L. (1991), *The Inoperative Community*. Translated by Connor, P. L. Garbus, M. Holland and S. Sawhney (Minneapolis: University of Minnesota Press).

Newman, J. (2014), Landscapes of antagonism: local governance, neoliberalism and austerity. *Urban Studies* 51: 3290–3305.

Phillips, D. (2006), Moving towards integration: the housing of asylum seekers and refugees in Britain. *Housing Studies* 21: 539–553.

Povinelli, E. (2011), *Economies of Abandonment: Social Belonging and Endurance in Late Liberalism* (Durham, NC: Duke University Press).

Rajaram, P.K. (2003), 'Making place' the 'Pacific Solution' and Australian emplacement in the Pacific and on refugee bodies. *Singapore Journal of Tropical Geography* 24(3): 290–306.

Robinson, V. (2003), Dispersal policies in the UK. In Robinson, V., R. Andersson and S. Musterd (eds) *Spreading the 'Burden'? A Review of Policies to Disperse Asylum Seekers and Refugees* (Bristol: Policy Press), 103–148.

Salerno, S. (2017), The politics of response to terror: the reshaping of community and immunity in the aftermath of 7 July 2005 London bombings. *Social Semiotics* 27(1): 81–106.

Sales, R. (2002), The deserving and the undeserving? Refugees, asylum seekers and welfare in Britain. *Critical Social Policy* 22(3): 456–478.

Salter, M. (2004), Passports, mobility, and security: how smart can the border be? *International Studies Perspectives* 5(1): 71–91.

Samuel, H. (2017), EU leaders offer support to Libyan coastguards, Chad and Niger to stem migrant flow at Paris summit. *The Telegraph* (28 August 2017) [online] http://www.telegraph.co.uk/news/2017/08/28/eu-leaders-offer-support-libyan-coastguards-chad-niger-stem/ [accessed 23 October 2017].

Scottish Refugee Council (2014), *The Extent and Impact of Asylum Accommodation Problems in Scotland* (Glasgow: Scottish Refugee Council).

Shapiro, M.J. (2010), *The Time of the City: Politics, Philosophy and Genre* (London: Routledge).

Sloterdijk, P. (2014), *Globes: Spheres II*. Translated by Hoban, W. (London: Semiotext(e)).

Tyler, I. (2013), *Revolting Subjects: Social Abjection and Resistance in Neoliberal Britain* (London: Zed Books).

Vaughan-Williams, N. (2015), *Europe's Border Crisis* (Oxford: Oxford University Press).

Wacquant, L. (2009), *Punishing the Poor: The Neoliberal Government of Social Insecurity* (Durham, NC: Duke University Press).

Weber, F. (2012), *Borderline Justice: The Fight for Refugee and Migrant Rights* (London: Pluto Press).

Williams, J.M. (2015), From humanitarian exceptionalism to contingent care: care and enforcement at the humanitarian border. *Political Geography* 47: 11–20.

Wilson, H.F. (2017), 'On geography and encounter: bodies, borders, and difference', *Progress in Human Geography* 41(4): 451–471.

Wilson, H.F. (2014), The possibilities of tolerance: intercultural dialogue in a multicultural Europe. *Environment and Planning D: Society and Space* 32(5): 852–868.

Wilson, H.F. and J. Darling (2016), 'The possibilities of encounter.' In Darling, J. and H.F. Wilson (eds) *Encountering the City: Urban Encounters from Accra to New York* (London: Routledge).

Whitlock, G. (2008), Letters from Nauru. *Life Writing* 5(2): 203–217.

Zetter, R. (2007), More labels, fewer refugees: remaking the refugee label in an era of globalization. *Journal of Refugee Studies* 20: 172–192.

10

Visibilising suffering or stealth humanitarianism? The perils of promoting durable protection in cities of the south[1]

Caroline Wanjiku Kihato and Loren B. Landau

Introduction: aid and accountability in a precarious, politicised world

Cities beyond the wealthy West – Johannesburg, Gaziantep, Peshawar, Amman and Beirut to name a few – are increasingly prominent theatres for humanitarian action. For many years, urban displaced people in 'the Global South' were people the humanitarian 'eye refused to see' (Kibreab, 1996). This changed in 2009 when the United Nations High Commissioner for Refugees (UNHCR) expressly recognised displaced people in urban areas as categorically entitled to assistance. Since then, a combination of growing awareness and the sheer numbers of urban displaced – from Haiti to conflicts in Iraq, Syria, the Horn of Africa and elsewhere – have generated multiple urban humanitarian engagements (see Lubkemann, 2010; also Polzer and Hammond, 2008). This presents practical and ethical challenges for organisations unfamiliar with urban institutional complexity and social diversity. Efforts to navigate these complexities reveals core characteristics and dysfunctions of a humanitarian system shaped through increasingly technocratic forms of global paternalism.

This paternalism has its roots in a confluence of developments in medicine, government and media technologies, a focus in law on universal humanity, and the growth of a scholarly interest in the 'suffering subject'. Through these, the displaced person has become a ubiquitous character in media imagery and global policy and scholarly debates. This is evident in humanitarians' approach to displaced people in urban areas. Rather than reconsider their approach, such engagements follow a familiar pattern of 'visibilising' targets of action in ways that legitimise humanitarian interventions. As objects of action, displaced persons' particular location, history, and desires are typically edited, standardised and mobilised with the intention of galvanising support for (or against) the displaced. In doing so, humanitarians, activists, media (Nachtwey, 1999; Salgado, 2005) and scholars (Agamben, 1995;

Arendt, 1973; Malkki, 1995; Malkki, 1996) oscillate between presenting displaced persons as an embodiment of 'bare life' – living but denuded of dignity and agency – or as agential heroes capable of overcoming adversity and contributing to all around them. The former reflects a tradition of refugees as 'speechless emissaries'(Malkki, 1996), silent figures employed to mobilise material aid and legitimise expert assistance. The latter is less infantilising, but is similarly essentialist. It too categorically visibilises individuals as 'displaced' in ways intended to mobilise political support, differentiating them as agential and entitled due to a specific, traumatic history (Feldman and Ticktin, 2010; Ticktin, 2014). Both strategies may produce short-term gains for the displaced and those self-nominated to assistant them. However, such approaches taint the displaced. It is a form of branding that potentially heightens potential for victimisation and marginalisation by host populations who, without external assistance, are navigating similar forms of precarity and exclusion.

This chapter explores the underlying ethos and consequences of urban humanitarian action as new practises. It demonstrates how inclinations towards political neutrality; technical fixes; and direct, targeted service delivery work against the long-term interests of those they ostensibly intend to help. The strategies they employ typically reify displaced persons' experience of suffering in ways that ultimately undermine their long-term protection in cities where host communities experience similar levels of socio-economic marginalisation. In these urban environments, building sets of entitlements around a 'displaced identity' is potentially hazardous, working against alternative forms of solidarity and the social negotiations necessary for navigating urban precarity.

Under the conditions of precarious potential offered by many 'Southern cities', the most effective forms of humanitarianism – those providing the safest and most durable forms of self-reliance – come from stealthily negotiating invisibility while expanding entitlements through horizontal solidarities. Promoting rights for displaced persons living among equally poor and vulnerable host populations requires tactical political alliances and solidarities with community-based organisations and local actors. Doing so means breaking from the visibilisation impulse. Instead, it requires complementing national and global appeals for funds and credibility with highly localised engagements. Doing so is predicated on comprehending intergovernmental relations and everyday bureaucratic practices and a willingness to work invisibly.

The following illustrate how those organisations employing forms of local literacy and back routes to rights – key components of 'stealth humanitarianism' – overcome overt and potentially costly political blunders while remaining effective advocates for the displaced. The stealth approach described here challenges the impulse to make displaced people's hardship hypervisible. In highlighting the tensions between effectiveness and existing practices, the chapter reconsiders the values of ethics and activism premised on rights and entitlements correlated with individual suffering. Similarly, it challenges the value of essentialising the 'displaced person' as victim or hero. Rather, it asks humanitarians to reimagine displacees as agentic figures embedded within historical and political contexts – contexts in which the possibility of navigating and negotiating inclusion exists.

Approach

This chapter brings together discussions of global humanitarian norms with a perspective rooted in the politics of local governance and humanitarian action. While there is little published work explicitly discussing the role of local authorities in addressing migration or displacement in the developing world, what exists nonetheless offers considerable guidance on the degree to which states and global legal norms govern local institutions (Edwards et al., 2014; Kimble et al., 2012; Landau et al., 2013). It is with these questions in mind that we have conducted our research and analysis.

This chapter is not another appeal for improved commitments from governments or humanitarians, but rather an effort to understand the institutional and political structures within which urban humanitarians and displaced people negotiate to forge new, secure lives. These operate at multiple scales, from the United Nations General Assembly to the neighbourhood chief or hood. While the latter often proves the immediate gatekeeper to protection, we nonetheless explore how the more formal processes of decentralisation, budgeting, vertical and horizontal cooperation and popular participation interact with displaced people's human security. In doing so, we follow displaced people into cities which serve as the tableau for diverse sets of actors, interests and institutions.

What follows is based on findings from original research in three African cities: Nairobi, Johannesburg and Kampala. We also draw on engagements with practitioners and policy processes from these sites and elsewhere in Africa and the Middle East. Our primary cases are trading and political centres which have become destinations and transit points for a broad range of people of concern. In both Kenya and Uganda, the primary focus of humanitarian attention was long on purpose-built camps and settlements. However, there are increasing activities oriented toward urban-based people of concern. In Nairobi these include longstanding and new refugee and asylum seeker populations from Africa's Great Lakes as well as from conflict and persecution across the horn: the Sudans, Ethiopia, Eritrea, Uganda and Somalia (see Campbell, 2006). Nairobi also hosts people internally displaced by ethnic conflicts, particularly those stemming from the 2007–08 post-election violence. Even if Kampala's urban refugee population is less well recognised and contentious, it too includes people from across the Great Lakes and Horn of Africa as well as considerable numbers of people displaced by longstanding conflict in Northern Uganda (see Bernstein and Okello, 2007; Hovil, 2007). Over the past two years, the humanitarian community has increasingly praised Uganda's willingness to allow displaced people to settle in urban sites.

South Africa is somewhat exceptional within Africa for maintaining no purpose-built refugee camps. Since the mid 1990s, it has instead relied exclusively on forms of temporary, local integration. For many years the world's leader in individual asylum claims, South Africa hosts asylum seekers and displaced people from across Africa and from parts of South and Southeast Asia and Central Europe. In the late 1990s and early 2000s, the humanitarian community looked to South Africa's camp-free policies as examples for elsewhere in the world. Heightening hostility and xenophobia have somewhat tarnished the country's global image, as have increasingly hostile asylum policies seeking to limit displaced people's access to labour markets.

In assessing how humanitarians and municipalities engaged within the municipalities described above, a research team evaluated the experience of urban displacement and humanitarianism on four fronts:

Who holds formal and *de facto* responsibility for people of concern.
The obstacles, abilities and incentives for local authorities and humanitarians responding to people of concern.
Non-state actors (e.g., NGOs, international organisations, religious bodies) who are (a) providing or prohibiting opportunities for people of concern and (b) working on behalf of people sharing similar interests with people of concern; and the consequences of varied forms of interventions (c).
The interests motivating the various actors identified in the mapping outlined above and the real and potential consequences of their actions.

To these ends, the research team conducted key informant interviews with local, national and provincial governments, as well as international NGOs and local community organisations, over a period of six weeks in each site.[2] The interviews assessed local government's formal and *de facto* responsibilities for the health, housing and economic development of displaced populations. In addition to interviewing sector officials, we examined local government budgeting, community participation, planning processes and intergovernmental relationships. In all cases we visited neighbourhoods rich in displaced people and spoke to representatives from both host and displaced populations. Looking within local governments revealed the cognitive, financial and political incentives that work for and against a positive, proactive protection response for displaced people.

Rather than offer city-specific overviews of the legislative and institutional frameworks and humanitarian practices likely to affect people of concern, we use the case material to extract more general observations. We do not intend the insights as blueprints for humanitarian action, although humanitarians might benefit from considering their implications. Instead the chapter intends to reveal the institutional and ethical imperatives and constraints shaping urban humanitarian action.

Protecting the urban displaced

We live in an urban age. The industrial revolution created the modern cities of Europe and North America, but it is in the 'developing world' – poorer and more loosely legalised spaces outside the wealthy West – that we now see the most rapid urban growth (UNDESA, 2014). Even if the global cities' literature is largely informed by the imperial metropolises – London, Paris, Tokyo, New York – and their nouveau riche cousins – Dubai, Shanghai, Jakarta – the focus of urban humanitarianism is elsewhere. In places like Kabul and Khartoum, cities surrounded by seemingly interminable conflicts, displaced people significantly contribute to cities' rapid population growth (Beall and Esser, 2005: 6). Jordanian and Lebanese cities will be forever changed by Syria's civil war and the displacements they have engendered.

While UNHCR long resisted calls to work in urban spaces – often citing expense and the efficacy of camps – the organisation and its partners have begun to embrace the need for urban oriented action.[3] As the UNHCR notes, over 53 million people worldwide – or 7 out of every 10 people displaced within or across international borders – seek refuge in cities. The implications of this in cities like Beirut, where one in five people is Syrian, is profound. Across Africa, there is growing awareness that the majority of displaced people live and seek protection in what are often deeply impoverished, unequal and under-capacitated but increasingly global urban centres.

Although it is unclear if displaced persons' presence in global cities is as novel as many suggest (see Cooper, 1992; Malkki, 1995; Rogge and Akol, 1989), strong normative, political and financial motivations have now captured the humanitarian imagination. The massive displacements from Iraq and Syria have contributed to framing urban displacement in crisis terms. Indeed, the continued focus on displaced persons' immediate needs and vulnerabilities limits the field's engagement with broader questions of urbanism, precarity and resilience and the potential dangers of visibilising potentially vulnerable populations. If nothing else, this chapter suggests there are compelling normative and intellectual arguments for sustained attention to both cities and the people seeking protection within them. However, as the remaining pages demonstrate, the city reveals how humanitarian neutrality and the new public management drive to quantification and efficiency single out and essentialise the 'refugee' in ways that are likely to compromise efforts to promote human security and refugee agency.

Humanitarian neutrality

Much of the need for visibilisation comes from one of the humanitarian system's founding principles: neutrality. Debates continue on whether humanitarians are political actors and if humanitarians can reconcile the necessity of political engagement with the demand for political neutrality (see Lischer, 2006; Rieff, 2003; Stein, 2005). At issue is whether humanitarians' original position of neutrality, impartiality and independence (Mills, 2005; also Barnett and Weiss, 2008) is realisable or even appropriate (Rieff, 2003). Many humanitarian organisations and humanitarians maintain that protecting relief workers and vulnerable people requires aloofness from warring parties' political interests. Amid polemic Cold War politics, relief organisations needed a neutral stance to be effective. Politics was considered a moral pollutant and practical obstacle (Barnett and Weiss, 2008: 4). Indeed, the United Nations High Commissioner for Refugees was founded on principles of neutrality and remains hesitant to publicly critique, let alone try to shape, domestic or local policies. What is important for present purposes is how humanitarians justify their actions in spaces where they are meant to be neutral. This often demands global, self-evident standards placed outside the political sphere, a position that immunises them from quotidian negotiation and compromise. As these exist outside 'normal' politics and law, the protections they offer can only apply to 'exceptional' populations: those demonstrating unique trauma or vulnerabilities. Moreover, the metrics of humanitarian success become technocratic material measures that largely exclude social or political indicators.

It is not only humanitarian neutrality that fosters visibilisation. The impulse also stems from the political economy of the global aid regime. In an era of increased competition for humanitarian resources, organisations are compelled to highlight particular forms of need. They must also define these needs in ways that can be addressed through external, technocratic interventions. This pushes humanitarians to visibilise displaced people in ways that highlight their vulnerabilities – or particular, material aspects that can be remedied through aid. Rarely does this analysis move beyond individual abjection, but where social structures are discussed they are presented as regressive, contrary to global human rights standards or norms of civility (e.g., protections of youth and gender). In this move we see the broader 'de-politicisation' of the spaces in which displaced people live and of displaced people themselves.

While organisations can be advocates for migrants and displaced people, they must do so in ways that that resonate with concrete universalised norms and standards of the vulnerable or their rights (see Barnett, 2005; Barnett and Snyder, 2008; Belloni, 2007; Leebaw, 2007; Mills, 2005; Minear, 2002; Rieffer-Flanagan, 2009; and Subotic, 2009). Backed by international laws and treatises, their work, like that of political activists and watchdogs, seeks to ensure state compliance in the protection of populations displaced in conflict. Yet this is an oddly standardising impulse. Their very presence and engagement in these spaces demands defining populations in particular ways – namely as displaced people – and with problems that can be resolved through at least the performance of humanitarian neutrality (cf. Fassin, 2012).

Quantifiable efficiency and new public management

Furthering the need to visibilise complex needs and structures in ways that conform to a neutral humanitarian ethos, the 'professionalisation' of humanitarian organisations promotes particular forms of visibilisation and essentialisation (Barnett, 2005). Following global patterns in public administration that might be loosely termed a shift to 'new public management', humanitarians have been increasingly asked to see the displaced as clients (see Kapucu, 2006). Furthering this are widespread efforts at 'standard setting' for service delivery in which humanitarian agencies' primary 'shareholders' (i.e., donor states) place pressure on them to improve the efficiency and timeliness of their operations. This in an environment in which increasing competition for ever-dwindling resources has meant that humanitarians have to ensure greater accountability to donors. This means shifting how they do business, with increasing demand on measurable outputs and outcomes, and a focus on standards, evaluation and reporting. The SPHERE initiative is not only an effort to improve the lives of the displaced, but also to ensure that humanitarian resources are used efficiently and effectively (see Dufour et al., 1994).

Shifting spaces and norms: navigating competing imperatives

The remainder of this chapter reflects on how various humanitarian organisations have sought to reconcile the competing imperatives and complications of working in new spaces and funding environments and the potentially dangerous by-products of their strategies of visibilisation and targeted intervention.

Humanitarians and human rights activists have sought to counter limited local political interest in assisting displaced populations by evoking international law and principles while peddling an essentialised discourse of the needy refugee. Justifying their presence means institutionally (if not physically) distinguishing their target population from other precarious populations. In instances of widespread scarcity, a condition characterising the majority of hosting municipalities globally, this is potentially dangerous. Unless there is a strong local constituency concerned with displaced peoples' rights and welfare, or strong political incentives such as global recognition or financing, politicians will do as little as possible to promote the welfare of displaced people. Where local populations are hostile to people of concern – as they are in Nairobi and Johannesburg – local authorities may win points through policies that explicitly exclude or deny them. Ironically, the more democratic and participatory local governments become, the less likely they may be to dedicate scarce resources to the displaced. Under such circumstances, overt or public demands for displaced persons' access to services and opportunities may only provide fodder for populist politicians.

Those managing to avoid such visibilisation and victimisation play a game with an alternative set of rules: one far less premised on externally imposed legal–bureaucratic categories. For the reasons outlined above, international humanitarian organisations are often poorly suited for effective engagement with the kind of precarity and politics that characterises many 'Southern' cities. Many remain trapped in the language of neutral humanitarianism, rights and technical efficiency that acts as an epistemic blinder. This limits their ability to see and engage with variations in institutional configuration, the language of urban development and the politics surrounding diversity, poverty reduction and immigration. While some local aid agencies may recognise this, many do not. International agencies that parachute staff from other emergencies are unlikely to have these skills. The remaining sections of this chapter discuss the principles of those organisations that are able to maintain a level of invisibility while still promoting the long-term protection of displaced populations in urban areas.

Investing in local literacy

No single approach allows humanitarians to navigate competing imperatives. However, humanitarians are often more successful when able to identify multiple entry points and mobilise support for the displaced by employing multiple logics. This demands a holistic assessment and understanding of the municipalities that those concerned with displaced people alone typically overlook. Moreover, it means recognising scaled variations. Even within a single country, municipalities and neighbourhoods are distinguished by the nature of their institutions, political priorities, resource bases, populations and geographies. Working across a region or on multiple continents further highlights the challenge of universal forms of engagement with varied institutions, interests and abilities likely to shape responses to people of concern. Those engaging effectively are unlikely to use the universal language of humanitarian neutrality or refugee vulnerability. Rather, rhetoric that can mobilise sympathy and support in one setting may prove ineffective or potentially harmful in another. Similarly, appeals to principles – rights, inclusivity, justice, efficiency, legal and ethical obligations – generate divergent results among planners and politicians steeped in different traditions, priorities and institutional or political incentives (see Donnelly, 2003; also Elias, 2008).

To illustrate the value of local literacy and a multiplicity of ethical appeals, we can take differences in political priorities between Johannesburg and Nairobi. For South African municipalities, authorities typically measure success by their performance in countering economic and social exclusion. While authorities may not universally consider people of concern among the marginalised groups as deserving of assistance, advocates have found ways of using the language of inclusion to help displaced people be inserted into policy. Rather than appealing to rights as displaced people, municipal authorities have responded to arguments about the displaced person's general economic and physical vulnerability.

Compare this with Nairobi. In the Kenyan capital – and to some degree in Kampala – officials have little direct responsibility and express little moral commitment to providing the kind of inclusive, transformative services available to some Johannesburg residents. As such, demands for inclusion or access to state services – even where residents may be legally entitled to such services – are unlikely to garner support or an effective response. Indeed, where displaced people are a low political priority and states provide little to their own citizens, few gains come from demonstrating that people of concern have unmet protection needs. Similarly, demonstrating that officials have fallen short of their legal obligations to people of concern accomplishes little where officials and citizens expect little. Rather, Kenyan officials see their role as fostering opportunities for business formation and self-reliance for everyone. Under such conditions, appeals to improve the conditions for entrepreneurialism – improved physical security, licensing and access to markets – are a more effective way of expanding the protection space. Organisations often continue to speak a rights-based language to donors and continue overt campaigns for improved health care, housing and other services, but even these are more effective when aligned with Kenya's largely laissez-faire, market-based ethos.

Moving beyond legal recognition towards de facto protection

While legal protection remains important, local practices often matter more. *De facto* protection is typically negotiated outside of refugee law and policies. It is in this kind of grounded negotiation for protection that the dangers of visibilisation are most apparent. Conversely, humanitarian adaptations and engagements most likely to result in improved protection for displaced people in urban areas may have little to do with engagements around migration, immigration or asylum per se. People moving into cities due to war or persecution are, by definition, 'displaced', but this status does not define them. Rather, displaced persons are also parents, traders, students, clients, service providers, consumers and potential investors. As such, their lives and economic impacts are shaped by the policies and practices that intersect with, but are not framed by, policies and practices explicitly oriented towards displacement and displaced persons. Addressing questions of public order policing, registration of new businesses, access to bank accounts, and regulations surrounding housing and health care (including physical and psychological care for gender-based violence) are often far more important than immigration or asylum policy in determining individual outcomes.

Even where the law explicitly entitles displaced people to a range of services – under South Africa's Refugees Act (1998) they are entitled to public health care, work opportunities and potentially public housing – claiming those rights may well require incentivising local authorities or modifying sectoral regulations and practices. In Johannesburg, displaced people may already be formally eligible for varied forms of subsidised housing but are excluded due to rationing or ignorance on the part of officials and advocates. Although it had not yet happened at the time of research, interviews suggested that by providing limited supported to the city's department of housing or even to specific housing schemes it may well be possible to negotiate access to secure accommodation. In Nairobi, a pool of resources dedicated to disaster management existed while there were no funds set aside for assistance to people of concern. Under such circumstances, research suggested that working with officials responsible for disaster management can unlock funding for refugee-related initiatives that would otherwise remain untouched. The more decentralised the institutional configurations, the more necessary it has become for effective organisations to engage across a range of administrative levels and policy sectors.

Where rights to services and/or markets are not clearly delimited in refugee legislation, authorities have been similarly persuaded to create environments in which people of concern are as empowered as citizens and long-term residents to access opportunities. This can be done through small-scale engagement to amend licensing or other regulations. Indeed, the most rapid changes in protection outcomes have often been achieved through highly localised, sectorally specific advocacy. In politically hostile or contentious environments, a stealthy approach may be the best one. Although it works against the grain of those striving for legal recognition and protection, positive change in local regulations or by-laws can be achieved without making explicit reference to the inclusion of displaced people or other people of concern. Removing provisions that provide free access to public services only to 'locals' (as is the case with Nairobi's public 'Iko' toilets) enables displaced people to access the service without making them overtly visible. In all three cities researched for this chapter, the most effective forms of protection are also those that rely on legal and social 'invisibility'. Understanding how people of concern integrate into markets and services may ultimately lead humanitarians to pragmatically adopt strategies of 'benign neglect': allowing people to negotiate their own ways into markets and services. This falls short of guaranteeing universal access, but it may be quicker, cheaper and more politically and economically sustainable than making such universal demands.

Aligning protection with local development objectives

Support for existing mechanisms can win political favour for a population that would otherwise be stigmatised or exploited. Where widespread decentralisation and deprivation occur, humanitarian organisations' explicit engagement with municipal authorities and urban populations demands a shift in both approach and language. This means humanitarians recognising local authorities' interests and incentives and developing strategies to align them with protection concerns within domestic or local politics and law.

Interest alignment may take the form of direct calls for resources to protect refugee rights, although such efforts will succeed where there is broad public sympathy (or at least a vocal constituency) for displaced people or human rights more generally. The Sanctuary City movement in the United States is perhaps the clearest illustration of this. More frequently it comes from demonstrating how the presence of displaced people can be a political or financial asset by providing enhanced revenue through taxes or attracting direct assistance to core government departments. It is this approach that Betts and Collier (2017) describe and which the World Bank has promoted in referring to refugee protection as a local and global 'public good'. In almost all instances, protection will likely be achieved by finding creative ways of inserting people of concern into existing programmes and policies or enhancing those programmes in ways that can accommodate people of concern. Yet even this strategy is risky as it essentialises displaced people as assets, almost legitimising the exclusion of those who are in need of help. Moreover, it premises access on a history of suffering. The strongest form of incorporation is that which does not 'mark' people or justify their rights based on their particular displacement histories. Through this kind of stealth or 'bureaucratic incorporation' (Marrow, 2009; also Ellermann, 2006) humanitarians may avoid complex and contentious public battles over rights, instead naturalising the presence of displaced people in their respective communities while building solidarities with marginalised constituencies.

Our research draws attention to the innovative work of RefugePoint in facilitating displaced peoples' access to Kenya's National Health Insurance Fund (NHIF) instead of promoting a parallel system of service delivery. Through a careful review of the insurance legislation, advocates determined that displaced people were legally entitled to insurance. Rather than making a public appeal, they worked quietly with a mid-level official to complete the paperwork required to enrol hundreds of displaced people at the minimal costs charged to citizens. While initially reluctant to enrol displaced people, RefugePoint was able to appeal to the official's performance targets of securing new members. While contexts vary, such appeals to local authorities' interests in programme implementation, revenue generation and business formation allows advocates to help align government action and opportunities with protection interests.

Such technocratic engagements also open multiple spaces for engagement. Rather than relying on rights to 'trickle down' from national policy pronouncements – although this may be required in centralised systems like Kampala – a sectorally-specific approach opens multiple spaces. Engaging with municipal or sub-municipal bureaucrats may do little to change national policy, but appeals to professional values can often do more and do it more quickly than high-level policy reform. Wherever possible, humanitarians will benefit from capitalising on 'bureaucratic incorporation'.

In summary, no strategy was guaranteed to produce results precisely because the particularities of municipality, neighbourhood and country militate against universal 'best practices' as commonly understood. Instead, best practice means finding ways of diversifying their expertise and points of engagement. Without abandoning efforts to sway national policies – an effort that is particularly important in centralised systems like Uganda – municipal savvy opened multiple spaces for engagement in ways that better avoided contentious public politics. Small shifts in by-laws, performance incentives or small-scale alignment of interests can produce immediate, positive effects. Such initiatives require considerable up-front effort and expertise, but they often do not require extensive or sustained expenditures. Rather they required urban nous and humility. They also mean getting into the trenches of urban politics in ways that play to local interests and incentives, not principles.

Conclusions: confronting the imperative to visibilise

The case study materials and analysis presented above suggest a complex and varied operational environment. Negotiating protection in purpose-built settlements or camps is neither simple nor straightforward, yet urban environments present both opportunity and risks for humanitarians. In spaces often characterised by fluidity and socio-political fragmentation, there can be no single 'best practice', although the demand for global solutions and technocratic expertise tends to push for 'solutions' premised on potentially hazardous forms of visibilisation. This despite evidence that appeals to universal rights, international law or even domestic refugee policy are often ineffective. Moreover, focusing legal instruments and internationally accepted protection principles may demand displaced people come forward to claim rights or access services based on their displacement histories. Using legal rights and policy pronouncements may interrupt the varied strategies people are already using to access protection. Demanding that displaced people be seen as economic assets similarly essentialises displaced people and introduces them into the marketplace as marked. Ill-informed interventions demanding clearly marked sub-populations may disrupt participation in market mechanisms, the benefits of bureaucratic incorporation or accessing non-legal claims. Indeed, a blunt appeal to rights or utility may disrupt *de facto* systems of protection while alienating the people and politicians needed for expanding protection and human security.

Recognising this, the most effective humanitarian action is likely to come from a kind of a complementary politics informed by a spatial, social and political understanding of rights violations and potential for protection. At the heart of this is the need to find 'back routes to rights' and social solidarity with locally legitimate actors – local officials, businesspeople, landlords, service providers – who have the power to bring about immediate positive change. As rights are increasingly negotiated 'horizontally' (see Kabeer, 2005) with neighbours, not states, a state-centred language of rights can be impotent and potentially perilous.

Our observations do not suggest that humanitarians who are effective are abandoning their traditional focus on documentation, legal status or reform to refugee and immigration laws. Rather, such campaigns remain important symbolically, even if documentation and formal rights translate into practical protection far less directly than advocates often presume (Landau and Duponchel, 2011). They are also critically important for appeasing headquarters and donors who often equate legal status with protection. However, the observations presented here suggest that the savviest humanitarians are those that look for opportunities to build solidarities with local populations by appealing to interest. To do this requires a new, spatial perspective; for as Soysal (1996: 21) noted long ago: 'all these trends imply that the nation state as a territorial entity is no longer the source of legitimacy for individual rights'. She had in mind the ceding of national competencies to supra-local bodies. However, Marrow's work on the bureaucratic incorporation of immigrants into the United States localises the claim. She speaks about how 'bureaucrats' responses to immigrants' interests precede those of elected officials and are driven by strong professional norms' (Marrow: 2009: 758). Elsewhere, appealing to more generalised interests, around housing, crime or other concerns – not rights – can help appeal to local political incentives in ways that do not draw lines or make references to discourses which are seen as foreign, threatening or unwelcome. In all cases, the language must resonate locally, the interventions be locally legitimate and the approach stealthy, gradual and cautious.

The paragraphs above outline the possibilities for working in urban areas and point to strategies that engage within the localised institutions and incentives that structure urban life. Such engagements are not, however, easy to reconcile with the imperatives for humanitarian neutrality and quantifiable outcomes tied to time-bound improvements among a subset of the urban populations. Indeed, the processes described above not only require a level of local literacy and knowledge, but will often demand engagement in political processes that are long, convoluted and have uncertain outcomes. They also mean surrendering the visibilisation imperative on which so much humanitarian work depends. This is an existential challenge for bodies responsible for quick, quantifiable actions undertaken in ostensibly neutral forms.

In some instances, the approach called for here may mean all but abandoning the language of rights and protection embedded in humanitarian law and guiding principles. Such instruments may continue to inform and guide humanitarians' work, but through locally appropriate language informed by a close reading of politics, interests and opportunities. This will not be easy for agencies and individuals steeped in the humanitarian status quo. As Fassin (2010) so trenchantly notes in discussing reforms to the humanitarian systems, there are great institutional and personal interests invested in preserving both the universal language and mechanisms long used in mobilising for rights. People have an almost religious faith in past approaches and principles and may be deeply unsettled by needing to think in new, more pragmatic shades of grey. Organisations built around a rights discourse may fear for their relevance and funding. Indeed, the kind of political approach called for here may be used against organisations like the UNHCR or its partners who are expected to remain politically neutral. But there is a place for all these strategies in the kind of advocacy strategies described in the pages above. The diversity of spaces in which we push for social justice demands as many strategies and appeals. As much as the humanitarian mindset may resist a break from norms of neutrality, it is perhaps the political economic of humanitarianism that continues to present the most thorough obstacle to effectively achieving urban protection.

Notes

1 This chapter elaborates arguments initially outlined in Kihato and Landau (2016).
2 The interview framework was developed by the Urban Institute in Washington DC, Jean Pierre Misago in Johannesburg, Caroline Wanjiku Kihato in Nairobi and David Obot in Kampala.
3 See, for example, (UNHCR, 2009) *Forced Migration Review*'s 2010 issue dedicated to urban refugees, along with a range of other studies conducted in Africa, Asia, the Middle East and Latin America by or on behalf of humanitarian organisations (Zetter and Deikun, 2010) and a series of studies by such high-profile organisations as the Women's Refugee Commission (2011a, 2011b) and the associated International Rescue Committee (Lyytinen and Kullenberg, 2013).

References

Agamben, G. (1995), We refugees. *Symposium* 49(2): 114–119.
Arendt, H. (1973), *The Origins of Totalitarianism* (Harcourt: Brace Jovanovich).
Barnett, M.N. (2005), Humanitarianism transformed. *Perspectives on Politics* 3(4): 723–740.
Barnett, M.N. and T.G. Weiss (eds) (2008), *Humanitarianism in Question: Politics, Power, Ethics* (Ithaca: Cornell University Press).
Barnett, M.N. and J. Snyder (2008), The grand strategies of humanitarianism. In Barnett, M. and T.G. Weiss (eds) *Humanitarianism in Question: Politics, Power, Ethics* (Ithaca: Cornell University Press), pp. 142–171.
Beall, J. and Esser, D. (2005), *Shaping Urban Futures: Challenges to Governing and Managing Afghan Cities* (Kabul: Afghanistan Research and Evaluation Unit).
Belloni, R. (2007), The trouble with humanitarianism. *Review of International Studies* 33(3): 451–474.
Bernstein J. and M.C. Okello. (2007), To be or not to be: urban refugees in Kampala. *Refuge* 24(1): 46–56.

Betts, A. and P. Collier (2017), *Refuge: Transforming a Broken Refugee System* (London: Penguin).

Campbell, H.E. (2006), Urban refugees in Nairobi: problems of protection, mechanisms of survival, and possibilities for integration. *Journal of Refugee Studies* 19(3): 396–413.

Cooper, D. (1992), *Urban Refugees: Ethiopians and Eritreans in Cairo* (Cairo: American University in Cairo Press).

Donnelly, J. (2003), *Universal Human Rights: In Theory & Practice*, 2nd edn (Ithaca: Cornell University Press).

Dufour, C., V. de Geoffroy, H. Maury and F. Grünewald. (1994), Rights, standards and quality in a complex humanitarian space: is SPHERE the right tool? *Disasters* 28(2): 124–141.

Edwards, B., Y. Serdar and J. Boex. (2014), *Local Government Discretion and Accountability in Sierra Leone* (Washington, DC: Urban Institute).

Elias, J. (2008), Struggles over the rights of foreign domestic workers in Malaysia: the possibility and limitations of 'rights talk'. *Economy and Society* 37(2): 282–303.

Ellermann, A. (2006), Street-level democracy? How immigration bureaucrats manage public opposition. *West European Politics* 29(2): 287–303.

Fassin, D. (2012), *Humanitarian Reason: A Moral History of the Present* (Berkeley: University of California Press).

Fassin, D. (2010), Heart of humaness: the moral economy of humanitarian intervention. In Fassin, D. and M. Pandolfi (eds) *Contemporary States of Emergency* (New York: Prospect Books), pp. 269–293.

Feldman, I. and M. Ticktin (2010), Introduction: government and humanity. In *In the Name of Humanity: The Government of Threat and Care* (Durham, NC: Duke University Press).

Hovil, L. (2007), Self-settled refugees in Uganda: an alternative approach to displacement. *Journal of Refugee Studies* 20(4): 599–620.

Kabeer, N. (2005), *Inclusive Citizenship: Meanings and Expression* (London: Zed Books).

Kapucu, N. (2006), New public management: theory, ideology, and practice. In Farazmand, A. and J Pinkowski (eds) *Handbook of Globalization, Governance, and Public Administration* (Boca Raton: CRC Press), pp. 889–902.

Kibreab, G. (1996), Eritrean and Ethiopian urban refugees in Khartoum: what the eye refuses to see. *African Studies Review* 39(3): 131–178.

Kihato, C.W. and L.B. Landau. (2016), Stealth humanitarianism: negotiating politics, precarity, and performance management in protecting the urban displaced. *Journal of Refugee Studies* 30(3): 407–425.

Kimble, D., J. Boex and G. Kapitova. (2012), *Making Decentralization Work in Developing Countries: Transforming Local Government Entities into High Performing Organizations* (Washington, DC: Urban Institute).

Landau, L.B. and M. Duponchel (2011), Laws, policies, or social position? capabilities and the determinants of effective protection in four African cities. *Journal of Refugee Studies* 24(1): 1–22.

Landau, L.B. and A. Segatti with J.P. Misago (2013), Planning and participation in cities that move: identifying obstacles to municipal mobility management. *Public Administration and Development* 33(2): 113–124.

Leebaw, B. (2007), The politics of impartial activism: humanitarianism and human rights. *Perspectives on Politics* 5(2): 223–239.

Lischer. S.K. (2006), *Dangerous Sanctuaries: Refugee Camps, Civil War, and the Dilemmas of Humanitarian Aid* (Ithaca: Cornell University Press).

Lubkemann, S. (2010), Past Directions and Future Possibilities in the Study of African Displacement. Unpublished Scoping Study. Stockholm: Nordic Afrika Institute.

Lyytinen, E. and J. Kullenberg. (2013), Urban Refugee Research: An Analytical Report. New York: International Rescue Committee.

Malkki, L.H. (1995), Refugees and exile: 'From "Refugee Studies" to the National Order of Things'. *Annual Review of Anthropology* 24: 495–523.

Malkki, L.H. (1996), Speechless emissaries: refugees, humanitarianism, and dehistoricization. *Cultural Anthropology* 11(3): 377–404.

Marrow, H.B. (2009), Immigrant bureaucratic incorporation: the dual roles of professional missions and government policies. *American Sociological Review* 74(5): 756–777.

Mills, K. (2005), Neo-humanitarianism: the role of international humanitarian norms and organizations in contemporary conflict. *Global Governance* 11(2): 161–183.

Minear, L. (2002), *The Humanitarian Enterprise: Dilemmas and Discoveries* (Bloomfield: Kumarian Press).

Nachtwey, J. (1999), *L'Inferno* (New York: Phaidon).

Polzer, T. and L. Hammond. (2008), Invisible displacement. *Journal of Refugee Studies* 21(4): 417–431.

Rieff, David. (2003), *A Bed for the Night: Humanitarianism in Crisis* (New York: Simon and Schuster).

Rieffer-Flanagan, B.A. (2009), Is neutral humanitarianism dead? Red Cross neutrality: walking the tightrope of neutral humanitarianism. *Human Rights Quarterly* 31(4): 888–915.

Rogge, J. and J. Akol. (1989), Repatriation: its role in resolving Africa's refugee dilemma. *International Migration Review* 23(2): 184–200.

Salgado, S. (2005), Migrations: humanity in transition. Interview with Nandy Madlin [online] http://pdngallery.com/legends/legends10/migration.pdf [accessed 3 November 2005].

Soysal, Y.N. (1996), Changing citizenship in Europe: remarks on postnational membership and the national state. In Cesarani, D. (ed.) *Citizenship, Nationality, and Migration in Europe* (London: Routledge), pp. 17–29.

Stein, J. (2005), 'Commentary: humanitarianism as political fusion. *Perspectives on Politics* 3(4): 741–744.

Subotic, J. (2009), Humanitarianism at a crossroads. *International Studies Review* 11(1): 187–189.

Ticktin, M. (2014), Transnational humanitarianism. *Annual Review of Anthropology* 43: 273–289.

UNDESA (2014), *World Urbanization Prospects* (New York: UNDESA).

UN High Commissioner for Refugees (UNHCR) (2009), *UNHCR Policy on Refugee Protection and Solutions in Urban Areas, September 2009* (Geneva: UNHCR).

Women's Refugee Commission (2011a), *Bright Lights, Big City: Urban Refugees Struggles to Make a Living in New Delhi* (New York: Women's Refugee Commission).

Women's Refugee Commission (2011b), *No Place To Go But Up: Urban Refugees in Johannesburg: South Africa* (New York: Women's Refugee Commission).

Zetter, R. and G. Deikun. (2010), Meeting humanitarian challenges in urban areas. *Forced Migration Review* 34: 5–7.

11

Onward pushes and negotiated refuge: theorizing the fluid national and urban regimes of forced migration in Southeast Asia

Pei Palmgren

In May 2015, thousands of Rohingya "boat people" fleeing violent persecution in Myanmar appeared throughout Southeast Asia's Andaman Sea and Strait of Malacca (Fuller and Cochrane, 2015). As the boats approached the shores of Indonesia, Malaysia, and Thailand, state authorities refused to allow them to dock, opting instead to push them back out to sea. Responding to international criticism, Thai Prime Minister Prayuth Chan-ocha signaled the pressures of states of first arrival, stating, "Everyone wants a transit country like us to take responsibility. Is it fair?" (AP, 2015). As states closed their borders, smugglers transporting the forced migrants[1] abandoned ship, leaving thousands stranded at sea. After continued outcry from media and human rights organizations, the countries agreed to stop rejecting boats, choosing instead to detain/shelter the passengers while emphasizing that they would not be allowed to work or settle. Though governments met to discuss the crisis, they put forth no binding plans for addressing impending forced migration situations, indicating a continued reliance on ad hoc measures.

Restrictive state responses to forced migrations at Southeast Asian borders (land or sea) also have reverberations at the urban level. In 2011, for example, a group of Khmer Krom asylum seekers from Vietnam (via Cambodia) detailed to me their daily fears of being arrested in Bangkok. That year they experienced a series of deportations, during which Thai police would arrest and then transport them to Cambodia. A few days later, they would pay a smuggler to bring them back into Thailand. Upon one arrest, one man called the United Nations High Commissioner for Refugees (UNHCR) Bangkok office seeking help, only to be told by the officer on the line to get deported and sneak back across the border to reapply for asylum. Just as state responses to forced migration include the deployment of ad hoc, informal, and even illegal (discussed below) practices, this humanitarian actor's advice reveals a working familiarity with the blurred boundaries of formal and informal, legal and illegal, in a context without codified frameworks for managing international displacement. Such muddled distinctions manifest in several ways as refugees encounter the state in urban settings.

Amid such disorder, how do regimes of forced migration – systems of power and interests that regulate the movement and activity of forced migrants – emerge and transform, and why do they take on different forms within and between countries? Much of the scholarship on forced migration governance, with its focus on formal refugee policies, offers little help in answering these questions, while a growing literature on informal modes of governance has yet to develop theories explaining the formation of control regimes. Drawing from advocacy and ethnographic fieldwork conducted intermittently between 2010 and 2015 with Rohingya and Kachin (among other) forced migrants in Malaysia and Thailand,[2] as well as from media and non-governmental organization (NGO) reports on forced migrations in Southeast Asia, this chapter puts forth a theoretical perspective for studying the formation and transformation of regimes of forced migration in contexts without refugee laws. To do so, it extends law and society scholarship on the relationship between formal law and types of legality constituted in everyday life to cases of forced migration governance in Southeast Asia. Attending to legal (formal/informal) and spatial (borders/cities) dimensions of such governance, the chapter unpacks the concepts of *onward pushes* and *negotiated refuge*, arguing that the patchwork of formal laws and informal regulatory practices states employ at national borders demonstrates a semi-legal governance framework that shapes regulatory relationships at the urban level. The chapter concludes with suggestions for theorizing the emergence and transformation of regimes of forced migration by studying their co-determination by local social relations and broader social forces at state and international levels.

Law, informality, and forced migration governance: a conceptual framework

Much of the literature on forced migration governance focuses on the institutional structures and policy instruments that states and humanitarian actors use to manage refugees. Several works analyze the development of the refugee regime through the 1951 UN Refugee Convention and its 1967 protocol and evolving institutional structures and complexes revolving around the UNHCR (Barnett, 2002; Betts, 2010; Feller, 2001; Goodwin-Gill and McAdam, 2007). Legal scholars have also assessed the design and effectiveness of regional refugee agreements in Africa and Latin America (Arboleda, 1995; Harley, 2014; Okoth-Obbo et al., 2000), noting the expansion of the refugee definition from its primary focus on persecution to also include those affected by generalized violence and disorder. Much research has analyzed national level asylum policies, including those related to protracted war-induced refugee situations in sub-Saharan Africa (Betts, 2010; Crisp, 2000; Milner, 2009), as well as how Global North states filter and receive refugees through asylum and resettlement programs (Hamlin, 2014; Loescher, 1986; Menz, 2009). With a primary focus on the design and implementation of formal laws, however, the literature neglects analysis of "weakly legalized spaces" (Landau, 2017: 166) and thus cannot explain state regulatory dynamics in the absence of these laws.

Studies of governance in specific spaces provide better analyses of the messy and changing processes through which state and humanitarian actors regulate forced migrants. A key strand of this research uses Agamben's (1998) notion of camps as "spaces of exception," in which refugees are reduced to "bare life" and subject to absolute and incontestable forms of control, to analyze how authorities govern camp populations (Hanafi and Long, 2010; Hyndman, 2000; Minca, 2015). Others have challenged this strand by identifying the pluralistic and networked governance structures (McConnachie, 2014a) and refugee politics (Sanyal, 2014) that emerge in and reshape camp spaces. Looking beyond camps, the growing literature on self-settled refugees focuses mainly on coping strategies in urban environments. Some apply a "livelihoods" framework, considering refugee assets and strategies used to achieve goals amid "vulnerability contexts" defined by institutional and legal structures (Jacobsen, 2006). Even in places with comprehensive refugee policies, refugees are not always able to attain protection due to a lack of "institutional prerequisites" to translate rights into entitlements (Landau, 2006), leading many to construct their own livelihoods and coping mechanisms (Campbell, 2006; Grabska, 2006). Self-settlement can also give way to informal settlements existing outside of cities, where aspects of refugee screening and control reminiscent of camps take place without the formal legitimacy of the state or humanitarian agencies (Sanyal, 2017: 118). While the self-settlement literature presents promising avenues of research interrogating the blurred boundaries of formal governance and informal modes of adaptation and control, it has yet to explain how regimes of forced migration that utilize (or are based on) these blurred boundaries emerge and transform in environments without refugee laws.

Though not yet applied to forced migration, the extensive law and society literature on everyday legality offers a fruitful theoretical orientation for studying regimes of forced migration. Eschewing top-down analyses of legal implementation for inquiries into people's understandings and uses of the law in everyday life (Merry, 1985; Silbey, 2010), such work conceives of legality as a "structure of social action" (Ewick and Silbey, 1998: 33–56) that is made up of cultural schemas and resources (Sewell, 1992) circulating through the "legal consciousness" of ordinary people in a variety of social settings. Rather than viewing law as merely an instrument that authorities impose on society, this perspective conceives of legality as continually made and recreated through conceptions and social actions that coalesce into "the meanings, sources of authority, and cultural practices that are recognized as legal, regardless of who employs them or for what ends" (Silbey, 2005a: 336). The hegemonic power of legality lies in its dialectical relation to formal law, as an array of schemas circulate through narratives that integrate understandings of varied local action with abstract, normative aspirations represented by legal concepts and institutions (Silbey, 2005b: 342, 2010: 476).

To advance a theoretical perspective for studying the formation of forced migration regimes in Southeast Asia, this chapter extends this literature in two ways. First, along a legal dimension, it moves beyond the interplay of formal law with informal negotiations of law by ordinary people to attend to higher levels of informality demonstrated in ad hoc state responses to forced migrations within a multilayered governance context. It refers to "illegal" practices as those that exist outside of or go against formal law. Here, the concept of "semi-legality" (Kubal, 2013), which denotes "legally ambiguous situations" of migrants existing within a "multidimensional space" between legal and illegal (Kubal, 2013: 556), is useful for characterizing not only the statuses and conditions of forced migrants but also governmental approaches to controlling them. Second, recognizing that regulatory practices and relationships vary between national and urban scales, constituting distinct yet related structures of control, the chapter avoids the "territorial trap" of the state (Agnew, 1994) and a sole focus on national governance while analyzing geographic scales and their politics in perpetual relationship with each other (Brenner, 2004). Attending to the spatial dimension, it thus analyzes the mélange of informal and codified approaches to forced migration at national borders as well as in urban environments hosting the unsettled and economically precarious "southern urbanism" of refugees (Landau, 2017), contributing to discussions on the link between informality and confinement (Pasquetti and Picker, 2017).

An overview of forced migration governance in Southeast Asia

Forced migration control in Southeast Asia is characterized by varied state responses to diverse migration flows, implemented amid competing legal concepts and normative frameworks. War displaced ethnic minorities and stateless people from Myanmar make up the bulk of contemporary forced migrations in the region, which also include those fleeing political and religious persecution in Laos and Vietnam, and a smaller number of refugees from outside of the region (McConnachie, 2014b; PEF, 2010). Though war displacement from Myanmar has decreased in recent years, the Rohingya crisis continues to produce refugees. Excluded by Myanmar's 1982 Citizenship Law, the stateless Rohingya continually face state oppression and ethnoreligious violence, leading hundreds of thousands of the Muslim minority to flee (Cheung, 2011; ERT, 2012; ICHR, 2010). Since the mid 2000s, the Rohingya have boarded boats leaving Bangladesh or Myanmar, in hopes of reaching Malaysia (via Thailand), a Muslim majority country with a sizable Rohingya population seeking resettlement (ERT, 2014b: 37–40; IRC, 2012). Such migrations spiked in 2009, 2012, and again in 2015 (AP, 2015; ERT, 2012, 2014b: 45–49), and at the time of writing, sustained military-backed violence in Rahkine State has compelled a steady exodus of Rohingya to neighboring Bangladesh.

A set of competing legal and normative frameworks influence state responses to these migrations. At the international level, UN agencies, international NGOs, and local advocacy and service organizations based in Southeast Asian cities assert international legal concepts and normative human rights frameworks as events arise. Foreign embassies also regularly raise refugee rights with host governments. In addition to NGO monitoring and reporting of government treatment of refugees, international media outlets regularly note government deviations from human rights norms in their reports on forced migrations. International norms and legal concepts related to refugees, however, are absent in regional and national legal frameworks. The Association of Southeast Asian Nations (ASEAN) has no refugee agreement, and its inter-governmental human rights commission lacks enforcement mechanisms to ensure state compliance to rights norms, which are secondary to principles of non-interference and state sovereignty (Ginbar, 2010; Petcharamesree, 2016). In addition, eight of the ten ASEAN countries are not signatories to the UN Refugee Convention (including the major destination countries of Malaysia and Thailand) and have no domestic refugee laws.

Instead, Southeast Asian states apply general immigration laws with rigid distinctions between legal and illegal migration to incidents of forced migration, reflecting priorities of national sovereignty and state security. States uphold these laws with varying degrees of stringency as events unfold, resulting in ad hoc modes of governance that can be grouped into three broad categories. First, states deny entry outright, as demonstrated in their deflection of Rohingya boats. While Thailand has porous land borders, police operate several internal roadside checkpoints, deporting those they catch without entry authorization. Malaysia runs similar internal checkpoints and is notorious for rooting out migrants in urban areas who have slipped through the border (Hedman, 2008). Second, states shelter forced migrants in enclosed areas, providing basic subsistence while prohibiting integration with local society. Thailand has housed thousands of "displaced persons fleeing fighting" from Myanmar in border camps since the 1980s (McConnachie, 2014b) and also held Laos Hmong refugees in a camp and warehouse for years before deporting them in 2009 (PEF, 2010). Thailand also detains asylum seekers for indefinite periods in immigration detention centers, at times yielding to pressure from origin states to return them (Wong and Amatatham, 2015). Finally, states tolerate the presence of refugees in urban areas, with the understanding that they will be resettled or repatriate. Bangkok has an estimated 8,000 refugees and asylum seekers (Asylum Access, 2017), and Kuala Lumpur hosts over 140,000 such migrants (UNHCR, 2017). Such tolerance is tenuous, as demonstrated by frequent arrests in Malaysia's cities and intermittent raids of asylum seeker residences in Bangkok (Fortify Rights, 2017).

Onward pushes at national borders

Focusing on Thai and Malaysian state responses to Rohingya boat arrivals from 2009–15, this section conceptualizes *onward pushes* as the informal, at times illegal, collaborations between state and non-state actors to facilitate movement of forced migrants out of the national territory. The section identifies two ways state authorities have accomplished these pushes: collusion with human smugglers to deflect boats or funnel passengers through shadow migration routes, and devolution of management to humanitarian actors working to resettle refugees to other countries.

In 2009, news stories exposed the Thai Navy's "push back" policy of towing intercepted boats of smuggled Rohingya migrants back out to sea, at times without food or working engines, and setting them adrift toward Malaysia (ERT, 2014b: 45; PEF, 2010). In subsequent years, Thailand replaced this uncodified policy with a new "help on" policy of first providing rations, fuel, and engine checks before towing boats out for onward travel to Malaysia (HRW, 2013). This new form of deflection was at times combined with "soft deportation" across land borders if boats were found to be unseaworthy. In early 2013, for example, the navy intercepted a boat of 73 Rohingya passengers near the shores of Phuket. After discovering cracks in the boat and the poor health of the passengers, they took the group ashore, and immigration police transported them by land to an area of Myanmar where smugglers were ready to take the deportees to Malaysia (HRW, 2013). Thai authorities have practiced this type of inconspicuous overland deportation in many other instances. In 2009, after intense criticism for initial push backs, the immigration bureau detained nearly 80 boat migrants in Bangkok for over two years before transporting them to Myanmar's Karen State, where many procured the services of smuggling agents to travel to Malaysia (ERT, 2014b: 46–48). The common thread in these stories is deportation to an area where smugglers are readily available to take them back into Thailand and on to Malaysia if desired.

Authorities have also entered into more direct, and patently illegal, collaborative practices with smugglers. Parallel to the emergence of the "help on" policy, state agents began bringing intercepted boats ashore and transferring passengers to smugglers who would detain them in jungle camps along the Thailand–Malaysia border and take those who could afford it to Malaysia (ERT, 2014b: 49; Sidasathian and Morison, 2012). In a 2013 Reuters report, a Royal Thai police officer acknowledged the existence of a covert "option two" policy of funneling arrivals through smuggling networks and confirmed the existence of "holding bays" in Southern Thailand (Szep and Marshall, 2013). In addition, an anonymous senior government official said that diplomatic sensitivities prevented Thailand from criticizing Myanmar for causing Rohingya displacement and that they did not have the capacity to prosecute all of the Rohingya for breaking immigration laws, so "option two" was their best solution (Szep and Marshall, 2013). Likewise, a Thai official admitted that working with smugglers was the only short-term solution to the refugee influx because Malaysia was better able to deal with them (Fisher, 2013).

The depth of such collusion was revealed further in a series of dramatic events, detailed in high-profile news stories. In 2015, over 30 graves of Rohingya and Bangladeshi migrants were found at the Thailand–Malaysia border (Fuller and Cochrane, 2015). In the aftermath, dozens of police officers and senior officials were charged with complicity in the trade of humans (Fuller and Cochrane, 2015). Indications of state involvement in human smuggling arose again when a senior investigator fled to Australia to seek political asylum out of fear of violent retribution by the high-level government, military, and police figures he was implicating in his investigation (Ramzy, 2015). After a temporary halt in the investigations, the US State Department's demotion of Thailand to tier three of its annual Trafficking in Persons report spurred the government to ramp up its anti-trafficking efforts, resulting in the 2017 conviction of over 60 people, including a former army general and former local politicians, on charges related to human trafficking (Bendix, 2017). This series of events indicates that systems of collusion between state agents and smugglers were in place and readily available for use in the management of forced migrants.

Compared to Thailand, Malaysia has been more lenient in allowing Rohingya boat migrants to disembark, but with the intent to push them onward through a UN resettlement program. While in 2015 authorities stated they would rescue boats in danger of sinking but not allow any seaworthy boats ashore (Calamur, 2015), international outcry prompted the government to continue its existing practice of detention upon arrival and release under the auspices of the UNHCR. Through this practice, authorities hold arrivals in immigration detention centers and allow the UNHCR to determine their "persons of concern" status. Those who receive this international status are then released into refugee communities to await resettlement without any lawful residence or work status from the host state (ERT, 2014a: 16). Those who do not face indefinite detention and deportation (ERT, 2014a: 53).

Though not as abrupt an expulsion as practiced by Thailand, detaining refugees and releasing them into urban areas is also oriented to onward migration and reflects an informal collaboration with non-state actors to accomplish this goal. In effect, the state tolerates the presence of refugees (if defined as such by the UNHCR) in urban areas without providing actual accommodation, instead allowing them to live among other refugees, migrants, and the urban poor, with the understanding that they will resettle or repatriate. The UNHCR does not provide accommodations or assistance but releases refugees into urban refugee/migrant communities through grassroots "refugee committees" that leaders have self-organized along ethnic lines to provide various forms of coping assistance. In the past, the UNHCR secured the release of Rohingya refugees to the Rohingya Society of Malaysia (RSM),[3] a committee with members in Kuala Lumpur and Penang. Others who sneak into Malaysia through land borders, such as war-induced refugees from

Myanmar, also find co-ethnic committees for various forms of support and assistance with advancing through the resettlement process (Palmgren, 2017). Moreover, while the forced migrants are not expelled immediately, they are not provided a secure stay and are only marginally distinguished from "illegal" migrants. In lieu of a formal agreement between Malaysia and the UNHCR to protect refugees, their tenuous security is based only on a "gentlemen's agreement" between the government and UN agency to not arrest refugees. This agreement, however, is not codified by law, and local adherence is spotty, leaving the refugees vulnerable to coercive practices that state agents wield regularly, reinforcing the ever-present threat of an onward push.

Onward pushes are collaborations between state and non-state actors and institutions to advance the onward movement of forced migrants. As the examples of Malaysia devolving population management to humanitarian agencies, and Thailand using smuggling networks to facilitate clandestine migration demonstrate, these pushes exist on a continuum from formal/legal to informal/illegal and reflect states' fluid, semi-legal governance approaches to forced migration in Southeast Asia. Furthermore, states implement these practices within an international context of competing norms and legal concepts. The state practices described above were seemingly motivated by attempts to mediate the tensions between national sovereignty and universal human rights frameworks that arise with pronounced incidents of forced migration, resulting in patchwork responses that uphold restrictive immigration laws and successfully shirk formal asylum accommodations while avoiding immediate charges of refoulement – the forcible return of migrants to countries where they face persecution. These onward pushes thus share conceptual similarities with the "neo-refoulement" practices of states that use geographical tactics (e.g., Australia's out-sourcing of detention and processing procedures) to prevent asylum seekers from reaching sovereign territory to make legal refugee claims (Hyndman and Mountz, 2008). Neo-refoulement arrangements, often between states, are more formal instances of onward pushes that, like the informal, even illegal, practices discussed in this chapter, "create a geographical game of hopscotch" for those seeking refuge (Hyndman and Mountz, 2008: 268). In Southeast Asia, urban environments are also part of this game.

Negotiated refuge in urban environments

The semi-legal governance approaches exhibited by state authorities at borders also shape regulatory practices and relationships at the urban level. This section looks at the interplay between formal law and everyday legality regarding forced migrants in Bangkok and Kuala Lumpur, parts of which resemble Landau's conceptualization of "Southern urbanism" – "the deeply fluid, often sociopolitically fragmented, and economically precarious spaces" where various migrants strive to survive, and where "national, municipal, regional, or international law confronts myriad formal and informal regulatory regimes"

(Landau, 2017: 165). The experiences of many living in these areas are shaped by their "semi-legality," or "in-between" statuses representing forms of legality that interact with formal immigration status in different ways (Kubal, 2013: 565). In these settings, the illegal status of the irregular migrant feeds a popular understanding of refugees as vulnerable and powerless vis-a-vis various urban actors, while the semi-legal status of the international refugee enables them to negotiate refuge. Though urban refugees are not cordoned off and controlled in camps, the informal processes of negotiated refuge nevertheless have marked confining effects.

The restrictive immigration laws that govern forced migrants in Malaysia and Thailand underscore a perpetual vulnerability that shapes their relationship with local authorities and frames their experience in urban areas. For one, threats of arrest and deportation continue to be a part of everyday life. A Rohingya man living in Bangkok told me that he had been arrested and deported thirteen times since moving to the city years earlier. [4] Similarly, Khmer Krom asylum seekers living on the outskirts of Bangkok described a common cycle of arrest, deportation, and (unauthorized) re-entry that made them live, as one woman put it, like "rats in a cage."[5] This vulnerability is popularly understood not only by migrants but also by local authorities and native residents. The most common problems Kachin refugees reported facing in Kuala Lumpur were being extorted by police and harassed by thieves. Police regularly extort refugees, often telling them, according a leader of a refugee committee, that they are "kosong" cases, meaning "zero" cases who have no rights. Police extort refugees on the street so often that sometimes locals present themselves as plain clothes officers, demanding money while threatening arrest. Other times, thieves wield weapons to rob refugees. Those in Kuala Lumpur are particularly cautious of robberies and extortions at the end of the month, as that is when they are carrying their newly earned cash wages, and perpetrators seem to know this. These examples reflect the pervasive notion, popularly understood and used to different people's advantage, that refugees are powerless urban inhabitants.

At the urban level, migrants acquire a semi-legal status through a mix of state, humanitarian, and grassroots procedures. In Kuala Lumpur, those who arrived by land, including most of the war refugees from Myanmar, first register with a co-ethnic refugee committee and wait for the UNHCR to accept asylum applications from committee member lists, after which those who gain international refugee status are supposed to be exempt from state coercion as per the "gentlemen's agreement." Here, the government does not bestow refugee status, but the migrant moves gradually from an illegal/irregular status to a semi-legal status, relying on grassroots co-ethnic assistance, international humanitarian mechanisms, and a verbal state assurance to respect a status that the refugee regime formally designates at the international level but state authorities only loosely recognize in national and urban arenas. In Bangkok, asylum seekers apply for refugee status directly with the UNHCR, but as several told me, police often do not recognize this status. A few Rohingya men I talked to in 2012 had procured a "white card" from district offices that allows legal residence for those without a nationality who have lived in the country for decades but prohibits employment. Their ability to obtain these cards, however, depended on the attitudes and actions of district authorities who grant the cards, and those with cards still only enjoyed a semi-legal status as they had to work illegally to survive.

Since forced migrants in Bangkok and Kuala Lumpur only ever reach a semi-legal status, they use cash earned in informal labor markets to negotiate their security with local authorities. Many Rohingya, for example, cook and sell roti on the streets of busy districts throughout Bangkok. In Kuala Lumpur, refugees appear to hold a unique position in the urban labor market based on their semi-legal status. Here, UNHCR officers, staff of migrant rights organizations, and several Kachin refugees told me that employers prefer hiring refugees over migrant workers recruited through formal channels because the former are not protected by labor regulations and thus work longer hours for less pay. In addition, refugees are less likely to be deported than "illegal" migrants because of the "gentlemen's agreement." Refugees thus constitute a large and exploitable labor force for local restaurants, retailers, and other manual labor and service businesses in Kuala Lumpur who benefit from the legal ambiguities that accompany refugee semi-legal status.

The wages earned from informal employment enable the refugees to continually negotiate their security with local state agents. Several Rohingya roti sellers told me identical accounts of paying police officers from three departments in their district 500 Thai baht (about 15 USD) each per month, for a total of 1,500 baht out of their monthly income in order to work without being arrested. In addition, they must also pay any police officer who enters their area and demands money at any time. Kachin refugees in Kuala Lumpur also told me common stories of frequently being stopped by police in the streets. When this happens, the officer threatens detention, demanding the refugee pay a fee to be released. If the refugee cannot afford it, he or she calls their refugee committee to intervene and negotiate a lower release price. One committee member told me that police are happy when their victim calls a committee, since they know it will ensure a payment. Leaders of refugee committees contend that paying these bribes is the best and most common way to prevent arrest, as police officers often ignore UNHCR cards, and a UNHCR refugee hotline is ineffective. "They never answer," one refugee told me. "I can say, it is worthless," another claimed.

Negotiated refuge in urban environments involves refugees acquiring semi-legal status and using cash bribes, in association with this status, to prevent state coercion. This type of refuge is shaped by the ambiguities of refugee semi-legal status in the cities. They are illegal vis-à-vis state immigration laws but given formal refugee status at the international level. At the urban level, however, any recognition of refugee status that the refugee regime and host government may have is often not translated to local state agents, necessitating the continual negotiation of refuge through status claims and cash bribes. Furthermore, the local governance practices that constitute negotiated refuge have significant confining effects, contributing to discussions about the relational dynamics between informality and confinement (Pasquetti and Picker, 2017). The requirement to bribe corrupt authorities has the effect of circumscribing refugees within the limits of local regulation, even though they have achieved a semi-legal status. While this status, particularly in Kuala Lumpur, provides certain assurances of protection (or exception) from state coercion, interactions with locals, employers, and police confine them to certain spaces, roles, and actions within the city. Importantly, such confinement is not the result of formally cordoned off spaces for those with state-recognized refugee status but rather of the local interactions among authorities, migrants, and their networks that take place within a poorly defined semi-legal context.

Conclusion: from the legality of forced migration to theorizing forced migration regimes

This chapter offers a theoretical perspective on forced migration governance in Southeast Asia, with the aim of moving toward a theory of how regimes of forced migration emerge and transform in contexts lacking refugee legal frameworks. Law and society literature has highlighted how the dialectical relationship between the concepts, institutions, and instruments of formal law and people's practical action in everyday life constitute legality, understood as a "structure of social action" consisting of cultural schemas and resources (Sewell, 1992) that determine and pattern social life. This chapter suggests that as a structure of social action, the legality of forced migration in Southeast Asia is fluid, made up of competing schemas and negotiated at different levels in different spaces, resulting in mixtures of formal laws and legal concepts and informal, at times illegal, regulatory practices. By introducing the concepts of *onward pushes* and *negotiated refuge*, the chapter offers two key extensions of the literature on everyday legality that are useful for theorizing regimes of forced migration in Southeast Asia.

First, state responses to forced migrations demonstrate that the interplay between formal laws and informal, practical action serve to constitute legality not only in the daily lives of ordinary people but also in dealings of the state. Thailand's collusion with the human smuggling industry, and Malaysia's loose agreement with the refugee regime, are both examples of state-level informality that are characteristic of forced migration governance in Southeast Asia. Such governance occurs within a multilevel context of competing schemas, which influence and draw from differential resources, giving way to blurred lines of formality and informality (and legality and illegality). States implement their responses within a primary national sovereignty framework, wielding coercive arms of the state to enforce strict migration laws, but they do so as "transit" countries within an international community that asserts universal human rights and humanitarian norms through media and diplomatic pressures. Amid this mixture of norms, legal concepts, and regulatory approaches, state responses reflect a patchwork of formal, informal, semi-legal, and illegal practices implemented in ad hoc fashion but with the consistent and resolute goal of pushing the migrants onward. As such, conceptions of forced migration regimes must incorporate the informal/illegal elements that are fundamental to state modes of control.

Second, this chapter introduces a spatial dimension to the analysis of formal law and informal legality by highlighting a constant interaction between scales of control. State actions aimed at advancing onward movement feed a popular conception of forced migrants as illegal, to be dealt with however the state deems necessary, and informs the everyday attitudes and social actions that constitute the legality of forced migration in the city. If legal consciousness is a social phenomenon resulting in the daily constitution of legality (Silbey, 2005a, 2010), then the legality of forced migration is significantly shaped by the pervasiveness of the ideas of refugee illegality, vulnerability, and powerlessness. The UNHCR officer who advises the refugee to get deported and return, the police who consider refugees "zero" cases, the local who robs the refugee without fear of repercussion, and the employer who sees opportunity for exploitation, all invoke these ideas in their everyday practices. Refugees and their allies in turn contest this notion by asserting the humanitarian schema of refugees as people in need of protection, drawing on semi-legal status as a resource to distinguish oneself from "illegal" migrants, as well as on cash earned in the informal economy to ward off state coercion. Here, the international scale that influences state responses to arrivals is also present at the urban level, as humanitarian actors and their partners assert internationally recognized refugee rights to state agents, with varying success. Attending to the spatial dimension of forced migration governance compels us to move beyond situated studies of legality in particular settings, and of national responses to refugee arrivals, to multi-sited studies that reveal how different scales of control shape and develop from particular forced migration regimes. Furthermore, the practical actions of refugees navigating the regulatory landscape and negotiating their refuge in urban environments suggests the need to incorporate the experiential dimension in conceptions of control regimes.

Theorizing regimes of forced migration in contexts without refugee laws requires an understanding of the mechanisms by which these regimes emerge and transform at different times and in different spaces. Such theorizing should thus explain why states vary in their responses to forced migrations as well as why they respond in certain ways sometimes and other ways other times. As this chapter suggests, broad social forces coming from both domestic and international/global arenas can inform competing sets of schemas and shape different resources that make up structures of forced migration governance. A theory of the emergence and transformation of regimes of forced migration in Southeast Asia, or other contexts lacking refugee legal frameworks, should thus come from comparative studies that analyze the co-determination of these control regimes by local social relations and broader social forces, with acute attention to how formal and informal actors, approaches, and practices work together to constitute modes of control.

Notes

1 This chapter uses "forced migration/migrants" to denote those who have fled violence, persecution, and other forms of unbearable hardship in their origin. Though legal/bureaucratic labels never map neatly to complex conditions and processes of migration, for the purposes of analyzing the interplay between formal law and informal regulation, the chapter uses the term "refugee" to denote someone who has gained this status from the UNHCR and "asylum seeker" for someone who is in the process of applying for such status. Following the language of states, the term "irregular migration" refers to those who have crossed (or attempted to cross) international borders without authorization.
2 See ERT (2014a), Palmgren (2017), and PEF (2010) for research output.
3 Discussion with RSM members in Kuala Lumpur and Penang, August 2010 and with UNHCR officers in Kuala Lumpur, July 16, 2015.
4 Interview with Rohingya refugee in Bangkok, June 24, 2012. Note that Thailand has a significant population of Rohingya refugees who came by land in the late 1990s and early 2000s, when traveling through Myanmar to reach the Thailand border was possible.
5 Interview with Khmer Krom asylum seekers in Bangkok, July 12, 2011.

References

Agamben, G. (1998), *Homo Sacer: Sovereign Power and Bare Life* (Stanford: Stanford University Press).

Agnew, J. (1994), The territorial trap: the geographical assumptions of international relations theory. *Review of International Political Economy* 1(1): 53–80.

AP (Associated Press) (2015), Malaysia and Thailand turn away hundreds on migrant boats. *The Guardian* (May 14, 2015).

Arboleda, E. (1995), The Cartagena Declaration of 1984 and its similarities to the 1969 OAU Convention – a comparative perspective part 2: protection of refugees, returnees and internally displaced persons. *International Journal of Refugee Law* 7: 87–101.

Asylum Access (2017), Urban refugees in Bangkok [online] http://asylumaccess.org/urban-refugees-bangkok/ [accessed December 31, 2019].

Barnett, L. (2002), Global governance and the evolution of the international refugee regime. *International Journal of Refugee Law* 14 (2/3): 238–262.

Bendix, A. (2017), Dozens found guilty in Thailand's largest human trafficking trial. *The Atlantic* (July 20, 2017).

Betts, A. (2010), The refugee regime complex. *Refugee Survey Quarterly* 29(1): 12–37.

Brenner, N. (2004), *New State Spaces: Urban Governance and the Rescaling of Statehood* (Oxford, New York: Oxford University Press).

Calamur, K. (2017), Malaysia says it will turn back migrant boats. *NPR.org* (May 12, 2015).

Campbell, E.H. (2006), Urban refugees in Nairobi: problems of protection, mechanisms of survival, and possibilities for integration. *Journal of Refugee Studies* 19(3): 396–413.

Cheung, S. (2011), Migration control and the solutions impasse in South and Southeast Asia: implications from the Rohingya experience. *Journal of Refugee Studies* 25(1): 50–70.

Crisp, J. (2000), Africa's refugees: patterns, problems and policy challenges. *New Issues in Refugee Research*, Working Paper No. 28, Geneva: UNHCR, August 2000.

ERT (Equal Rights Trust) (2014a), Equal only in name: the human rights of stateless Rohingya in Malaysia. Equal Rights Trust.

ERT (Equal Rights Trust) (2014b), Equal only in name: the human rights of stateless Rohingya in Thailand. Equal Rights Trust.

ERT (Equal Rights Trust) (2012), Burning homes, sinking lives: a situation report on violence against stateless Rohingya in Myanmar and their refoulement from Bangladesh. Equal Rights Trust.

Ewick, P. and S.S. Silbey. (1998), *The Common Place of Law: Stories from Everyday Life. Language and Legal Discourse* (Chicago: University of Chicago Press).

Feller, E. (2001), The evolution of the international refugee protection regime. *Washington University Journal of Law & Policy* 5(1): 129–139.

Fisher, J. (2013), Burmese refugees sold on by Thai officials. *BBC News* (January 21, 2013).

Fortify Rights. (2017), Thailand: release asylum seekers detained in raids last week. [online] http://www.fortifyrights.org/publication-20171106.html (November 6, 2017) [accessed December 30, 2019].

Fuller, T. and J. Cochrane. (2015), Rohingya migrants from Myanmar, shunned by Malaysia, are spotted adrift in Andaman Sea. *New York Times* (May 14, 2015).

Ginbar, Y. (2010), Human rights in ASEAN – setting sail or treading water? *Human Rights Law Review* 10(3):504–518.

Goodwin-Gill, G.S. and J. McAdam (2007), *The Refugee in International Law* 3rd edn (Oxford; New York: Oxford University Press).

Grabska, K. (2006), Marginalization in urban spaces of the Global South: urban refugees in Cairo. *Journal of Refugee Studies* 19(3): 287–307.

Hamlin, R. (2014), *Let Me Be a Refugee: Administrative Justice and the Politics of Asylum in the United States, Canada, and Australia* (Oxford: Oxford University Press).

Hanafi, S. and T. Long (2010), Governance, governmentalities, and the state of exception in the Palestinian refugee camps of Lebanon. *Journal of Refugee Studies* 23(2): 134–159.

Harley, T. (2014), Regional cooperation and refugee protection in Latin America: A 'South-South' approach. *International Journal of Refugee Law* 26(1): 22–47.

Hedman, E-L.E. (2008), Refuge, governmentality and citizenship: capturing 'illegal migrants' in Malaysia and Thailand. *Government and Opposition* 43(2): 358–383.

HRW (Human Rights Watch) (2013), Thailand: don't deport Rohingya 'boat people' [online] https://www.hrw.org/news/2013/01/02/thailand-dont-deport-rohingya-boat-people (January 2, 2013) [accessed December 30, 2019].

Hyndman, J. (2000), *Managing Displacement: Refugees and the Politics of Humanitarianism* (Minneapolis: University of Minnesota Press).

Hyndman, J. and A. Mountz. (2008), Another brick in the wall? Neo-refoulement and the externalization of asylum by Australia and Europe." *Government and Opposition* 43(2):249–269.

ICHR (Irish Centre for Human Rights) (2010), Crimes against humanity in Western Burma: the situation of the Rohingyas. Irish Centre for Human Rights.

IRC (International Rescue Committee) (2012), In search of survival and sanctuary in the city: refugees from Myanmar/Burma in Kuala Lumpur, Malaysia. International Rescue Committee.

Jacobsen, K. (2006), Refugees and asylum seekers in urban areas: a livelihoods perspective. *Journal of Refugee Studies* 19(3): 273–286.

Kubal, A. (2013), Conceptualizing semi-legality in migration research. *Law & Society Review* 47(3): 555–587.

Landau, L.B. (2017), Southern urbanism, legalization, and the limits of migration law. *AJIL Unbound* 111: 165–171.

Landau, L.B. (2006), Protection and dignity in Johannesburg: shortcomings of South Africa's urban refugee policy. *Journal of Refugee Studies* 19(3): 308–327.

Loescher, G. (1986), *Calculated Kindness; Refugees and America's Half-Open Door, 1945 to the Present* (New York; London: Free Press; Collier Macmillan).

McConnachie, K. (2014a), *Governing Refugees: Justice, Order and Legal Pluralism* (Abingdon: Routledge).

McConnachie, K. (2014b), Forced migration in Southeast-Asia and East Asia. In Fiddian-Qasmiyeh, E., G. Loescher, K. Long, and N. Sigona (eds) *The Oxford Handbook of Refugee and Forced Migration Studies* (Oxford: Oxford University Press), pp. 626–638.

Menz, G. (2009), *The Political Economy of Managed Migration: Nonstate Actors, Europeanization, and the Politics of Designing Migration Policies* (Oxford; New York: Oxford University Press).

Merry, S.E. (1985), "Concepts of law and justice among working-class Americans: ideology as culture." *Legal Studies Forum* 9: 59–70.

Minca, C. (2015), Geographies of the camp. *Political Geography*, Special Issue: Historical Geographies of Internationalism, 49 (Supplement C): 74–83.

Milner, J. (2009), *Refugees, the State and the Politics of Asylum in Africa* (Basingstoke: Palgrave Macmillan).

Okoth-Obbo, G., A-S. Georges, J. Crisp, R. Ramcharan, and M.F. Tinta. (2000), Thirty years on: a legal review of the 1969 OAU Refugee Convention. *African Yearbook of International Law* 8: 3–180.

Palmgren, P. (2017), Survival and integration: Kachin social networks and refugee management regimes in Kuala Lumpur and Los Angeles. *Journal of Ethnic and Migration Studies* 43(13): 2247–2264.

Pasquetti, S. and G. Picker (2017), Urban informality and confinement: toward a relational framework. *International Sociology* 32(4): 532–544.

PEF (People's Empowerment Foundation) (2010), Refugee protection in ASEAN: national failures, regional responsibilities. People's Empowerment Foundation, Thailand.

Petcharamesree, S. (2016), ASEAN and its approach to forced migration issues. *The International Journal of Human Rights* 20(2): 173–190.

Ramzy, A. (2015), Fleeing Thailand, top investigator of human trafficking says he fears for his safety. *New York Times* (December 10, 2015).

Sanyal, R. (2017), A no-camp policy: interrogating informal settlements in Lebanon. *Geoforum* 84 (Supplement C): 117–125.

Sanyal, R. (2014), Urbanizing refuge: interrogating spaces of displacement. *International Journal of Urban and Regional Research* 38(2): 558–572.

Sewell, W.H., Jr (1992), A theory of structure: duality, agency, and transformation. *American Journal of Sociology* 98(1):1–29.

Sidasathian, C. and A. Morison. (2012), Thailand lists boatpeople arrested or assisted along Phuket holiday coast. *Phuket Wan News* (March 18, 2012).

Silbey, S.S. (2010), Legal culture and cultures of legality. In Hall, J.R., L. Grindstaff, and M-C. Lo (eds) *Handbook of Cultural Sociology* (London and New York: Routledge).

Silbey, S.S. (2005a), After legal consciousness. *Annual Review of Law and Social Science* 1(1): 323–368.

Silbey, S.S. (2005b), Everyday life and the constitution of legality. In Jacobs, M. and N. Hanrahan (eds) *Blackwell Companion to Sociology of Culture* (Oxford: Blackwell Publishing).

Szep, J. and A. Marshall (2013), Special report – Thailand secretly dumps Myanmar refugees into trafficking rings. *Reuters* (December 5, 2013).

UNHCR (United Nations High Commissioner for Refugees) (2017), Malaysia global focus page [online] http://reporting.unhcr.org/node/2532#_ga =2.250208966.1327743233.1514445944–1092853737.1422166725 [accessed December 30, 2019].

Wong, E, and P. Amatatham (2015), Ignoring protests, Thailand deports about 100 Uighurs back to China. *New York Times* (July 9, 2015).

Index

EU authorised representative for GPSR:
Easy Access System Europe, Mustamäe tee 50,
10621 Tallinn, Estonia
gpsr.requests@easproject.com

www.ingramcontent.com/pod-product-compliance
Lightning Source LLC
Chambersburg PA
CBHW050641280326
41932CB00015B/2736